The Edinburgh Companion to Scottish Traditional Literatures

Edinburgh Companions to Scottish Literature

Series Editors: Ian Brown and Thomas Owen Clancy

Titles in the series include:

The Edinburgh Companion to Robert Burns
Edited by Gerard Carruthers
978 0 7486 3648 8 (hardback)
978 0 7486 3649 5 (paperback)

The Edinburgh Companion to Twentieth-Century Scottish Literature
Edited by Ian Brown and Alan Riach
978 0 7486 3693 8 (hardback)
978 0 7486 3694 5 (paperback)

The Edinburgh Companion to Contemporary Scottish Poetry
Edited by Matt McGuire and Colin Nicholson
978 0 7486 3625 9 (hardback)
978 0 7486 3626 6 (paperback)

The Edinburgh Companion to Muriel Spark
Edited by Michael Gardiner and Willy Maley
978 0 7486 3768 3 (hardback)
978 0 7486 3769 0 (paperback)

The Edinburgh Companion to Robert Louis Stevenson
Edited by Penny Fielding
978 0 7486 3554 2 (hardback)
978 0 7486 3555 9 (paperback)

The Edinburgh Companion to Irvine Welsh
Edited by Berthold Schoene
978 0 7486 3917 5 (hardback)
978 0 7486 3918 2 (paperback)

The Edinburgh Companion to James Kelman
Edited by Scott Hames
978 0 7486 3963 2 (hardback)
978 0 7486 3964 9 (paperback)

The Edinburgh Companion to Scottish Romanticism
Edited by Murray Pittock
978 0 7486 3845 1 (hardback)
978 0 7486 3846 8 (paperback)

The Edinburgh Companion to Scottish Drama
Edited by Ian Brown
978 0 7486 4108 6 (hardback)
978 0 7486 4107 9 (paperback)

The Edinburgh Companion to Sir Walter Scott
Edited by Fiona Robertson
978 0 7486 4130 7 (hardback)
978 0 7486 4129 1 (paperback)

The Edinburgh Companion to Hugh MacDiarmid
Edited by Scott Lyall and Margery Palmer McCulloch
978 0 7486 4190 1 (hardback)
978 0 7486 4189 5 (paperback)

The Edinburgh Companion to James Hogg
Edited by Ian Duncan and Douglas Mack
978 0 7486 4124 6 (hardback)
978 0 7486 4123 9 (paperback)

The Edinburgh Companion to Scottish Women's Writing
Edited by Glenda Norquay
978 0 7486 4432 2 (hardback)
978 0 7486 4431 5 (paperback)

The Edinburgh Companion to Scottish Traditional Literatures
Edited by Sarah Dunnigan and Suzanne Gilbert
978 0 7486 4540 4 (hardback)
978 0 7486 4539 8 (paperback)

The Edinburgh Companion to Liz Lochhead
Edited by Anne Varty
978 0 7486 5472 7 (hardback)
978 0 7486 5471 0 (paperback)

Visit the Edinburgh Companions to Scottish Literature website at
www.euppublishing.com/series/ecsl

The Edinburgh Companion to Scottish Traditional Literatures

Edited by Sarah Dunnigan and Suzanne Gilbert

EDINBURGH
University Press

© editorial matter and organisation Sarah M. Dunnigan and Suzanne Gilbert, 2013
© the chapters their several authors, 2013

Edinburgh University Press Ltd
22 George Square, Edinburgh EH8 9LF

www.euppublishing.com

Typeset in 10.5/12.5 Adobe Goudy by
Servis Filmsetting Ltd, Stockport, Cheshire

A CIP record for this book is available from the British Library

ISBN 978 0 7486 4540 4 (hardback)
ISBN 978 0 7486 4539 8 (paperback)
ISBN 978 0 7486 4541 1 (webready PDF)
ISBN 978 0 7486 8459 5 (epub)

The right of the contributors
to be identified as author of this work
has been asserted in accordance with
the Copyright, Designs and Patents Act 1988.

Contents

Series Editors' Preface		vii
Acknowledgements		viii
	Introduction	
	Sarah Dunnigan and Suzanne Gilbert	1
1	The Roots of Living Tradition	
	Margaret Bennett	7
2	Genre	
	Emily Lyle, Valentina Bold, Ian Russell	14
3	Folk Belief and Scottish Traditional Literatures	
	Lizanne Henderson	26
4	Transmission	
	James Porter	35
5	'Tradition' and Literature in the Medieval Period	
	John McNamara	42
6	Vernacular Gaelic Tradition	
	Robert Dunbar	51
7	The Early Modern Period	
	Sarah Dunnigan	63
8	The Heroic Ballads of Gaelic Scotland	
	Anja Gunderloch	74
9	Eighteenth-Century Antiquarianism	
	Valentina Bold	85
10	Lowland Song Culture in the Eighteenth Century	
	Katherine Campbell and Kirsteen McCue	94
11	Tradition and Scottish Romanticism	
	Suzanne Gilbert	105
12	Nineteenth-Century Highland and Island Folklore	
	Jason Marc Harris	114

13	Tradition and Innovation in Twentieth-Century Scottish Gaelic Literature	
	Michael Newton	123
14	The Politics of the Modern Scottish Folk Revival	
	Corey Gibson	134
15	Continuing the Living Tradition	
	Margaret Bennett	144

Endnotes 153
Further Reading 199
Notes on Contributors 206
Index 209

Series Editor's Preface

In the preface to the first tranche of volumes in this series, the series editors argued that, while recognising that some literary canons can conceive of a single 'Great Tradition', there is no such simple way of conceiving of Scottish literature's variousness. This year's tranche, the fifth, illustrates that variousness in two ways.

The subject of this year's author volume, Liz Lochhead, currently Scotland's Makar, illustrates the variousness of her talents as poet, playwright and, in a broader sense, figure of cultural significance. As she moves between poetry and playwriting, her work brings lessons from each genre to the other, highlighting the generic slipperiness and interpenetration that is such a feature of Scottish literature. Her work also illuminates relationships between Scotland's languages and dialects, particularly between the Scots and English languages – but also the varieties of dialect and register in Scots usage – as she brings her sharp eye and insightful wit to bear. In her art, Lochhead exemplifies even wider artform interaction as her painting, poetry and playwriting each shape aspects of her creative output.

The second volume this year is one of the series' topic volumes. In its own way, it also illustrates the variousness of the elements in the canon of Scottish literature, sliding between the oral and literary traditions – and their interaction – and voyaging among a wide variety of genres, including story, song, ballad and poetry. This is part of the reason it is entitled a Companion not to 'Scottish Traditional Literature', but to 'Scottish Traditional Literatures'. It considers the impact of traditional literatures in Scotland's several languages both on one another and on what is often more commonly, if in a more limited (and limiting) sense, defined as the Scottish literary tradition. In fact, this volume, like the rest of the series, challenges just what is meant by such a term. The volume pays particular attention to the role of tradition-bearers and those who collected traditional material and made it available to us. In doing so, it raises important and pressing questions about the nature of collecting and the conception of authenticity of tradition.

          Ian Brown   Thomas Owen Clancy

Acknowledgements

We would like to thank the General Editors and all at Edinburgh University Press for their guidance and support in bringing the volume to fruition, and especially Ian Brown for his endless advice and patience. We are very grateful to all our contributors; to Linden Bicket for compiling the Further Reading; to Michael McVeigh for allowing us to use his painting; to Rob Dunbar for his kind readiness to advise and help; and to Margaret Bennett for her generosity and wisdom.

Introduction
Sarah Dunnigan and Suzanne Gilbert

Writing of fairy tales, the late Angela Carter, a dazzling fabulist herself, remarked on their 'user-friendliness'. So too, we might add, does this characterise the rich seam of ballad, song and folktale traditions seeded deep in the varieties of Scottish cultural heritage. Like Carter's cherished *Märchen*, Scots ballads are 'powered by' a 'narrative drive' which asks '"What happened then"?',[1] accommodating and reeling us into their distinctive emotional and verbal worlds. Rather ironically, then, this volume devoted to what we have called 'Scottish traditional literatures' needs to begin with a variety of qualifications and definitions in order to encompass the subject's multifariousness. We are dealing with a multiplicity of modes and forms – folk narrative; folk poetry and song; folk drama; folk language or folksay; and these in turn can encompass ballads, folktales, and songs; jests, riddles, jokes and other types of oral material; wonder tales, heroic stories, fables, Jack tales; lullaby, lament, chant and work-song. After all, that the much-loved fairy abduction narrative, 'Tam Lin', should exist as an allusion in an obscure sixteenth-century Scots allegory ('the tayl of the yong tamlene'), as a ballad communicated by Robert Burns to James Johnson, compiler of the *Scots Musical Museum* and as a song recorded by the 1960s English folk rock band, Fairport Convention (to choose only three of its incarnations) suggests the kind of historical and cross-cultural hybridity of this field in which categories and terms need to be used with care. If this Scots ballad heritage of beautiful, powerful and ribald songs belongs to what is commonly called 'oral tradition', how can it then be subsumed into a category that invokes 'literature' (i.e. what is written; printed)? If oral tradition means transmission by word of mouth, how can we understand an oral culture that would seem to have no record, documentation, or sources? And before we even begin to qualify or refine the categories of 'orality' or 'the folk', what is meant by the term 'tradition' itself? The 'bardic tradition' in Gaelic culture, for example, is spoken of, but refers to formal, professional, court or religious poetry written in an artificial, learned language, rather than the narrative poetry of Gaelic ballad tradition (see Chapter 8). 'Tradition' has been frequently a debateable and politicised term – in the context of

European Romanticism, often viewed as a touchstone of an 'authenticity' used to shore up cultural nationalism or, in the context of the mid-twentieth-century folk revival, which saw the establishment of the Edinburgh People's Festival Ceilidhs and the School of Scottish Studies in 1951, part of a diverse process of cultural and political recovery led in Scotland by Ewan MacColl, Hamish Henderson and others. Traditional culture and its expressive range is also shared as a subject of scholarly interest between a range of disciplines such as ethnology, history, folklore, linguistics, or musicology. Whilst these have some overlapping preoccupations, each field is also defined by its own critical and interpretative terminology, approach and methodology to what might best be described as 'living tradition'.

Some of this tangled web of definitions and assumptions is unpicked by the essays here. This volume hopes to restore a more dynamic, inclusive and holistic understanding of the subject whilst working outwards from a core starting point of literary history. It is our contention that in bringing back traditional modes and cultures of expression into the 'fold' of Scottish literary history we can uncover relatively unexplored layers within what we understand as 'literature'. The intermingling of folk and literary traditions in Burns, Scott and Hogg, for example, is often noted, but their use can be more widely and illuminatingly contextualised. We can become more alert to the 'layering' in medieval and early modern literature – its folkloric and mythopoeic materials and heritage as well as its more familiar classical and scholastic aspects. Awareness of what we might call 'popular culture' within these periods opens up its parameters to include more neglected subjects such as saints' lives, legends, otherworld visions and the origin legends (in essence marvel tales) embedded in historiographical works. The volume is designed so that key aspects or genres of traditional literature are discussed chronologically from the later medieval period to the present. In that way, it offers historical perspectives, providing narratives running parallel to literary histories, with chapters focusing on key engagements with tradition. Interspersed at relevant points are chapters that deepen and extend some of the theoretical or conceptual aspects raised in the historically-based analysis and, in so doing, introduce the work of some key scholars in the field. A number of different perspectives are encompassed that also reflect key questions of performance and different expressive modes such as music, and the influence of popular belief and culture on traditional expression.

Our retention of the term 'literature', and use of the plural, is deliberate. There is no single 'culture' on which the volume is based but rather a variety of linguistic cultures – Scots Gaelic; Scots; English – as well as dialects, each of which in turn is shaped by factors such as historical period, locality, region and the very medium of transmission. Traditional expression itself arises out of local and indigenous traditions, but also reaches out to, and is caught up in, wider cultural inter-relationships: the Irish cycle of Fenian hero tales, romances and ballads crosses to Scotland so that the deeds of the great warrior Fionn mac Cumhaill are partly 'indigenised' or 'relocalised'. Recent developments in Scottish studies have underlined the importance of empire and emigration to the nation's cultural production; the migration of Scottish stories, songs and music to Canada and North America, the Caribbean, Australia and New Zealand is vital to an understanding of these diasporic cultures.

Many of the materials here also challenge conventional or intuitive assumptions that we bring to literature. In part, we are encountering a form of communication or transmission between a singer or storyteller and an audience or group of listeners – a social, communal experience, in other words. It is often impossible to chart a date or origin of composition, and we rarely know the 'author' of a song or ballad or narrative (indeed, its 'teller' or 'performer' frequently chooses to remain anonymous). The extraordinary range of variants or versions by which a single ballad or tale can be known destabilises any assumptions about textual stability or uniformity, and nurtures our awareness that behind every textual variant frequently lies a different singer or teller, a 'tradition-bearer' or 'informant'. It is important to recognise that tradition-bearers are not homogenised or undifferentiated, but that cultural, social, or political backgrounds influence an individual's repertoire. Anna Gordon (Mrs Brown of Falkland) famously gave songs to Scott and other ballad collectors, but as the daughter of an Aberdeen classics professor, who learned songs in childhood from a family maidservant, as well as her mother and aunt, she obviously inhabited a different socio-cultural world from another important female tradition-bearer, Agnes Lyle, the daughter of a Renfrewshire weaver. Lyle's choice of, and interpretation of, ballad repertoire is powerfully shaped by the political radicalism of the weavers' agitation in the face of the Industrial Revolution, war and the manipulations of the political elite. Furthermore, a particular singer inflects a story or song with their own emotional colouring, texture and performance style. Norman Buchan described the great ballad-singer Jeannie Robertson as being 'always inside the song and moving it out to her listeners'.[2] The recovery, recording, or appreciation of an individual voice is a vital, indeed emotionally compelling, aspect by which traditional literature is experienced. The immediacy and intimacy of oral narration can still survive even on the printed page, and even when the closure is formulaic, as here in the familiar 'end-run' of the tale of 'Lasair gheug, the king of Ireland's daughter'. After relaying the king's wedding, the narrator (previously invisible within the narrative) intrudes:

> I got shoes o paper there on a glass pavement, a bit of butter on an ember, porridge in a creel, a greatcoat of chaff and a short coat of buttermilk. I hadn't gone

far when I fell, and the glass pavement broke, the short coat of buttermilk spilt, the butter melted on the ember, a gust of wind came and blew away the greatcoat of chaff. All I had had was gone, and I was as poor as I was to start with. And I left them there.[3]

The materials explored in this volume also enable us to see a more nuanced picture of the interdependence of oral and written cultures, challenging the perception, as Adam Fox puts it, that the written word is 'the natural antidote to oral culture'.[4] John MacInnes notes that the renowned Gaelic bard, Duncan Ban MacIntyre (1724–1812) dictated his poems to the Rev. Donald MacNicol, an Argyllshire minister who was himself a noted collector of poetry. This formed the basis of printed editions of the poet's work, of which Duncan Ban saw three in his own lifetime.[5]

But these also circulated as songs in the oral tradition, some of which exactly mirror the book versions, so that we fascinatingly see how 'the printed text has stabilised the oral version'.[6] In the eighteenth and nineteenth centuries in particular, print becomes the medium for the transmission of traditional songs, ballads and stories, not only through the published editions of collectors, but through an extraordinary variety of broadsides and chapbooks. A broadside ballad can be defined as a song text (or texts) that was printed on one side of a single sheet of paper, and 'hawked' by itinerant ballad sellers at a range of public, social spaces such as fairs, markets and public meetings. Tunes were often cited by name rather than specific music, suggesting their popular currency, and their subjects, frequently dictated by their topicality, could be polemical and even seditious. A chapbook was longer, also eclectic in subject matter, but frequently printed popular tales and rhymes; it was sold by a chapman in the streets of towns and cities, or taken into the countryside, to 'scattered farms and hamlets' by '"flying stationers"', itinerant pedlars or chapmen.[7]

The connection between traditional expression and the material circumstances from which it comes reinforces the importance of the places, peoples and cultures that foster it. Many song and ballad traditions, for example, spring out of a rooted, concrete world of work – the labour of waulking, or furling cloth, as in the Gaelic tradition of waulking songs; the fishing and herring industries; the north-east farming and agricultural communities from which 'the bothy ballad' tradition comes; or the Perthshire berry-picking industry (the famous ballad singer Belle Stewart and her husband, Alex, a piper and storyteller, whose daughter Sheila Stewart is a renowned tradition-bearer, had their own berry farm in the 1950s). The collective, ritual activities of work and song or storytelling bind groups of people and communities together just as interior domestic and social spaces provided a forum for familial and other smaller groups: 'this story, Isaac, that I'm goin to tell you, Isaac, is the story that my grandfather used to tell me an all the rest o the bairns aroon the fireside on a lang summer's nicht to keep us quiet and to pass the time by'.[8] Traditional expression can enable the articulation of strong emotional, social and political ties; a heritage or store of particular materials can preserve and sustain identity, community and memory. In Scotland, this has been especially important to the culture of the travelling people to which some of the most powerful modern tradition-bearers have belonged: for example, Jeannie Robertson, Jimmy MacBeath, Belle Stewart, Willie MacPhee, Duncan Williamson. The Traditional Music and Song Association was founded in order to organise the Blairgowrie Festival in 1965 where Scotland's travelling community gathered for the annual fruit picking.

In addition to the lived realities and lives that surround this extraordinary variety of creative and cultural material, there is a range of interpretative scholarly and critical approaches. We have not privileged any in particular though they are alluded to in some essays: for example, the notion of a 'tale type' (famously based on Stith Thompson's motif-index and his work with Antti Aarne on the classification of folktale in the early part of the twentieth century); the ways in which a narrative adheres to basic structures that characterise the genre or type, including stylistic motifs, settings and characters. Whilst the formulation and patterning of ballads, for example, might relate to their 'memorability' for a singer, it also creates a distinctive 'aesthetic'. Though this term might seem inappropriately literary, there are affinities between the kinds of receptivity or responsiveness – to rhythm, structure, pattern, narrative momentum and so on – nurtured in both listener and reader, though their social and cultural contexts may differ. A ballad, song, or story may need to be directly felt and experienced: Jeannie Robertson described a singer who sang without 'the richt feelin' in't' as 'like an egg without salt'.[9] But it can still be refelt and re-experienced, opened up to new communities of readers, who were not the original or intended audience, and who lie beyond the conventional disciplinary boundaries of the field. Though a volume such as this cannot be fully comprehensive or encyclopaedic, it hopes to nurture a more sharply attuned and informed cultural awareness of why and how Scottish literary writers have borrowed and been inspired by traditional genres, modes and motifs. This is not inevitably a form of appropriation, but can be creatively regenerative in a spirit that is true to the materials' identities. The supernaturalism of ballad tradition has been reworked, for example, by two twentieth-century Scottish women writers – the poet Marion Angus, in powerfully imagined lyrics of the interior life, and the novelist Elspeth Barker, in her Gothic fable. We are also in the midst of a revival of traditional arts and storytelling through the proliferation of events, festivals and clubs in many regions of Scotland, and in the development of new media. Traditional culture has not been curtailed or made finite by contemporary life; like the tale recorded in 1977 from the Shetland storyteller, Tom Tulloch, 'accordin to the imagination o the story-teller an the patience o the bairn 'at they were telling it til, it could ha' gone almost indefinitely'.[10]

CHAPTER ONE

The Roots of Living Tradition

Margaret Bennett

Stories and songs heard in childhood have inspired Scottish 'makars', bards, poets, song-makers, storytellers and writers for centuries. The power to connect one generation to the next in the performance of a story or song extends also to the printed page, exemplified by books and manuscripts from all parts of Scotland. Thus, the 'living tradition' continues breathing life into new singers, tellers and writers.

Reflecting on what inspired him, Robert Burns spoke of his mother's fine singing voice and large repertoire of songs, adding that it was their old housemaid who fired his imagination:

> She had, I suppose, the largest collection in the country of tales and songs concerning devils, ghosts, fairies, brownies, witches, warlocks, spunkies, kelpies, elf-candles, dead-lights, wraiths, apparitions, cantraips, giants, enchanted towers, giants and other trumpery – this cultivated the latency of poesy.[1]

Walter Scott, too, regarded his early years in the Borders, rather than his formal schooling in Edinburgh, as having the strongest influence on his imagination and skill as a writer. Though a twist of fate made his parents decide to leave him in the care of his grandparents at Sandyknowe, Scott recalled being 'fed with the legendary lore of the Borders as with a mother's milk [. . .] My grandmother, in whose youth the old Border depredations were matter of recent tradition, used to tell me many a tale of Wat of Harden [. . .] Jamie Telfer of the fair Dodhead [. . .]'. Like Burns, he also enjoyed reading from an early age: 'two or three old books lay in the window seat and were explored for my amusement in tedious winter days [. . .] Ramsay's *Tea-Table Miscellany* [was] my favourite'.[2]

Scott and Burns both acknowledged Allan Ramsay (1686–1758) as enriching their appreciation of the 'living tradition' as did Alexander MacDonald (Alasdair mac Mhaighstir Alasdair, c. 1700–70), son of an Ardnamurchan minister and educated at Edinburgh University in Ramsay's time. The Gaelic bard began his 'Oran an t-Samhraidh' (Song for Summer) with a verse inspired by Ramsay's 'Through the Wood, Laddie', from the *Tea-Table Miscellany*.[3] Ramsay, who co-founded the 'Easy Club',[4] had himself been so inspired by the vitality of the poems and songs he heard that he not only composed poems and songs for this anthology, but also collected the ones he heard for another four volumes, *The Ever Green, Being a Collection of Scots Poems Written by the Ingenious before 1600*. Both sets were published in 1724. The following year, reflecting his great interest in theatre, he composed and published a *pastorale*, 'The Gentle Shepherd', which gave rise to a new form, the ballad opera.[5] Though Ramsay died the year before Burns was born and the *Tea-Table Miscellany* was in its twelfth edition when the young Walter Scott came across it, yet Allan Ramsay's influence is of such significance that, to this day, he is regarded as a leader in international ballad scholarship.

From youth, Scott had acquired a repertoire of Border ballads that would take 'several days in the recitation' and he was familiar with their exact locations, having often explored them on horseback. At the age of twenty-one, he began collecting ballads during expeditions made with fellow Borderers and ballad enthusiasts, William Laidlaw, John Leyden and James Hogg. They too contributed to the collection, as Scott had impressed upon them his intention of writing down as much as possible from the living tradition lest it should be lost. Even partly recalled fragments were noted as well as background history, traditions and local anecdotes, which went into the preparation of Scott's *Minstrelsy of the Scottish Border*. Published between 1802 and 1803, this contained 112 ballads, more than a quarter of which were claimed not to have appeared hitherto in print.[6] They included 'Clerk Saunders', 'The Douglas Tragedy', 'Johnnie o' Bradislee', 'Proud Lady Margaret', 'The Cruel Sister', 'The Wife of Usher's Well' and, widest known of all, 'The Queen's Maries'.

Scott's collection became the catalyst for other enthusiasts and new collections soon followed. To mention but a few: in Dumfriesshire Charles Kirkpatrick Sharpe produced an anthology of stories remembered from his nursemaid; in the north-east, historian and printer Peter Buchan (1790–1854) collected local folk songs and folk tales;[7] and, in Edinburgh, a young publisher, Robert Chambers (1802–71), gathered 'Fireside Nursery Stories' for his *Popular Rhymes of Scotland* (1826), in turn influencing every succeeding generation of social historians, folklorists and general readers, both Scots and Gaelic as well as Norn.[8]

The nineteenth century saw a blossoming of folk-song and folk-tale collection in many countries, particularly after the publication of two volumes of German folktales, *Die Kinder- und Hausmärchen* (1812–15), written down from local storytellers by Jacob Grimm (1785–1863) and his brother Wilhelm (1786–1859). The work of the Grimms, besides the popularity of tales still enjoyed in over 150 languages, was seminal to international narrative scholarship, as readers interested in literature, language and anthropology soon noticed striking similarities in folk tales of other countries. Aschenputtel, for example, known generally in the English-speaking world as Cinderella, turns up as 'Rashie Coatie' in Scotland, while Rumpelstilzchen, or Rumpelstiltskin, is told as 'Whuppity Stoorie' in the Lowlands and as 'Peerie Fool' in the Orkney Islands.

The folk tale, 'Der Froschkönig oder der eiserne Heinrich' ('The Frog King'),[9] in which a frog asks a princess to marry him, has long enjoyed popularity among Gaelic storytellers whose frog naturally speaks Gaelic. When he reminds the princess of the promise she made to him, he says:

A chaoimheag, a chaoimheag, an cuimhneach leat
An gealladh beag a thug thu aig an tobar dhomh, a ghaoil, a ghaoil?

[Gentle one, gentle one, do you remember
the promise you gave me beside the well, my love, my love?][10]

Collected in the mid-1800s by John Francis Campbell of Islay – Iain Òg Ìle (Young John of Islay) as the 'son of the big house' was known – the story is one of several hundred folk tales written down from the Gaelic tradition. What began in 1847 as a hobby turned into a project in 1858 when, as a British government diplomat, he happened to discuss story-telling with a colleague, Sir George Webb Dasent who had met Jacob Grimm in Stockholm in 1842.[11] Dasent, whose passion was Norse folk tales, and had meanwhile been hoping to find an 'English Grimm' to take up the study in Britain, encouraged Iain Òg Ìle to begin in his native area of Scotland, the Gaelic-speaking West Highlands.

Shortly afterwards, and with financial assistance from the Duke of Argyll,[12] Campbell recruited Gaelic-speaking collectors, requesting that, as far as possible, the exact words of the teller should be written down.[13] He also specified that they should collect folk tales rather than legends. Within two years Campbell and his small team had written down almost 800 tales from Gaelic Scotland.[14] In preparing a selection for publication, Campbell added his own translations and scholarly notes with international comparisons, as he was conversant with over a dozen languages. He also noted several Scottish variants of the Frog King, including 'Wearie Well at the Warldis End' from Robert Chambers,[15] adding that 'There are many versions still current in Scotland, told in broad Scots; and it can be traced back to 1548.'[16] In his extensive travels, Campbell combed the literature of Scandinavia, Russia, France, Germany, America, Korea, India, the Philippines, Ceylon (as Sri Lanka was then called) and beyond, adding annotations to his four-volume collection *Popular Tales of the West Highlands* (1860–2). Critically acclaimed as 'the Arabian Nights of Celtic Scotland' (*The Times*, 5 November 1860),

Campbell's work stands not only as a milestone in international narrative scholarship to this day, but also as the model for many collections of the living tradition of storytelling.

Every story, no matter how long, short, ancient or modern, consists of a series of 'motifs': single elements such as 'milk-white steed', 'golden apples' or 'lily-white hands', woven together to depict characters and create the plot of a story. The phrase 'spinning a yarn' seems apt, as motifs are the raw material out of which any story can be woven. The content can vary as widely as the setting; general descriptions such as 'by the fireside' might evoke a specific location or none at all. It could, however, be a cottage, castle, council house, chieftain's hall, taigh cèilidh, bothy, caravan, traveller's tent, pub, workman's hut or school playground. Within each story there will be differences from teller to teller, group to group. Those inclined to classify differentiate between kinds of stories told, recognising key elements that distinguish one group from another; thus they may refer to a particular story as myth, folk tale, legend or anecdote. As these terms have gained international currency and are not interchangeable, they are summarised here. If in doubt, however, they may simply be referred to as 'stories'.[17]

Myths belong to the remote past. More often than not there are sacred elements and characters such as gods and demi-gods, giants, wondrous animals, birds, people and places. Despite incredible motifs such as 'a giant with three heads and flames shooting out of them' or 'food that is provided miraculously', a myth should not be regarded as untrue; it is an ancient story that attempts to explain the mysteries of nature, creation or cultural tradition.

Folk tales, such as those collected by Campbell of Islay, may share some motifs with myths (for example, giants and magical plants), but they are told primarily for entertainment, without the expectation of belief. As the plot unfolds, anything can happen: a skull can speak, animals can talk, or the princess can talk only if she meets someone who can perform impossible tasks or solve impossible riddles. As the characters emerge and the plot unfolds, the folk tale often shines light and hope on aspects of real life: a desperate situation, extreme poverty, a moral dilemma are all dealt with time and time again. Some folk tales with a transparently didactic purpose are called 'fables', such as 'The Fox and the Crow', famously included in the collection by Aesop.

The distinguishing feature of legends is that they are told as true, regardless of whether listeners believe such a story or not. Legends may be about secular or sacred subjects, dating back to a time that may be identified as being in a certain century or simply 'some time' in the past. The plot revolves around human (therefore credible) characters though the appearance of supernatural beings such as ghosts, witches or fairies, broonies, and trows, is common as they are all encountered in human experience.[18]

Religious legends about saints are often connected to a particular place, for example, Kilmaluag in Skye, which takes its name from St Moluag. Far from being localised, however, such legends were often relocalised:[19] there are legends about Moluag in Argyll where he is regarded as the patron saint; he also appears in Aberdeenshire and Perthshire legends, and in the Isle of Lewis, where Moluag, known for his gift of curing madness, gives his name to the church near Ness, Teampull Mholuaidh. Glasgow has its St Mungo (or Kentigern) while Fife's St Andrew belongs to all of Scotland. The legend of how Andrew became the patron saint may vary from telling to telling but its significance to the nation lies more in its symbolic truth than in provable historical facts of the story.

There are also religious legends explaining why some plants and animals are connected with a saint or deity. For example, the 'thumb-print' on the haddock is attributed to St Peter, from the time Christ told his disciples to 'let down their nets'.[20] Tradition has it that the first fish Peter pulled from the heavily laden net was a haddock, which, ever after, bears the mark of the sacred thumb-print. In Scotland the story varies from area to area and some children who hear it at an early age remember how to tell the difference between a haddock and a whiting: only the haddock has Peter's thumb-print. Legends about why the aspen quivers, the dung-beetle lives in such an undesirable place, or the robin has a red breast are usually heard in childhood and stay with listeners till they in turn tell them to a new generation. Although such legends are sometimes said to be 'from the Bible', on closer examination only an occasional motif can be found: for example, Peter is, indeed, asked to let down his net, but where is there mention of a haddock? The legend is entirely from oral tradition as are certain maxims cited as 'biblical truths' such as, 'a whistling woman and a crowing hen makes the Devil come out of his den'.[21]

Scotland shares with Ireland a large repertoire of medieval legends about Celtic heroes remembered from approximately the first century AD. As the sea between the two countries was a main highway, it is not surprising that many adventures of Irish heroes and heroines were acclaimed in Gaelic stories and songs. One legend has Cù Chulainn, the warrior and champion of Ulster, trained in the art of combat by a formidable Albannach (Scottish) woman, later localised to Skye, called Scáthach, and he, in turn, bringing his warriors there to learn such skills. The poignant legends of Deirdre come down through fifteen centuries of Scottish, as well as Irish, tradition, as do legends and songs about the great warrior, Fionn mac Cumhaill, who led the king of Ireland's soldier-warriors, the Fians or Féinn.[22] Testifying to the remarkable strength of oral tradition, many of these stories survive to the present day, like the story of Diarmaid and Gràine, told by Donald Sinclair of Tiree to John MacInnes who recorded it for Edinburgh University's

School of Scottish Studies in 1960. The legend tells how Fionn's young wife, Gràinne, fell in love with his handsome nephew and one of his loyal warriors, Diarmaid. When Diarmaid resisted Gràinne's efforts to lure him, she enlisted the help of the fairies.

More recent legends include accounts of clans, their strong family ties, feuds and battles. Many are connected with musicians, such as MacCrimmons, MacArthurs, MacKays, or the Clarsair Dall (Blind Harper) and they weave together a colourful tapestry of clan history connecting not only past to present but also the natural and supernatural. There are no sharp dividing lines between the world of clan chiefs, musicians, landowners, crofters, ministers and priests and the world of fairies, ghosts, haunted places, witches and broonies, and the legends that recount them are simply stories 'told as true'.

The printed page as a reflection of living tradition has a long history not only among storytellers and singers, but also among spinners of yarns, jokes, conundrums and other verbal forms. Even the latest book of riddles can be found to echo elements of anthologies as old as Poggio Bracciolini's fourteenth-century collection from the Papal Court of Rome. For centuries the living tradition has been influenced by print, often to the surprise of literary scholars, folklorists and collectors, like America's Alan Lomax who, at the end of his world tour of folk-song collecting in 1951, remarked:

> What most impressed me was the vigour of the Scots folksong tradition, on the one hand, and its close connection with literary sources on the other [. . .] The Scots have the liveliest folk tradition of the British Isles, but, paradoxically, it is the most bookish.[23]

Nevertheless, what is commonplace 'at home' is often taken for granted, as with generations of Scottish singers who have treasured a favourite book, such as Cameron's *Lyric Gems*, Scott's *Minstrelsy*, Hogg's *Jacobite Relics*, Sinclair's *An t-Òranaiche*, MacKenzie's *Sàr-Obair* or MacLeod's *Clàrsach an Doire*.[24] Learning a song from oral tradition, however, does not require the singer to be able to read music or even words, as most traditional singers sing what they hear, regardless of what is 'in the book'. Curious as it may seem to anyone outside such singing traditions, very often the satisfaction of owning the book, especially in a time when they were not readily available or accessible, was in seeing the song in print. Among many examples recorded by folklorists was a Gaelic-speaking octogenarian Allan MacArthur (b. 1881) whom I recorded in 1970. After singing one of his favourite songs, 'Òran na Cailliche', which he learned from his mother and grandmother, he left the room and returned with 'the book', to show me the song.[25] The ensuing conversation revealed, however, that he was unable to read Gaelic, but could recognise that what he saw in print corresponded to the song he had learned from his maternal grandmother, who emigrated from Moidart in the early 1800s.[26] While he regretted not being able to read his mother tongue, he took pleasure in seeing the song in print and in being able to read (in English) about the bard who composed it.[27]

Until the appearance of mechanical and electronic recording devices, particularly the wax cylinder recorder of the early 1900s, books and manuscript collections were the mainstays of scholars the world over. There may be no song scholar in the world more significant to the study of the ballad than polymath Francis James Child (1825–96), son of a Boston sail-maker, who graduated from Harvard College in 1848. On a two-year study leave in Europe pursuing research in German philology, he found himself in such a creative and intellectually stimulating environment that, despite the many callings of academia, he would take it upon himself to do for the ballad what the Grimms had done for the folk tale. Returning to America as Harvard's newly appointed Professor of Rhetoric, Child began compiling the work which became the 'bible' of every ballad scholar: *The English and Scottish Popular Ballads*. In carrying out his aim 'to include every obtainable version of every extant English or Scottish ballad, with the fullest possible discussion of related songs or stories in the popular literature of all nations', Child amassed an enormous collection of books, manuscripts and letters including over twenty from John Francis Campbell of Islay.[28]

Having studied song collections in many languages,[29] Child identified 305 international ballads, assigning each a general title and an identification number that would become as vital to the ballad scholar as Linnaeus's Latin plant-names to the botanist. His main texts are from the British Isles (from the books, manuscripts and letters of earlier collectors such as Ramsay, Herd, Scott, Hogg and Motherwell) with comparative versions and notes reflecting an exhaustive search of every available source. Child's work became a lasting reference for ballad scholars, who, like botanists, continue their quest for new 'species', sparing no effort to compare their findings with others.

CHAPTER TWO

Genre

Emily Lyle, Valentina Bold, Ian Russell

Ballad
Emily Lyle

Although ballads can be firmly identified as songs, there has been considerable dispute about how exactly to define the ballad genre within this broad category. In the context of studies of Scottish traditional literature, however, we can assume a special concern with the Scottish ballads, one of the finest expressions of Scottish culture, with international importance. A particular category of ballad, which could perhaps be called the Scottish classical ballad, has had this high level of impact. Ballads of this type treat topics like feuds and border-raiding, for example, 'The Bonnie House o Airlie' and 'The Battle of Otterburn'; young lovers and the happy or tragic results of their attempts to marry, for example, 'Katharine Jaffray' and 'The Braes o Yarrow'; and contacts with supernatural beings, e.g. 'Tam Lin'. They treat them in a particular manner with powerful aesthetic effects. There are some humorous pieces, e.g. 'The Keach i the Creel', but in general they are marked by emotional intensity rather than comic perceptions of the human condition.

The word 'ballad' can be used loosely to refer to any kind of song: its strict definition rests on a distinction the poet William Shenstone made in the eighteenth century. He wrote to Thomas Hull in connection with Thomas Percy's proposed edition of the *Reliques*:

> I know not how far I am *singular*; but as I love to avail myself of different Words, to bundle up Ideas in different Parcels, it is become habitual to me, to call *that* a *Ballad* which describes or implies some Action; on the other Hand, I term that a *Song*, which contains only an Expression of *Sentiment*.[1]

This is remarkably exact. It would have been easy to say simply that ballads describe some action and accordingly are narratives, but Shenstone observes that they may simply 'imply' some action. Ballads are not all good-going narratives unfolding stories. The emotional response to events is often present and may dominate to the point where the actual story is lost altogether.

Historically, ballads started out as narratives, but their whole development seemed like a denial of that origin as they moved towards the expression of their emotional core,[2] as in the lingering on the sadness of the execution of a young woman in 'Mary Hamilton', in a verse remembered by Robert Burns who provided the first known record of this ballad in 1790:

> Little did my Mother think,
> That day she cradled me,
> What Land I was to travel in,
> Or what death I should die![3]

Other versions contain poignant stanzas when Mary Hamilton contrasts her life as one of the queen's four waiting maids in the court's splendid setting with the death coming to her and, finally, contemplates the absence her death will leave, as in this verse recorded from Nancy Hamilton and Mrs Gentles in 1825:

> Yestreen the queen had four Maries,
> This night she'll hae but three;
> There was Mary Beaton, and Mary Seaton,
> And Mary Carmichael, and me.[4]

The change of treatment from narrative to more lyric mode leads to consideration of what can be meant by movement of ballads through time. Ballads occur in multiple versions. They are anonymous as we have them, the end result of a process whereby narratives, composed by individuals whose names we do not know, were sung for centuries by people in oral environments with no sense of a fixed text and where modifications were constantly made. In the case of 'Mary Hamilton', for example, we meet a radical variation where the young woman escapes being hanged and there is no tragic outcome.[5] Although we do quite often know the names of the singers from whom our various versions were derived and we sometimes know the names of those from whom they learned the ballads, these are simply single points of information out of an accumulation of singers and listeners about whom we know nothing.

Towards the end of the eighteenth century and at the beginning of the nineteenth, as part of a wave of interest in Scottish national song,[6] many ballad texts and tunes were taken down from singers. Some collections of ballads were published in Scotland in the nineteenth century,[7] but none had enough scope to do full justice to the key concept of variation. It was Francis James Child of Harvard University, as Margaret Bennett has observed in

Chapter 1, who initiated a sufficiently large-scale project to allow this. His five-volume collection, *The English and Scottish Popular Ballads*, appeared in 1882–96. He aimed to publish all the versions of the 305 ballads he selected, expending much energy in tracing Scottish manuscript collections he had heard of in order to include their contents.[8] Today, the versions from two additional major nineteenth-century collections that he missed, those in the Crawfurd and Glenbuchat manuscripts,[9] can also be taken into account when studying this period. Child agonised about what to include and not to include in his set of ballads, but there were no firm criteria at the periphery of his collection and we need not follow him in his cut-off points in the continuum of narrative song. However, it is customary to attach Child numbers to ballads as a means of identification – something especially useful since versions of the same ballad may go by quite different names. Another American scholar, Bertrand Bronson, was responsible for adding the missing musical dimension in his four-volume collection *The Traditional Tunes of the Child Ballads* (1956–72), which followed Child's schema.

Interestingly, the end result of collecting activity is a body of different versions for a single ballad, which allows people nowadays to immerse themselves in a considerable range. This situation has some similarity to that in the oral culture from which the versions were taken: there, it was quite likely that a person would hear a ballad sung in a variety of different ways. An individual eventually singing a ballad, heard from a variety of sources, put a personal stamp on it, selecting from those, as well as modifying text in the ways available even when there was only a single source. It seems likely that in most cases the singer initially experimented and then settled on a preferred text, which remained generally stable, although not totally fixed. A singer was, of course, totally free to pick another version of the same ballad and sing that as well.

Linguistically the ballads are in 'thin Scots', largely comprehensible to Standard English speakers, with occasional words that might require glossing. The ballad, typically, launches straight into its story, and intersperses its third-person narration with passages of direct speech, which may or may not be explicitly assigned to a speaker. Ballad narrative in one way is swift, calling on the active participation of the recipient to fill out such things as the passage of time and the details of a setting, while it concentrates on key events. In another way, it has a slow tempo as, for instance, when it pauses to devote two or three verses to saying much the same thing in largely identical wording. The latter effects a shift into a contemplative mode of reception.

The ballad stanza is a quatrain made up of alternating four-beat and three-beat lines with the second and fourth lines rhyming (an abcb rhyme-scheme).[10] We might think only this metre defines a ballad, but things are not so simple and the positing of the idea of a core formulation can be valuable.[11] At the core of the ballad concept is a narrative in ballad metre. And we can add another dimension to the core concept – such a narrative has its paradigmatic existence when it is being sung. This, of course, implies the existence of melody to which it is sung. Again, the position is not simple and clear-cut: a specific ballad text may have a distinctive tune (and can be said to be sung 'to its own tune') or may be sung to a variety of tunes. Even when it has a distinctive tune wedded to it, there is no proprietary right that means the tune could not be used with a different ballad, or indeed with another kind of song. So the ideal ballad form being constructed is a sung narrative in ballad metre. Clearly there is a limitation here not to be taken literally. When the ballad is not actually being performed, it still may exist in written or printed form or in memory. The singing voice actualises it fully, but there may be partial actualisations if the ballad is spoken or read silently, and there is the interesting point that, when the ballad is read silently by someone who is aware of 'the' tune, or 'a' tune selected for the reading, the inner experience can be one of silent performance.

Part of the definition of the ballad genre lies in the existence of multiple versions brought about in the course of transmission. We can see to some extent how modifications came about, but where did the ballads being reshaped come from, and when did they arise? A genre can have horizons and one of these is set by the English/Scots ballad metre stanza form, which was first available in the thirteenth century and became more common in the centuries that followed.[12] This is to say that ballads do not have extreme antiquity. Although the motifs found in them (such as the 'singing bone' that reveals the murderer in Child 12 'The Twa Sisters') may go back to a much more ancient level of culture, the ballads themselves do not, coming from late medieval and early modern times. The earliest Scottish historical ballad that can specifically be dated is Child 178 'Captain Car, or, Edom o Gordon' which relates to the burning of Corgarff Castle in Aberdeenshire in 1571 and is found in a sixteenth-century manuscript where its opening runs:

> It befell at Martynmas,
>   When wether waxed colde,
> Captaine Care said to his men,
>   We must go take a holde.[13]

There is no metrical change to define another horizon and it can be argued that we have not reached one. James Porter in particular sees a future for the ballad genre,[14] but it is clear that aspects of the ballad died with the coming of modernity. The world of the classical ballads was a distinctive one that already seemed old in the late eighteenth century. Nearly all of the classical ballads were known by 1820, giving us something of an end-point for the generative oral tradition of the classical ballads as a separate phenomenon, although ballad metre and narrative continued to be fruitful in parody and political song.

Porter rightly points out that the ballads come alive in a performance context where both singers and hearers experience what he calls 'presence',[15] and it should be noted that the refrains and last-line repeats found in a number of ballads lend themselves to audience participation. A refrain may come at the end of a stanza or single refrain lines may alternate with the narrative lines, as in Child 11 'The Cruel Brother':

> She leand her oer the saddle-bow,
>   With a hey ho and a lillie gay
> To give him a kiss ere she did go.
>   As the primrose spreads so sweetly
>
> He has taen a knife, baith lang and sharp,
>   With a hey ho and a lillie gay
> And stabbd that bonny bride to the heart.
>   As the primrose spreads so sweetly[16]

A refrain may be detached in sense from the narrative line. Clearly, in this case, the nonsense syllables and flower references of the refrain do not echo the harsh theme of a vengeful brother's murder of his sister on her wedding day, but rather contrast with it. It should be mentioned that, although in modern performances singers of ballads often employ instrumental accompaniment, the tradition of ballad-singing in Scotland, so far as we can reach back in time, has been for the unaccompanied solo voice, with the possibility in some cases of the support of other voices in refrains.

The ballad has continued to have presence in Scotland. The singing tradition's preservation, especially in the traveller community up to and beyond the period of the folk-song revival of the latter part of the twentieth century, has averted any danger of its becoming a bookish phenomenon.[17]

Folk Narrative
Valentina Bold

> This is a culture that bonds [. . .] There's so much beauty on the earth if we look for it.   Stanley Robertson[18]

Folk narrative, to appropriate John Hodgart on ballad, is 'as hard to define' as 'easy to recognise'.[19] Many would assume it is primarily oral in character; however, it cannot be isolated from the literary, whether at point of origin, or the point of capture/collection. Perhaps 'folk narrative' could be understood as any narrative 'belonging' to people in Scotland, in whatever folk group to which they show allegiance at a particular time (national, regional, ethnic, family, gender, religiously- or occupationally-based).[20] Perhaps a sense of possession, by teller and audience, is more marked with folk narrative than with literary texts. Then, there are the related issues of language choices (including English, Scots or Gaelic) and transcription (as it affects reception) along with interrelationships with folk drama,[21] custom and song. Here, folk narrative is considered in four ways – as collected item; performed text; generically related; and subject for analysis.

Scotland has a long and distinguished record of collecting folk narratives in manuscript and recorded forms (for private or archival use), printed anthologies and within biographical or place-based materials. Martin Martin's pioneering *Description of the Western Isles of Scotland, c. 1695*, for instance, includes a wealth of information, from a Gaelic speaker, about the narrative traditions of this area. Robert Chambers's *The Popular Rhymes of Scotland* (1826) and *Scottish Jests and Anecdotes* (1832) are groundbreaking. Hugh Miller's *Scenes and Legends of the North of Scotland* (1835) is important, along with J. F. Campbell's *Popular Tales of the West Highlands* (1860–2). As a survey of the historical development of collection in Scotland, Donald Smith's *Storytelling Scotland* (2001) is an excellent introduction.

In terms of concerted national collecting, the 1951 foundation of Edinburgh University's School of Scottish Studies (now part of Celtic and Scottish Studies) has played a substantial and continuing role, from the pioneering work of Hamish Henderson and Calum MacLean onwards (the latter particularly with Gaelic material) to Alan Bruford, John Shaw and others. In terms of diaspora traditions, too – again, too sizeable a topic to consider in any depth here – there is a long tradition of collecting; for instance, that of Helen Creighton in Nova Scotia or that represented by the Western Australian Folklore Archive.[22] The Scottish Storytelling Centre has become a forum for the transmission and enjoyment of orally-performed texts; the Scottish Storytelling Festival, first held in 1989 in Edinburgh, has become a crucial arena for the promulgation of the artform. Recently, a wide range of material has become available on-line, often with useful, contextual support materials. For instance, *Tobar an Dualchais/Kist o Riches* offers free access to 26,000 oral recordings made in Scotland from the 1930s onwards. Its predecessor, the *Pearl* website, offers access both to archived folk narratives in Gaelic, Scots and English, and also to those already published in the journal *Tocher*. Regionally focused sites that include manuscript and printed forms of folk narrative include *Am Baile. Highland History and Culture* and NEFA (The North East Folklore Archive). The SCRAN website is another rich access point, including sound and video recordings of storytellers.[23]

Even though they can be read as autonomous, stories should not simply be separated from their tellers, or creators, whether individuals or community – the transmission process makes them, in effect, joint efforts. As a form, folk narrative is far more adaptable than the fixed literary text; manner of delivery, for instance, can sometimes (if not always) vary in response to storyteller or audience demands, needs or preferences. Each occasion generates a different experience and the storyteller's art depends on understanding this process: a story told in an intimate family setting will be delivered and received in a context-driven way (this allows, for instance, the storyteller to explain resonances to children as the story continues); the same tale retold in a festival, or printed in a book, will lose much of its intimacy, although, arguably, it may gain from a more theatrical framing.

Performance contexts have certainly changed dramatically over the past millennium, as interactions between the oral and print (from chapbooks and literary retellings of folk narratives to film and television contexts) have widened and deepened. From the purpose-specific website (too many to list), to the tweeted joke, circulation can be instant and (arguably) superficial. The proliferation of local clubs and storytelling circles[24] again establishes new contexts for transmission. The Scottish Storytelling Centre website[25] includes a register of people from diverse cultural and ethnic backgrounds, places of residence and interests, whilst also providing resources, education and advocacy for the art form as a relevant activity for all age groups and needs. Publicly commended individuals include James Hogg's grandfather, Will o' Phaup, allegedly the last man to see the fairies in Scotland, and certainly benefiting from his grandson's ability to highlight his skills. The collecting work outlined above has highlighted the incomparable work of traveller storytellers, from Jeannie Robertson and her family, including her nephew, the late and peerless Stanley, to Alexander Stewart of Lairg, the Williamsons (particularly the great Duncan Williamson), Betsy Whyte of Montrose, Sheila Stewart of Blairgowrie and others too numerous to mention.

Broadly speaking, folk narratives are usually grouped into 'minor' (proverbs, riddles, sayings, anecdotes, jokes) and 'major' genres (anecdotes, tall tales, folk drama, legends and myths, *Märchen* and oral histories).[26] The latter include animal tales (Scotland holding a distinguished record in fables through, for instance, Henryson; see Chapter 5); tales of local worthies; and, most recently, the 'chat show' anecdote, employing its own distinctive idioms. Then there is legend, whose main characteristic is often referred to as verisimilitude – these are stories told as if they are true, with validating details (dates, names, places). Categories within include the historical (legends about the past) and origin myth, as well as the contemporary legend – the urban 'myths', often circulated in print and internet media. Jan Harold Brunvand categorises a series of these from the 'Phantom Hitchhiker' to 'the Hook'; in a Scottish context, the work of Sandy Hobbs is also important, along with insights in the *Perspectives on Contemporary Legend* series (1984–90).[27] Contemporary legends are often said to express social fears, for instance about the vulnerability of the young (particularly women).

Probably the best known and certainly the most studied of the major genres is 'Märchen' (a technical term adapted from the 1812 *Kinder- und Hausmärchen* of the brothers Wilhelm and Jacob Grimm), also known as wonder, or fairy tales, although they do not always feature fairies. The Märchen is an adventure tale: coming from humble beginnings, the hero/ine endures a series of challenges (supernatural and natural) which s/he meets, often in opposition to the older and supposedly wiser siblings who precede him/her on their journey, winning, by the end, a throne and a wealthy, attractive partner: this, it is implied, is his/her just deserts for being pure at heart, even if simple in demeanour.

In terms of analytical techniques, folk narrative offers many possibilities. Particularly from the nineteenth century onwards, there was an attempt to classify their national and international dimensions, often for political ends. The Grimms said tales with close resemblances, found worldwide, were part of an Indo-European tradition, rooted in antiquity. This premise informs the two major reference collections for tales: Antti Aarne and Stith Thompson's *The Types of the Folktale* (1964) and Stith Thompson's *Motif-Index of Folk-Literature* (1955–8).

Folk narratives are generally seen, too, to be non-linear in structure: events are ranked by importance, rather than when they chronologically happened. They have been presented, from the early twentieth century onwards, as structurally predictable, as indicated in Vladimir Propp's influential *Morphology of the Folktale*. Equally, they have been seen as psychologically revealing, from Freud's study of *Jokes and their Relation to the Unconscious*, to Jung on dream narratives, to the more recent work of Alan Dundes. Equally, they have been seen as socially relevant and gender-significant (Marina Warner) by a variety of critics, academic and otherwise.[28] They have been seen as quasi-political too: defining a nation or, at the micro-level, a region, from Ernest Marwick's *The Folklore of Orkney and Shetland* to Alan Temperley's *Tales of Galloway*.[29]

Folk Song in Scotland
Ian Russell

Scottish folk song is not a single genre, but multifaceted and multi-formed. It is impossible to produce a simple definition of the term, or suggest that 'authenticity' in terms of Scottish origins is a yardstick. Gavin Greig and James Bruce Duncan realised, as they undertook their mighty collection of north-east folk songs in the early twentieth century that variants of almost half the songs they noted were also found in English and/or Irish tradition.[30] Folk-song scholarship categorises the repertoire by thematic content – 'Songs of Love' or 'Songs of War', for example – but this cuts the singer from the song, and the song from its context in time and place. This chapter, therefore, explores characteristics or key elements of folk song grounded in performance, taking account of tradition's dynamic nature.

The relationship between the lyrical songs of the late eighteenth and early nineteenth centuries and the narrative ballads that pre-dated them is a useful starting point. When John MacDonald of Elgin sang 'The Roving Ploughboy' in the 1950s and 1960s, not only did he perform a song redolent with the romance of agricultural life in the north-east lowlands prior to mechanisation, but it resonated with this earlier repertory.

> Come saddle tae me my auld grey mare
> Come saddle tae me my pony O
> An I'll tak the road an I'll go far away
> After my rovin ploughboy O.

The song relates directly to part of 'The Gypsy Laddie' (Child 200), but it sits more naturally as part of the bothy ballad tradition, albeit from a female perspective. The process whereby a lyrical song is created from a longer narrative has been explained in terms of the singer's desire to hold onto a memorable 'emotional core'.[31]

Each of these songs exists side by side as part of a traditional repertoire characterised by oral transmission – the same song can exist in multiple variations, set to different tunes or different versions of the same tune. When Elizabeth Stewart, a member of the Aberdeenshire Fetterangus Stewart family, performs 'The Butcher Boy',[32] she is singing a deeply disturbing murder ballad that exists in countless variations in the English-speaking world under such titles as 'The Wexford Miller' in Ireland and 'The Prentice Boy' in England.[33] Hallmarks of orality include motifs, such as 'ye shine whaur ye stand'[34] in praise of place, repetitions as in the verse above of 'The Roving Ploughboy', epithets such as 'milk-white steed', commonplaces such as 'Come all ye [. . .]', and the so-called 'floating verse', e.g. 'I wish, I wish, but I wish in vein, / I wish I were a maid again, / But a maid again I'll never be, / Till apples grow on an orange tree.'[35]

Another important element concerns the relationship of orality to print culture. Many songs in the traditional repertoire, such as 'Blooming Caroline o Edinburgh Toon',[36] were printed in popular vernacular media – broadsides, chapbooks, or in songsters – at some point in their existence. A notable example is the Poet's Box press.[37] This form of transmission often aided the song's distribution. A healthy interaction existed between the printed and oral versions of the same song, such that some of the characteristics of oral tradition, for example, textual variation, have been shown to exist in broadside versions, albeit to a lesser extent.[38]

Poets, song makers and song collectors of the eighteenth and nineteenth centuries from Allan Ramsay (1686–1758) to Robert Chambers (1802–71) (see Chapter 9) published collections of folk song and ballads, often refining and 'polishing' them for their genteel audiences. As David Buchan has noted,[39] they tried to write their own songs in the same style, but these remained contrived imitations and never achieved vernacular currency or appeal. There are, however, some notable exceptions that crossed freely from literary to oral contexts, especially the songs of Robert Burns (1759–96), particularly 'Ae Fond Kiss' and 'Willie Brewed a Peck o Maut',[40] and Lady Nairne (1766–1845), such as 'The Laird o Cockpen' and 'Caller Herrin'.[41]

Geographical provenance and historical development are key, though it is not enough to note that John MacDonald's 'The Roving Ploughboy' had a nineteenth-century origin in the north-east of Scotland. We need to take account of the significance of the song in the Scottish folk-song revival of the 1950s and 1960s, its contextual and performative dimensions, as well as current status in, for example, the Curriculum for Excellence in contemporary Scottish education.[42] It is also helpful to think in terms of prevalence and prominence; vernacular as opposed to high arts; and performance, by individuals from groups and communities who value and nurture such songs over generations, as distinct from the mass marketing of popular music – bottom up as opposed to top down. We should not, though, ignore the ways in which a song such as that of Roy Williamson of the Corries, 'Flower of Scotland' (dating from 1965), has reflected and contributed to national identity.

The performance of a folk song is essentially about communication of meaning, emotions and values, within relationships. One of the foremost traditional singers who has regularly performed at traditional music festivals and clubs for over forty years is Sheila Stewart (b. 1937), a member of the well-known Traveller family from Perthshire. When she performs 'The Berry Fields of Blair',[43] a widely-known song which her mother, Belle, wrote, not only does she do so in memory of her mother (1906–97), but also as a celebration of the gathering of migratory workers, especially Scottish Travellers, and with a certain nostalgia for seasonal harvesting events. Such events were witnessed and vividly documented by the foremost post-World War Two Scottish folk-song collector, Hamish Henderson (1909–2002) (see Chapter 14).[44]

The question of known authorship of songs has caused debate; some scholars maintained that this automatically disqualified a song from the 'canon' of folk song.[45] This is plainly nonsensical and numerous examples exist to rebut such a statement. One of the best known is 'The Wild Mountain Thyme'[46] and the many other variants recorded in Scotland and the north of Ireland of 'The Braes of Balquhidder',[47] which was written by Robert Tannahill (1774–1810), the Paisley weaver poet. A contemporary example is 'Yellow on the Broom', based on the life of Betsy Whyte (1919–88), a Traveller woman from Perthshire and Angus, which is widely sung both in Scotland and beyond.[48] The words were written by Adam McNaughtan and set to a traditional tune, 'The Female Drummer Boy'.[49] Another recent example of a 'composed' song becoming a part of contemporary song tradition, particularly in the north-east coastal villages, is 'Come A' Ye Fisher Lassies', which was written by Ewan MacColl for the BBC Radio Ballad, *Singing the Fishing*.[50]

In the early 1950s the man who energised the Scottish folk-song revival and collected songs alongside Hamish Henderson was the American, Alan Lomax (1915–2002).[51] His brief was to record for Columbia Records' World Library of Folk and Primitive Music, and in the north-east through the offices of a well known singer and entertainer, John Mearns,[52] he met and recorded the Buchan farmer John Strachan (1875–1958), and from the opposite end of the social spectrum two itinerants, Jimmy MacBeath (1894–1972) and Davie Stewart (1901–72), all three of whom were fine singers of 'bothy ballads'.[53] These essentially occupational songs, relate, often with wry humour, to working conditions on the farms, as well as diet, the character of the employers and fellow farm-workers, and the social life such as it was. Lomax described Strachan's singing:

> He sang [. . .] with the rant of the old-time singer of tales. His eyes sparkled, his face flushed with pleasure, his burry Scots voice romped through the verse as he swung his powerful arms in time to the beat of a ballad.[54]

While at John Mearns's house in Cedar Place, Aberdeen, Lomax heard children playing in the street and within minutes he was recording their songs and singing games.

The most obvious marker of Scottish identity is the use of vernacular Scots language, as in the drinking song 'Hame Drunk Cam I' and in bothy ballads, such as Davie Stewart's 'Tarves Rant' – 'So come aa ye jolly ploughrin lads, a warnin tak by me, / If ye gang doon tae Tarves, noo dinna get on the spree.'[55] Although Scottish folk songs share many themes with English and Irish repertoires, there are distinct characteristics in terms of place, people, occupation and allegiance. Thus singers perform songs of military provenance, for example, 'The Stoutest Man in the Forty Twa'[56] and 'The Forfar Soldier'[57]; in praise of place, 'Bonnie Udny'[58] and 'Tramps and Hawkers'[59]; songs of hardship, 'Jute Mill Song'[60] and 'Shift and Spin'[61]; songs that express disaffection, 'McCafferty'[62] and 'Jamie Raeburn'[63]; and songs of disasters including 'The Blantyre Explosion'[64] and 'The Donibristle Disaster'.[65]

In the early twenty-first century we are well resourced with regard to Scottish folk song. Not only is there the eight-volume *Greig–Duncan Folk Song Collection*,[66] but an equally significant set of volumes is to be published over the next nine years, *The James Madison Carpenter Collection*.[67] Some very useful collections have been published since the Second World War, including two edited by Norman Buchan[68] and two edited by Sheila Douglas.[69] Recordings of source singers on CDs have been well provided, with the inclusion of many tracks on the Topic Records twenty-volume *The Voice of the People* series and the series taken over by Greentrax for the School of Scottish Studies, *Scottish Tradition*. Two excellent web resources are *Tobar an Dualchais/Kist o Riches*[70] and Learning Teaching Scotland.[71] Moreover, there are many fine singers and interpreters of Scottish traditional folk song on the touring circuit, besides songwriters working in a traditional register.

CHAPTER THREE

Folk Belief and Scottish Traditional Literatures

Lizanne Henderson

This chapter concerns supernatural belief systems and traditions, like witches, fairies, brownies and second sight, and the ways they have manifested in various forms of Scottish traditional literatures. It focuses primarily on folk narrative, which can be split into two main genres – folktale and legend – and further divided into various sub-genres. Folk tale, for instance, includes the *Märchen* or wonder tale, animal tale, novella, jocular tale (numbskull or noodle tale), *Schwänke* or merry tale, and the tall tale. Legend can incorporate the aetiological, religious, supernatural, historical, personal (anecdote and memorate) and place-related. Within these broad categorisations there is much overlap and inter-relatedness.

Like folk literature, folk belief has undergone several scholarly attempts towards a definition. In the sixteenth and seventeenth centuries, when arguably folk belief was under attack as never before, the agenda was primarily concerned with separating 'supernatural or magical beliefs, as held by the folk, from supernatural or magical beliefs, as expressed in religion'.[1] By the eighteenth and nineteenth centuries, the focus was redirected predominantly towards debasing folk beliefs as relics of superstition and signs of backwardness, no longer befitting the enlightened and civilised world. Somewhat contradicting this view was the concomitant rise in folklore collecting, well under way by the mid-nineteenth century. The term 'folklore' was itself invented by William Thoms in 1846, in part a response to the fear that folkloric customs and traditions were fast dying out and had to be saved for posterity. Regrettably, in Britain at least, 'folklore' often carried a pejorative sense, a problem that has far from vanished from current usage.

Folk literature's multiformity is one of the characteristics marking it out from high literature. While the latter exists as a set version of a specific text, written by an acknowledged author, the former can exist in multiple variations and is multi-authored. Indeed the 'author', as such, is generally unknown and it can be fruitless trying to establish the date of original composition or geographical provenance. In the early days of folk literature collecting, which picked up pace in the nineteenth century, the historic-geographic method was favoured. This was basically an attempt to recover all known versions of a story in pursuit of the archetype, or Ur-text, of the tale. A highly comparative approach, it attempted to trace the story's international path back to its original source. By the mid-twentieth century, the pursuit of origins was mostly abandoned in favour of a contextualist approach, emphasising instead social context and the tale's performative aspects. There are also certain structural characteristics that have been detected in folk literature, by such pioneering folk narrative scholars as Axel Olrik – who noted the tendency of folk tale to concentrate on a single plot strand, patterning and repetition, and the 'law of three' – and Vladimir Propp, who discerned twenty-one character functions in folk tale.[2] Reidar Christiansen's list of migratory legend, as well as Stith Thompson's motif-index, and his work with Antti Aarne on the categorisation of folk tale into basic types, have also been hugely influential in how we understand and interpret folk narrative.[3]

Antiquarians and folklore collectors of the eighteenth to early twentieth centuries often lamented what they perceived as the death of folk beliefs, customs, traditionary tales and legends in the wake of rising literacy rates and educational advancements, as if folklore were innocent victim of progress and the civilising process. William Motherwell harkened back to past days when 'it was a common country pastime of a winter's night to while time away by repeating proverbs, telling tales, and reciting songs and ballads; but these old fashions are fast disappearing since the schoolmaster and politics were let loose upon the country'.[4] Robert Chambers (1802–71), from Peebles, described the folktales he collected 'of a simple kind, befitting the minds which they were to regale [. . .] they breathed of a time when society was in its simplest elements, and the most familiar natural things were as yet unascertained from the supernatural'. The material he collected was, he said, 'the production of rustic wits' or 'the whimsies of mere children, and were originally designed for no higher purpose than to convey the wisdom or the humours of the cottage, to soothe the murmurs of the cradle, or enliven the sports of the village green'. He cautions his reader 'not to expect here anything profound, or sublime, or elegant, or affecting [. . .] the absence of high-wrought literary grace is compensated by a simplicity coming direct from nature'.[5]

David Buchan thought that in comparison with other European nations, Scotland had been neglectful of studying its traditional literature, though he admitted the 'vineyard has not been empty', reserving particular praise for Chambers's work; his *Popular Rhymes of Scotland* (1826; rev. edn 1870) was considered an early attempt to present a 'multi-generic view of Scottish folk literature'.[6] The ballad collections of men such as William Motherwell (1797–1835) and the American scholar Francis J. Child (1825–96) are relatively well-known, as are the legends and tales assembled by Sir Walter Scott (1771–1832) and J. F. Campbell (1821–85). Other names, however, are less familiar, such as James Napier (1810–84) on the west of Scotland, Walter Gregor (1825–97) on the north-east and Galloway, Allan Cunningham (1784–1842) on Dumfries and Galloway and Hugh Miller (1802–56) on Cromarty.

The earliest Scottish publications to enquire into the supernatural and folk belief concerning witches and fairies include Robert Kirk's *The Secret Common-Wealth* (1691), George Sinclair's *Satan's Invisible World Discovered* (1685) and Martin Martin's *Description of the Western Islands of Scotland* (1703). A remarkable forerunner of such literature, by about a century, was James VI's *Daemonologie* (1597) in which the king warned that accused witches would try to pass off their diabolical experiences as encounters with fairies, in the hope of avoiding the ultimate penalty. In fact, the testimony emerging from witch trials often had the appearance of folk narratives, as I have suggested elsewhere.[7] The Ayrshire witch Bessie Dunlop, found guilty of witchcraft, consorting with fairies and a ghost, was executed in 1576. Her testimony almost certainly contains evidence of folk narrative plots and motifs now recognised as folk tale and local legend, reported by Dunlop as a personal experience narrative, especially under the pressures of actual or threatened interrogation. Such evidence might also be detected in other witch trial confessions, such as that by Jonet Boyman (1572) who conjured forth a fairy man near Arthur's Seat in Edinburgh in order to procure medicinal cures from him. Alison Peirson (1588) acquired her healing skills from her uncle, who visited her from Fairyland. Among her clients was Bishop Patrick Adamson of St Andrews, a controversial figure in his own right, a detail that did not escape the attention of his most fervent critic, the poet Robert Sempill, who mercilessly satirised them both:

> sorcerie and incantationes,
> Reasing [raising] the devill with invocationes,
> With herbis, stanes, buikis and bellis,
> Menis members, and south rinning wellis;
> Palm croces, and knottis of strease [straws],
> The paring of a preistis auld tees.[8]

There is good internal evidence that writers such as Robert Kirk and Martin Martin relied to a considerable extent upon oral informants and tradition-bearers. Kirk, the Episcopalian minister of Aberfoyle, composed his treatise, *The Secret Common-Wealth*, 'to suppress the impudent and growing Atheisme of this age' for, as his argument goes, if the existence of such phenomena as fairies is put into question then so too is the existence of angels and, ultimately, God. In the process, he preserved invaluable evidence of local, mainly Gaelic, folk beliefs and narratives, chiefly about fairies, but also second sight, brownies, ghosts and witchcraft.[9]

The dangers that fairies posed to humans was well understood in Kirk's lifetime: 'Women are yet alive who tell they were taken away when in Child-bed to nurse ffayrie Children,' while others reported attacks upon their livestock, 'usually said to be Elf-shot'. He reports having met a woman who had been repeatedly abducted and abused by the fairies. She was 'melanchollious and silent, hardly ever seen to laugh' and 'she took verie litle, or no food for several years past, she tarry'd in the fields over night, saw, and convers'd with a people she knew not'. The onset of the attacks could be traced to an occasion when the woman had wandered off in search of her sheep, become tired and fallen asleep on a small hill. She was then 'transported to another place befor day'. The assumption here was that the woman had inadvertently put herself in danger by falling asleep atop a fairy residence; 'there be manie places called fayrie hills, which the mountain-people think impious and dangerous to peel [interfere with] or discover'. It is of note that Kirk is the first writer known to have used the term 'fairy tale'.[10]

Martin Martin, a physician from Skye, wrote eloquently about the *lusbartan*, or 'little people' but he was more interested in the second sight, a subject on which he was a peerless authority, and the reality of which he did not doubt. He had himself been the object of visions and he strenuously defended the integrity of seers. Like Kirk, Martin, a Gaelic speaker, drew upon his deep knowledge of the oral culture. Indeed he was, for long, one of the few Gaels to write in English about Gaeldom; most commentators were outsiders.

Apart from the testimony of witch trials, Martin and Kirk come closest to preserving supernatural folk narratives from the earlier period.[11] Folk belief is often apparent in the destructive legislation of the church or the censorious records of kirk sessions. Despite the best efforts of the godly, as well as the rise of reason during the Enlightenment, much popular 'superstition' survived into the eighteenth and nineteenth centuries when collectors began to harvest the beliefs of the folk at large, convinced that such beliefs were on the point of extinction. However, although more folk narratives were being recovered, there were additional concerns about authenticity.

Allan Cunningham produced a prodigious number of publications, including an edition of Robert Burns's *Works* and *The Songs of Scotland, Ancient and Modern* (1825). He also wrote several short stories involving tales of fairy abduction, 'The Haunted Ships' and 'Elphin Irving: The Fairies' Cupbearers' for his book, *Traditional Tales of the English and Scottish Peasantry* (1822). Notoriously, when Robert Hartley Cromek produced his *Remains of Nithsdale and Galloway Song* (1810) it contained many of Cunningham's own compositions fraudulently passed off to both Cromek and the book-buying public as ancient ballads and traditional songs. It should be noted that Cromek's work is still frequently plundered by folklorists unaware of the possible dubious origin of the content. Cromek thanked Cunningham for having 'beguiled the tediousness of his toil' and for drawing 'from obscurity many pieces which adorn this collection, and which, without his aid, would have eluded my research'.[12] If Cunningham was an enthusiastic fraudster, Cromek was a gullible dupe. It was not unknown for eighteenth- and nineteenth-century writers, antiquarians and folklorists to present their own compositions as authentic folklore – James Macpherson's *Ossian* and Thomas Percy's *Reliques*, after all, had shown them the way.

The appendix, supplied by Cunningham, in the *Remains of Nithsdale and Galloway Song*, devotes quite a large section to the history of witchcraft sketched, as he claims, from 'the popular tales of the peasantry of Nithsdale and Galloway'. Cunningham returned to the subject in 1822, in *Traditional Tales of the English and Scottish Peasantry*, but once again, caution must be exercised for there was probably very little that was truly 'traditional' in this two-volume compendium, much having apparently been derived from his own creative imagination. There is a lively account of a witch who specialised in cursing ships which, by its very verbosity, has more of a literary flavour than of an orally communicated story.[13]

Cunningham collected a story about 'The Witches Tryst' – a meeting better known elsewhere as a sabbat or coven – where 'witches and warlocks of a county were assembled' and 'are yet remembered among the peasantry with terror'. He suggests that, even in the early nineteenth century, witch belief was not yet dead among the folk of this region:

> The noted tryste of the Nithsdale and Galloway warlocks and witches was held on a rising knowe, four miles distant from Dumfries, called 'Locher-brigg Hill'. There are yet some fragments of the witches' Gathering Hymn, too characteristically curious to be omitted.
>
> > When the grey howlet has three times hoo'd,
> > When the grimy cat has three times mewed,
> > When the tod has yowled three times i' the wode,
> > At the red moon cowering ahin the cl'ud;
> > When the stars ha'e cruppen' deep i' the drift,
> > Lest cantrips had pyked them out o' the lift,
> > Up horsies a' but mair adowe,
> > Ryde, ryde for Locher-briggs-knowe![14]

According to him witches liked to travel to these frightful gatherings on broomsticks fashioned from murdered men's bones, while others preferred to change humans into animals – specifically, in this region at least, into horses. This they did by using a magic bridle made from the shredded skin of unbaptised infants 'with bits forged in Satan's armoury'. The bridle worked by shaking it above the head of the intended victim. Two young lads of Nithsdale, Cunningham tells us, once served a widow woman who was in possession of such a magic bridle. One of the lads was plump and merry, but he suddenly became very skinny and sad. The other lad asked what ailed him, to be instructed, 'lie at the bed stock an' ye'll be as lean as me'. When Halloween came, the second lad decided to try this out to find out what would happen. He struggled to stay awake, but when the midnight hour arrived his mistress approached the bedside and proceeded to shake the charmed bridle over his face while speaking the words 'Up horsie'. To his complete surprise he was transformed into the shape of a grey horse. The bridle was put over his head and the bit was put in his teeth, while the old widow mounted his back and dug in her spurs. They took off like the wind and arrived, within minutes, at Locherbrigg Knowe. The lad was fastened tightly with the bridle to a tree and there he recognised others similarly transformed into horses. What ensued was a sight that terrified him; a hellish party of witches, engaged in lewd dancing and unspeakable obscenity. The lad prayed to Heaven to help him escape his bondage and his prayers were answered. He shook off the bridle and resumed his human shape. When the sun began to rise, the witches returned to their transport after a night of debauchery. The young lad's mistress approached him and he quickly grabbed the bridle and shook it over her head this time. She was instantly transformed into a gray mare. He got on her back and rode her back with great speed, digging the spurs into her sides until they bled. When they returned to the stable, he removed the bridle and his mistress was returned to her own shape, her feet and hands now lacerated. He swore never to tell of his night's adventure and her part in the witches gathering; in return he was allowed to keep the bridle.[15]

Cunningham relates this tale as a local legend, though stories of the magic bridle are fairly widespread and by no means specific to Nithsdale, or indeed Scotland. There is a Moray version and another from the Borders, 'The Blacksmith's Wife of Yarrowfoot'.[16] Elements of the story also appear in folk tale, such as the tale-type of 'the youth transformed into a horse', and 'the magic bridle' which gives the owner power over horses.[17] However, although the sources attest that witches frequently rode on stalks, bundles of straw or on the backs of animals, they do not mention, so far as I am aware, broomsticks made from the bones of murder victims.

Elsewhere Cunningham refers to the 'insensible marks, which the second sighted searchers of witchcraft called "little uncommon figures of strawberry leaves" found on the human frame'. This is a reference to the Devil's Mark, received after the witch entered into a demonic pact. This signature of a diabolical contract occurs in several witch accusations. He is also on much better attested and verifiable ground in his story of 'The Pawkie Auld Kimmer':

Kimmer can milk a hale loan o' kye,
Yet sit at the ingle fu' snug an' fu' dry.[18]

The idea here is that the kimmer, meaning witch, possessed a magical milking peg which could extract milk from any cow in the parish. This is an example of where folk narrative merges with documentation, for one of the crimes with which Elspeth McEwen (1698), a convicted witch from Balmaclellan, Galloway, was charged, was using a wooden pin to steal milk from her neighbours' cows by placing the pin on their udders.[19]

Cunningham also discusses fairies and brownies. Unlike the fairies, who were notably gregarious, the brownie was a solitary creature, usually male, 'living in the hollows of trees, and recesses of old ruinous castles'.[20] In appearance, brownies were variously described, as squat, shaggy, naked creatures at one extreme, but tall, handsome and well-proportioned, at the other. They had a dislike of clothing or excessive gifts and, for all their hard work, only wanted a bowl of cream. Some traditions state brownies were ordained by God to be helpers of humankind in the drudgery of their toil and labour brought on by sin; thus, they must not receive any form of payment for their assistance.[21] There was also a notion that brownies were particularly helpful to women, assisting them with everything from household chores to childbirth, and that they attached themselves to particular households or families. Among Cunningham's tales is one suggesting that family prosperity was brownie-dependent. At 'Liethin Hall', in Dumfriesshire, a brownie confided to an old woman that he had lived there for some three hundred years; when the new heir arrived he made the fatal mistake of giving the brownie meat, drink and a new outfit to wear. In great lamentation, the brownie was forced to remove himself, and with him the family's good fortune:

Ca', cuttie, ca!
A' the luck o' Liethin Ha'
Gangs wi' me to Bodsbeck Ha'.[22]

Brownies were popularised in the early nineteenth century by such publications as the story by James Hogg (1770–1835), *The Brownie of Bodsbeck* (1818), in which the 'brownie' is a persecuted covenanter, and the poem by William Nicholson (1782–1849), 'The Brownie of Blednoch' (1825). Nicholson's brownie, Aiken Drum, was so admired that he entered, in tale form, the oral tradition of Galloway. He 'lived in a lan where we saw nae sky [and] dwalt in a spot where a burn rins na by' and was, like most of his species, hard-working and helpful around the household, asking for no more than a dish of brose in return for his labours. However, in the poem, this did not prevent a modest wife, offended by his nakedness, from leaving out an old pair of her husband's trousers for him, forcing Aiken Drum to depart.

Let the learned decide, when they convene,
What spell was him and the breeks between;
For frae that day forth he was nae mair seen.[23]

The polymath Hugh Miller, better known for his geological discoveries, was the first person systematically to record the folklore of the north-east of Scotland, notably in *Scenes and Legends of the North of Scotland* (1835). He was, like so many collectors of his generation, concerned that the stories and traditions that he learned as a child were fast dying out and considered it his duty to preserve them for posterity. Growing up on the Black Isle, he had direct experience of the oral tradition and was exposed to storytelling, thus he acquired his knowledge by the fireside rather than in libraries, placing him alongside people like James Hogg rather than Charles Kirkpatrick Sharpe or John Graham Dalyell.[24] Unlike modern folklorists, he was not interested in versions, motifs or performance contexts, but simply wished to share his stories with the wider world, so ensuring their survival for future generations. In this endeavour, he collected hundreds of legends, folk tales, personal narratives and much local history. Miller did not particularly go in for formal fairy tales or *Märchen*; most of his narrations fall under the umbrella of local legend. At the time Miller was writing, when folklore, as a discipline, was in its infancy, there were few models to follow save Walter Scott and Alan Cunningham, both of whom, to varying degrees, were known to 'improve' or modify the stories and songs they collected. It is difficult to ascertain to what extent Miller did the same, in hopes of making the stories more cohesive or interesting, or simply to make them suitable for wider audiences.[25]

There are many examples where Miller presents a story as local legend, as a memory of some past event or personage. Take, for instance, his account of the witch Stine Bheag o' Tarbat; 'her history, as related by her neighbours, formed, like the histories of all the other witches of Scotland, a strange medley of the very terrible and the very ludicrous'. Miller reports that she was blamed for raising a storm at sea that killed her husband and son, allegedly to prevent them from reporting her engagement in 'orgies', presumably a reference to the Witches Sabbat, to the authorities. As might be expected, living in a coastal area, she was believed to be behind other problems at sea, wrecking ships and creating storms. She was also credited with annoying a farmer by assuming the shape of a black beetle, though despite her great powers, the farmer succeeded in capturing her while in beetle form, keeping her imprisoned in his snuff-box for four days. Miller cites another incident that he dated to 1738, when a crew of fishermen, unable to return to Cromarty due to bad weather, consulted Stine Bheag for she was 'famous at this time as one in league with Satan, and much consulted by seafaring men when windbound in any of the neighbouring ports'. When the fishermen entered her cottage they allegedly saw Stine sitting on a stool in front of the fire performing a spell and muttering a 'Gaelic rhyme'. The description of her 'ruinous and weather-beaten' cottage, atop which croaked a raven, is vivid and full of detail. The flames 'glanced on the naked walls of turf and stone, and on a few implements of housewifery which were ranged along the sides, together with other utensils of a more questionable form and appearance'. In the corner stood 'a huge wooden trough, filled with water, from whence there proceeded a splashing bubbling noise, as if it were filled with live fish [. . .] sentinelled by a black cat, that sat purring on a stool beside it'. Other objects in the room included a bundle of dried herbs, the skeleton of some animal partially moulded with red clay and a staff 'with the tail of a fish fastened to one end, and the wings of a raven to the other'. She obligingly performed a spell on the ship. The next day the men set sail for home.[26] Miller claimed that this last encounter was related by one of the fishermen involved, though given the date of the events (1738) he would not have heard it first-hand. It cannot be known definitively if Miller embellished these local stories in any way, but because of the level of detail he imparts, and the style in which it is retold, perhaps his own storytelling techniques can be observed. Strangely, he does not seem to question parts of the accumulated legends surrounding Stine Bheag, which venture into rumour and gossip. How could it have been known, for instance, that her son and husband had intended to report her for witchcraft and attendance at a Witches' Sabbat if she murdered them before they could do so? In these legends, however, there is much that is verifiable from witchcraft lore. Witches attended Sabbats, just as they were known to control the wind, and were consulted about such matters long after 1738. The witch's ability to shape-shift into animal form was relatively prevalent, while the cat made a suitable pet. In normal circumstances the cottage's furnishings and fish-tank could be seen as innocuous, but perhaps not in the case of a suspected witch. Herbs, skeletons and even the staff could be seen as traditional witch equipment. Stine was, in many ways, the recognisable witch of legend.

There have been many assumptions made over the years about what constitutes 'folklore'. This has in turn, to some extent, predetermined what is understood as 'folk literature', namely that it shares a close bond with orality. Further questions have arisen as to what folk literature's relationship might be with the written variety. Another approach has been to trace evidence of orally-based 'folklore' within literary and printed sources.[27] Kirk and Martin drew upon folk material just as Burns incorporated local legend in 'Tam o Shanter', as did Scott relentlessly. Perhaps, in conclusion, the relationship is best summed up as reciprocity, to the enrichment of both.

CHAPTER FOUR

Transmission

James Porter

In folklore study ('folkloristics'), as in anthropology and sociology, the concept of transmission has recently been challenged by the competing idea of 'communication'. Formerly, transmission was conventionally understood to convey the notion of 'passage of traditional lore over [a lengthy] time'.[1] This notion dominated until the 1960s, when younger North American folklorists began shifting the research focus into a synchronic mode, focused on single moments, emphasising, for example, 'folklore and communication', 'communicative storytelling events', 'performance and event'.[2] Basing their perspective mainly in sociolinguistics, these to some extent pushed folklore study away from its traditional humanities base and towards social sciences, as a branch of cultural anthropology. While terms like 'transmission' and 'communication' seem superficially synonymous, both involving sender and receiver, recent practice has tended to divide folklorists, some maintaining diachronic perspectives and others preferring synchronic views of traditional folk knowledge and art.[3]

This division – and folklore studies' notorious terminological problems – caused disciplinary arguments and fractures. Initially, 'transmission' was often equated with 'tradition' in its various meanings, although it generally had a more 'active' sense.[4] Recently, folklorists, facing challenges to their study's validity, have attempted to ring-fence it, with limited success. Folklore's subject matter clearly overlaps other subject areas (like history, language, medicine and music), while the compound term ('folk', 'lore') has accumulated, over more than two centuries of study and usage, meanings complicating neat definition. Further, from their discipline's nineteenth-century beginnings, folklorists have ventured physically and intellectually into territory simultaneously staked out by anthropologists and sociologists.[5] In contrast to North American colleagues, European ethnologists have largely preferred the idea of transmission over time: historically, their field has been grounded in both regional and long-term studies of the continent and its peoples.[6]

Transmission of Oral Literature

Another, literary, view of transmission emerged in the study of 'oral literature', a term conceived as a branch of folklore and literary history.[7] This was used from the turn of the twentieth century, when ballad scholars like Harvard University's G. L. Kittredge employed it.[8] Associated concepts of 'orality' and 'literacy' were later, from the 1960s, hotly debated: the equally problematic 'traditionality' in time superseded the former, while 'textuality' similarly replaced 'literacy' – all these terms overlapping in opacity and needing careful delineation in context of use.[9] A special strand of enquiry into 'oral composition' stemmed from A. B. Lord's influential *The Singer of Tales* (1960), addressing the problem of Homeric epics and their composition through reference to modern South Slavic epic traditions and the illiterate Bosnian singers enacting them.[10] Lord's work, emphasising verbal formulae's structural role as building blocks in oral composition and performance, in turn influenced some balladry students, notably David Buchan and William McCarthy, who conjoined this theory of oral composition 'in performance' to structural studies of Scottish ballad texts in historical context.[11]

Transmission, thus seen, was part of a process where 'oral composition', 'oral creation' and 'oral performance' were all the same thing. Traditional ballad singers, parallelling epic singers, recreated 'each story at each performance, during each performance'.[12] Critics, however, adducing modern as well as older recorded sources, strenuously objected that memorisation was the basic vehicle of oral tradition. As a genre, further, epics with their textual freedom and open-ended, quasi-improvised melodic style aim at expansion, while ballads aim at contraction. The ballad tune in particular, with its closed four- or eight-line form, is a potent aid to memorisation.[13] Ballad singers may have re-created ballads at a single sitting before the advent of general literacy, but in the modern world they generally memorise specific texts and tunes. Even in the later eighteenth century, Anna Brown of Falkland (1747–1810), the notable ballad singer originally from the north-east of Scotland, sang two somewhat different versions of the ballad 'The Lass of Roch Royal' seventeen years apart. The differences in the recorded ballad texts, though, arose because she learned the ballad from two separate relatives, not because she re-created them at each sitting.[14] Nevertheless, there is some evidence from Travellers' culture in Lowland Scotland that a rhapsodic style can sometimes involve elements of spontaneous re-creation.[15]

Written texts, of course, also perform this aide-memoire function. Literate members of a traditional society with an eye for written texts as well as an ear for oral versions and a mind to write both types down – from memory or from other sources – have contributed significantly, if paradoxically, to 'oral literature'. Writing as a means of transmission, often in personal diaries or manuscripts, is well documented in Scottish tradition.[16] Moreover, broadsides and chapbooks have contributed to the dissemination of popular ballads and tales: the nineteenth-century collector Robert Ford could discuss song traditions making no distinction between oral and written, or traditional and commercial forms.[17]

One example may help illustrate this concept of 'oral literature'. Cameron Turriff, a singer from the north-east village of Fetterangus, deep in the Buchan farmlands, struggled to remember the final verse of a song he heard at a farm where he worked, around 1927:

> No, I never heard my father at that one. I was sixteen years old, and I worked at a farm at Creemond [Crimond], what they call Moss-side o Creemond. There was a chap, Bill Junnor, foreman at that place, that learned me that song [. . .] Aye but as the years rolled on I forgot the last verse [. . .] Bit there was a vanman, a baker, come tae this house. He came from Longside, an I says til him: I hear it's a chap called Bill Junnor at Longside [. . .] you ask him if he remembers a chap Turra [Turriff] at worked there (I was a young boy working horse) if he remembers learning me this song, as I have forgot the last verse. So back he comes with that last verse o the song. I never spoke to that man since I was seventeen and I never met him. He was foreman at Moss-side o Creemond. He heard his father sing it. Yes, he got it from his father. He was twenty-seven when I was sixteen [. . .] I jist needed somebody [. . .] whit I could get that song, in a book, would come forward till I got every verse. There was a long time I lost that verse, it left my memory [. . .] [quoting vanman] Aye, he minds on ye. But he has the song in a kist, and he has tae rake in this kist to find it.[18]

From this, it is evident that song transmission, at least, is not a simple matter of oral and written texts, but one involving passage of time, place, occupation, family, memory, narrative appeal, memorable tune and aesthetic sense of completeness or wholeness. Significantly, Turriff's view of the song was that it was 'incomplete' without the final verse even though the penultimate stanza concludes the 'story'. For him, born in 1911 as son of a north-east farm servant, knowing the 'complete' song pulled him back to the world of his youth between the World Wars. It drew him again into the web of relationships among farm workers whose disciplined life, tending horses and livestock, had normally begun at 5 a.m.[19] Songs of this type, composed by men working on Scottish farms between c. 1850 and 1950, circulated freely in oral and written versions. In as much as one can talk about bounded communities where song-writing flourished, in those of the farm workers and their bothy songs creativity, performance, transmission, context and values merged in competitive unity. When that community ended after World War Two, some more memorable songs survived with the people who had sung them, as well as younger singers who learned them in the informal context of 1960s folk festivals.[20]

Tradition, Context, Genre

'Transmission', then, was normally understood as the 'handing down' or 'handing on' of traditional knowledge and art, primarily but not exclusively by oral means. Defenders of this concept argue it remains valid despite attempts to wrest folklore from dominant and lingering notions of history, tradition or the past and assign it a present free from such conceptions.[21] On the other hand, forms or genres like personal experience narratives, or memorates, do not depend on passage through the generations, and for that reason were distinguished by the Swedish folklorist Carl von Sydow from legends belonging to the community (however one defines 'community').[22] The modern proliferation of such personal narratives, given telecommunication devices, mobility and cultural pluralism, has led the study of narrative from definitional delusions and turf wars among ethnological disciplines toward a broader view of transmission: something that can transcend boundaries of time, space and community and be assimilated into a more comprehensive theory of cultural communication.[23] This transformation of the idea of 'context' would complicate that distinction between the two main types of context in which culture is transmitted: the broad historical and the immediately specific.[24]

It would also complicate the conception of genre. Some folklorists, borrowing from Bakhtin's concept of the dialogic, have suggested ways in which folklore genres are in dialogue, interdependent and ultimately inseparable. A generic text, in this view, can hold a variety of relationships to comparable texts and genre categories that precede it. A song containing a narrative might be considered narrative, song, lullaby, or sum of contextual meanings.[25] The interpretation brought to bear can then transform the concept of genre and, with an expanded view of context, bring into focus multiple avenues by which traditions are transmitted or disseminated.

Performance Theory

Meantime the development of 'performance theory', seen as a breakthrough theory of 'verbal art', did not become a substitute field for folkloristics.[26] Emphasising narrating, reflexivity and aesthetics, this model of 'storytelling events', according to its critics, does not correspond to folklore's reality in a scientific, industrial and technological age. Face-to-face performances are only one way in which transmission is effected. Critics particularly observed that focus on oral performance's action distorts narrative traditions' true nature. By concentrating on a relatively narrow part of tradition's spectrum, performance theory ignores or downplays the dynamics of transmission through mass media, including sound, film and print. In reaction, an alternative focus has emerged on issues like narrative memory, stability of tradition, memorates and discourse analysis.[27] Yet other issues have recently caught the attention of folklorists: class, gender, nationalism, community institutions and economy.[28]

When the 'verbal art' movement was in full flow in the 1970s, a symbolic concept of 'performance' emerged in anthropological circles, examining other modes of cultural expression like ritual and display events.[29] This view of performed social drama has been criticised for losing local and particular meanings.[30] Nevertheless, these analyses of enactment fulfilled an important function in emphasising folklore's semiotic nature, whether publicly presented in open spaces or in more restricted arenas like homes or theatres. Gesture, dance and bodily movement are traditional and non-verbal ways of transmitting or dramatising narrative or song. These in turn involve aural, tactile and visual transmission systems. Performances of this type, playing out conflicts underpinning daily life, have an essential role in binding communities together.

As noted earlier, 'transmission' as a concept has been supplanted in some recent studies by 'communication'. The question then arises: communication from, to and for whom; in what contexts; and over what span of time? Performance theorists have seemed eager to place boundaries on transmission's time and space, for the sake of 'event analysis'. More recent commentary shows transmission can involve more than a unidirectional chain in a single context bounded by time and space. It would be unimaginably narrow, in these days of assiduous fieldwork, to think of transmission or communication taking place within the confines only of a traditional community.

In such societies men have often been linked, typically, to public, instrumental and modern solo performances of musical forms, women to domestic genres, dance forms or choral performance, and older types of music.[31] Now, however, newer forms of popular culture have contributed to breaking down gender barriers. This can lead to fruitful studies of people's interaction in transmission and communication of traditional forms.[32] Because women's repertoire has often been directed towards children, the former have been traditional lore's key transmitters. For their part, children, in play and cultivation of forms like the urban legend, have shown creativity that often depends on or refers to traditional models for effect. Contrasting with recent institutionalisation in teaching and learning of traditional forms, informal performances of children show them as creative catalysts of traditional culture.[33]

Tradition-Bearer, Ethnographer

Considering transmission as cultural performance, scholars have often focused on the tradition-bearer's role. The ethnographer, too, as observer and interpreter, has come increasingly under scrutiny as ethical dilemmas in the ethnological sciences emerged. It is not just in ethnography's 'writing', for instance, that falsifications and biases appear, but in the entire stance of the ethnographer entering a traditional community, attempting to record its culture and conveying it, through interpretation, to the outside.[34] Ethnological sciences, indeed, have been accused of racism, colonialism and distortion for personal or political purposes; the ethnographer's very presence changes the community, often in unforeseen ways. Exploitation for the sake of ideology, academic promotion, or commercial gain have sometimes been hidden motives.[35]

The hermeneutic turn in fieldwork has affected the notion of traditional culture and its transmission. Following Herder and others, fieldworkers have often attempted an empathetic understanding of 'others' by imaginatively changing places with them. This has usually meant living among people in a traditional society: the early twentieth-century anthropologist Bronislaw Malinowski among the Trobriand Islanders, for instance, or closer at hand, Hamish Henderson with Travellers in Perthshire in the 1950s. More rarely, some have adopted a hermeneutics of observation where the interpreter deliberately stands apart from the cultural production under investigation and interpretation. Here, experience of cultural transmission or communication is others', conveyed by those 'others', captured through metaphor by an observer in a privileged position to understand.[36] At times, of course, the observer or 'outsider' has been partly a perceptive 'insider', born into the community, but for some reason separated from it in order to analyse it.

So the process of culture change, accelerated by the ethnographer, overtakes 'transmission', even understood in the broadest sense. Songs in Lowland Scotland that the traditional community formerly designated 'auld sangs' now become 'ballads' or 'muckle sangs' because folklorists, eager to find rarities, told the singer what kind of song he or she was really singing. Ethnographers, no matter how sympathetic to traditional societies under investigation and ethically scrupulous, introduce their value system, not just in discourse or 'collecting' language, but by their presence. A self-aware ethnographer must base the approach to culture interpretation in the reflexive relationship with co-workers (a term preferable to the unsatisfactory 'informants', which suggests a depersonalised source of cultural information).[37] This involves conversation on equal terms where 'truth' is negotiated through discourse, not 'transmitted', 'received', or 'recorded'. The ethnographer too belongs to a tradition, acquiring a world view perhaps at odds with the co-worker's, the source of knowledge in a field situation. Admitting biases and preconceptions aims at removing barriers that hinder understanding.[38]

Choices the ethnographer or student of oral literature makes affect how folk tradition is interpreted and transmitted – when, where and how communicated. Who is approached in seeking to study traditional knowledge and art? Why? The ethnographer's gender – and that of the subject of enquiry – is often critical. Possible reasons for choosing a particular individual might include stature in the community, mastery of a particular genre, the need for acceptance and approval, or simply strength of personality. Nothing is predictable about how the relationship between researcher and 'object' will develop. 'Subject' and 'object' can change places, and the interviewer find character and beliefs under unexpected scrutiny. When researchers are candid about their choices, however, adopting a modest, self-conscious (but not self-effacing) stance in their fieldwork, understanding of such central topics as transmission and communication can only be strengthened.

CHAPTER FIVE

'Tradition' and Literature in the Medieval Period

John McNamara

This chapter explores four key facets of the complex relationship between 'tradition' and literature in medieval Scotland. In the present context, this is defined as the period when Middle Scots developed through contact with the northern dialect area of Middle English and emerged into cultural dominance by the fourteenth century as a spoken and literary language, especially in the Lowlands. It is important to observe that the boundaries between manifestations of 'tradition' are not carefully demarcated, and that the energy behind them derives from cultural politics: who 'owns' (or acquires) it, under what conditions and for what purposes. Claims to tradition are clearly tied up with the politics and rhetoric of identity, which are linguistically and culturally complex in late medieval Scotland.[1]

First, there is the substantial body of ballads, folktales and legends that circulated orally in what Carl Lindahl calls the 'traditional, informal culture of communities'.[2] This is the living heritage of a people by which they preserve the memories and values that define their identity. Such traditional culture develops, circulates and grows among ordinary members of communities without having been imposed by official leaders or institutions 'from above'. Second, there is the construction of tradition for some purpose – cultural, religious or, in Scotland, often nationalist. Barbour's *Bruce* and Hary's *Wallace* both incorporate folkloric elements from oral tradition, thereby appropriating its authority and appeal for a wide popular audience, but they shape this legendry to promote their politics of patriotism. Third, some writers appropriate a prestigious tradition from outside Scotland, reshaping it to enhance Scottish literature's cultural capital (for example, and as explored in more detail later, Robert Henryson's *Moral Fables* recast the medieval Latin Aesopic tradition, but in Scots and its social registers). To these we could add a fourth kind of cultural politics, seen in the genre of saints' lives: these resituate into a learned, high register language (Latin) popular lore circulating earlier in a variety of vernaculars including Old English, North Brythonic and Old Gaelic (for example, Aelred's *Life of Ninian*, Jocelyn's *Life of Kentigern* and Adomnán's *Life of Columba*).

Some of the most important source material derives from the large body of ballads, at least some of which survive from the Middle Ages, though dating the origin of ballads has generally proved problematic, even highly controversial. A central problem is the fact that most ballads come to us in the forms in which they were collected in the eighteenth and early nineteenth centuries in collections like Thomas Percy's *Reliques of Ancient English Poetry* (1765) and Sir Walter Scott's *Minstrelsy of the Scottish Border* (1802–3); their versions were often 'improved' to fit modern tastes – itself an exercise of cultural power. Moreover, as ballads travel and develop over time, it is often difficult to define what is specifically Scottish in them. As Hamish Henderson pointed out,

> Ballad-Scots merges into Ballad-English, for the simple reason that England and Scots-speaking Scotland – and indeed English-speaking Ireland – really form one single great ballad zone. The narrative songs moved around with astonishing ease, and breached dialect and language boundaries like an underground army.[3]

He goes on to speak of 'the multi-ethnic origins of Scottish folk culture' being one of its strengths and concludes that '[t]he hybrid is often more resourceful and resilient than the pure-bred'. Even so, it is sometimes possible to establish the provenance of a ballad whose subject is a historical event. As Michael Chesnutt has pointed out, such is the case with 'The Battle of Otterburn' and 'The Hunting of the Cheviot', both of which relate their versions of a battle between English and Scottish forces on 19 August 1388 – one from an English point of view and the other the Scottish.[4] Each version focuses on the heroic qualities and actions of its own national hero; when the two ballads are taken together, they provide a telling example of cultural politics.

A rather different relation to tradition may be found in medieval epic. In their appropriation of written and oral cultures – including folk memory – to promote their great goal of shaping Scottish identity, works such as *The Bruce* by John Barbour (1330s-95) and *The Wallace* attributed to 'Blind Hary [Harry]' (c. 1440–92), embody another dimension of the relationship between cultural politics and 'tradition'. Barbour himself acknowledges his reliance on oral sources in numerous references – 'men still say', 'as I heard tell'[5] – indicating how widespread and long-lasting were the legends about King Robert as national hero (indeed, Barbour's extraordinary apostrophe to freedom against all odds – A! Fredome is a noble thing' – remains a *locus classicus* in Scottish literature).

There are also strong elements of romance here, made popular by French romances from the Continent, but the work as a whole adopts the rhetoric of chronicle with its concern for the truthfulness of its account, beginning with the opening lines:

Storys to rede ar delatibill	[delightful]
Suppos that thai be nocht bot fabill,	
Than suld storys that suthfast wer	[truthful]
And that war said on gud maner	
Have doubill plesaunce in heryng.	
The first plesaunce is the carping	[telling]
And the tother the suthfastnes	
That shawis the thing rycht as it wes,	
And suth thyngis that ar likand	[entertaining]
Till mannys heryng ar plesand.	
Tharfor I wald fayne set my will	
Giff my wyt mycht suffice thartill	
To put in wryt a suthfast story	
That it lest ay furth in memory	[last forever forth]
Swa that na tyme of lenth it let	[length of time prevent it]
Na ger it haly be foryet.	[cause it to be wholly forgotten]
(Book 1, lines 1–16)	

Later, when recounting the story of Bruce's killing his rival Comyn, Barbour seeks to justify this act at the high altar of a church, though he recognises Bruce committed sacrilege. As a careful reporter of this controversial event, Barbour notes that still 'sum men sayis / At that debat [quarrel] fell otherwayis' (Book 2, lines 39–40), acknowledging both the continuing life of the legend in oral tradition and his willingness as a truthful chronicler to include contrary opinions in his account. Moreover, his claim to truthfulness is further enhanced by the unflinching realism of his descriptions of brutality in warfare. Such is the case with the legend of 'the Douglas lardner' [larder], which Barbour describes as a country tale, in which King Robert's lieutenant Douglas beheads his enemies and mixes their dismembered bodies with the wine and victuals of the larder of the castle he has captured to keep these provisions from being used by further enemies (Book 5, lines 395–410). Historians such as A. A. M. Duncan, however, have demonstrated in great detail how Barbour altered historical fact to suit his own narrative vision. A notable example is the conflation of Robert Bruce with his grandfather at the beginning of the plot, apparently to elide some of the hero's own early unfortunate lapses. Even so, Barbour not only creates a masterful epic romance out of his written and oral sources, but in the process a great – and greatly influential – construction of Scottish national identity.

Scarcely a century later (c. 1477), the epic of William Wallace provides another example of the construction of tradition for patriotic ends. Wallace

(1272–1305) was a Scottish patriot who, in the poem's narrative, rose against the English, who had usurped the power of the king they had appointed (John Balliol), was outlawed by them, united his people as a national hero against their oppressors, won spectacular victories, was eventually defeated, driven into exile, betrayed, captured and executed. Although Wallace suffered a horrifying and humiliating execution at the hands of the English, his fellow Scots came to regard his death as a heroic martyrdom for their cause and, time and again over the centuries, his legends have been invoked by Scots in their struggles for national identity and freedom. After his brutal execution, Wallace was reviled as a barbarian outlaw by English chroniclers and largely ignored in the 'official' memory of his countrymen. While it is true that Andrew of Wyntoun's poetic chronicle (1420s) and Walter Bower's *Scotichronicon* (1440s) refer to him in their historical narratives, they do not recount his deeds in detail, nor treat him as a central figure in the Scottish Wars of Independence. Barbour's *Bruce* (1375) does not even mention Wallace, presumably in order to focus entirely on King Robert's great achievement without the embarrassment of his shifting alliances during the period when Wallace was Guardian. It was not until around 1477, more than 170 years after Wallace's death, that Hary – known to later tradition as Blind Harry – wrote the first full version of Wallace's life as an epic poem. He claims to base his work on a Latin life by John Blair, Wallace's chaplain, who had been commissioned by Bishop Sinclair of Dunkeld to do so in order that Blair's work could be sent to the pope, perhaps as hagiography to seek papal authority for a growing cult of Wallace in Scotland. Most historians are doubtful that such a Latin source ever existed and it was, of course, commonplace in medieval literature to claim the authority of 'sources' even when there were none. Nevertheless, whether or not there ever was a Latin account, Hary claimed that he used many stories about Wallace that had long circulated in oral tradition. Andrew of Wyntoun relates that

> Of his good deeds and manhood
> Great gestes and songs are made

though Wyntoun says they are too numerous for him to recount in his own work.[6] This tradition of 'gestes and songs' suggests Wallace lived on in folk memory as a national hero and Hary would have had abundant material for his own life of Wallace, whose popularity as epic, according to Elspeth King,[7] was for some centuries second only to the Bible as the most widely owned book in Scotland.

Early accounts say that this blind poet gave live performances of his *Wallace*. In the work itself, there are numerous references to oral presentation, though there are also several references to its being written down. Internal evidence shows that Hary was familiar with events of Wallace's career related in chronicles, but there is so much in the *Wallace* that is not in earlier texts that most of the narrative appears to have developed in legends to which Hary, as traditional teller, significantly contributed himself. The poetic narrative itself is a long praise-poem about Wallace as Scotland's national hero: first as outlaw, then as warrior chieftain, and again as outlaw who became national martyr through his execution. (Its extreme anti-English sentiment should be understood not only within the context of Wallace's time, but also Hary's own, as an attack on the pro-English policies of the Scottish King James III (reigned 1460-88).) Some of Hary's most memorable legends include Wallace's various disguises, sometimes as a woman, while an outlaw evading capture by the English; his being literally nursed back to health by a young mother who suckled him at her breast after he nearly died in prison at Ayr; his beheading the laggard Fawdon while being pursued by the English and later, in a harrowing scene, being haunted by the headless Fawdon at night in a dark wood.[8] Much attention is given to the dream vision in which he was given his sword by St Andrew, the patron saint of Scotland, and has his face crossed by the Blessed Virgin Mary with the saltire (the diagonal cross of St Andrew adopted for the Scottish flag), and to his numerous feats in battle, the most historically important of which was Stirling Bridge (1297). His ascent to heaven is foretold to a holy monk by a spirit from Purgatory, while the grisly details of Wallace's actual execution were passed over – he was hanged, cut down and disembowelled while still alive, and then quartered – in order to foreground instead his confessing his sins and focusing his vision on the Psalter while dying. Clearly, several of these details are the stuff of hagiographical legend.

A rather different form of appropriating – and in this case 'Scotticising' – traditional culture appears in the *Moral Fables* of Robert Henryson (c. 1435–c. 1505). While little actual information about him survives, it is generally accepted he was university-educated and master of the school at Dunfermline. As such, it is no surprise that he would take up the Latin tradition of Aesop's fables, often used as teaching texts in the medieval curriculum. Even so, Henryson transforms this tradition, usually associated with Latin learning, by resituating its tales in Scottish physical and social contexts, registering not only elite culture, but also the daily folk-life of ordinary people in rural settings. Different social classes and occupational groups employ distinctive linguistic registers, or ways of communicating, not only conveying meaning but also signifying membership in the classes or groups to which they belong and with which they identify. Thus, there are sociolinguistic registers that define membership in the worlds of physicians and ploughmen, of theologians and fowlers, of lawyers and shepherds, each register marking a border that identifies who is 'inside' or 'outside' a particular social group. (And, of course, someone may 'belong' to more than one group and thus be at home in more than one register.)

In the fables there is constant shifting from a register signifying 'high culture' to the culture of those 'below' or on the margins. For example, 'The Cock and the Jasp' begins with a cock 'upon ane dunghill' whose barnyard existence contrasts ironically with the aureate poetic style that Henryson puts in the creature's mouth when he finds the jasp (a jewel). But even more strikingly in the tales of 'The Two Mice', 'The Lion and the Mouse', 'The Fox, the Wolf, and the Husbandman' and 'The Wolf and the Wether', readers encounter Henryson's 'Scotticising' of his Latin sources, moving into registers in which various folk groups live and interact. Here are registers of farming, fowling, country folk distinguishing themselves from the town, people whose livelihood depends on knowing the ways of animals, the clever outsmarting those in power who seek to oppress them, the law from the perspective of those against whom it may be used. What is remarkable is Henryson's ease in shifting from one cultural group or class to another. In 'The Preaching of the Swallow', for example, he not only shows his learning in references to theology, Aristotle's *Metaphysics* and the flowers of rhetoric, but he can display intimate knowledge of flax-making as well:

> The lynt ryipit, the carll pullit the lyne,   [flax pulled up]
> Rippillit the bollis and in beitis set,   [combs pods; sheaves]
> It steipit in the burne, and dryit syne,   [soaks; brook]
> And with ane bitill knokkit it and bet   [mallet]
> Syne swingillit it weill, and hekkillit in the flet;   [scraped; combed out]
> His wyfe it span, and twynit it in to thread,
> Off quhilk the fowlar nettis maid in deid.
>   (lines 1825–31)

As the glosses suggest, Henryson is using the technical terms of fowlers and their wives in their everyday task of making flax into strong enough twine for nets to hold the birds they catch. Such registering of Scottish folk-life eludes even the moralising reflections that follow this and the other fables.

Equally bold, though in a different way, is the work of one of the greatest poets of the later Middle Ages, William Dunbar (c. 1469–c. 1520). Though he wrote 'the finest religious poems to survive from pre-Reformation Scotland', according to Priscilla Bawcutt,[9] he is best remembered for his playful, satirical works. A minor member of James IV's brilliant court, he could burlesque the pretensions of the elite, as in his depiction of a dance in the queen's chamber featuring the court physician stepping like a cobbled horse, the queen's almoner breaking wind 'like a bullock' and the poet himself jigging like a colt.

He could also produce serious court poetry, like 'The Thistle and the Rose' celebrating the marriage of James to Margaret Tudor.

In his justly famous 'Dance of the Sevin Deidly Synnis', he appropriates two popular medieval traditions – personifications of the deadly sins (pride, anger, lechery, envy, gluttony, avarice and sloth) as actors in the 'dance of death'. The sinners include not only harlots and frauds, but also clergymen and devious politicians. But Dunbar provides some of his most vivid imagery in his depictions of the personified sins. Thus, 'the fowl monster Glutteny' leads an equally foul train to the dance:

> Him followit mony fowl drunckart
> With can and collop, cop and quart,   [tankard, cup]
> In surffet and exces.
> Full mony a waistles wallydrag   [good-for-nothing]
> With wamis unweildable did furth wag   [paunches unwieldy]
> creische that did incres.   [blubber]
> 'Drynk!' ay thay cryit with mony a gaip. [gasp]
>   (lines 91–100)

Next appears a band of 'savage' Highlanders ('Erschemen') who 'Full lowd in Ersche [Gaelic] begowth to clatter / And rowp [croaked] lyk revin and ruke' (lines 116–17). The Devil is so annoyed by this barbaric uproar that he smothers the Highlanders with smoke in the deepest recesses of Hell. Along with his mischievous play with popular traditional forms, Dunbar here concludes with the Lowlanders' traditional satire on Highlanders' culture – and even language. The same kind of satirical sparring with Gaelic culture also appears in his famous *Flyting betwyxt Kennedie and Dunbar*, in which the popular tradition of the flyting – a verbal duel between adversaries – becomes the vehicle through which Dunbar dissociates himself from the Gaelic poetic tradition. While William Kennedy (c. 1460–c. 1508), a poet from the Lowland Gaelic-speaking country of Carrick defends his tongue as 'the gud language of this land', Dunbar rails against its 'Heland' noise.

Equally memorable, though in an earthier tone, is the poem that some regard as his masterpiece, 'Tretis of the Twa Mariit Wemen and the Wedo'. It begins with the language of courtly love, associated with the widely diffused and immensely popular genre of medieval romance. The audience is thus led to expect a conventional *demande d'amour*, in which various aspects of, or views about, love are discussed and perhaps debated. But such an expectation is soon thwarted as the women discuss love with a frankness about sex, together with a kind of pragmatism about marriage, quite foreign to the world of Lancelot and Guinevere. Once again, Dunbar shows his genius for manipulating tradition with ironic twists and turns.

All in all, then, there is great variety in the ways medieval Scottish writers and their works participate in, or appropriate, traditions. Beyond those already discussed, some of the most interesting cases may be found in saints' lives, among the most popular productions of traditional culture throughout the entire period, though they were largely neglected after the Reformation. The lives of SS Ninian (or Nynia), Kentigern (or Mungo) and Columba (or Colum Cille) are filled with the legendry common in folklore. And yet, although there are Gaelic lives of Columba and a Scots life of Ninian contemporary with Barbour, they largely come down to us in a Latin literary culture that, in appropriating them, confers on this legendry a new cultural authority – following such diverse models as the lives of SS Antony of Egypt, Martin of Tours and such Irish notables as Patrick and Brigid.

According to Aelred of Rievaulx (1110–67) in his 'official' biography of St Ninian (d. 432?), there was a long oral tradition of relating the life and miracles of the saint, though some of this tradition may have come down to him in writing. But Aelred expresses disgust at the 'barbaric style' in which the tradition was conveyed, with its 'rustic language' obscuring the greatness of the saint. Thus, Aelred claims, he was compelled to save Ninian's memory by bringing it 'out of darkness into the light of Latin prose'.[10] This is a commonplace among many Latin saints' lives, but in the context of Scottish tradition is clearly a rejection of the native language. Thus, Aelred, *pace* the later cultural politics of Gavin Douglas, argues that the native tongue cannot possibly approach the dignity of Latin, but that Latin will confer dignity on the oral tradition. Likewise, Jocelyn in his *Life of Kentigern* (c. 1180),[11] relies on earlier tradition that came to him in 'the Scottic style'. Given the greatness of his subject, Jocelyn promises to 'season with Roman salt [Latin] what had been ploughed by barbarians'.

There are countless Celtic saints, not to mention those from south-east Germanic-speaking areas like Cuthbert and Baldred, commemorated in early tradition, and their sanctity is assured by accounts of their miracles, both those performed while living and the post-mortem miracles performed through their relics. Such tales of wonder-working include St Ninian's exoneration of a presbyter falsely accused of fathering an illegitimate child with a woman in his congregation. Through the power of the saint, the child, born just the night before, speaks in an adult man's voice clearing the clergyman of blame. In the *Life of Kentigern*, a queen gives her lover a ring given to her by her husband, the king, who, while the lover is sleeping, removes it from his finger and throws it into the River Clyde. When the king later commands the queen to show him the ring, she faces execution for adultery. However, she becomes contrite and implores help from Kentigern. The saint orders a recently caught salmon cut open, revealing the ring, so restoring it to the queen and preserving her honour. This story is a Scottish version of a traditional tale whose diffusion reaches back to Ireland – for example, to the seventh-century *Life of Brigid* by Cogitosus, itself based on oral tradition. Its importance for Scottish tradition is shown by the incorporation of the salmon and the ring in the arms of the city of Glasgow. In the case of Adomnán's *Life of St Columba* (c. 700) there is an example of traditional lore, given the authority of one of the greatest medieval saints' lives, which still has power in modern times. According to Adomnán's account, the saint was travelling in Pictland by the River Ness and came upon a group of local folk burying a man who had been mauled and killed by a water monster. Columba ordered Luigne, one of his followers, to swim across the river to fetch a boat from the opposite shore. When the monster charged at Luigne, the saint made the sign of the cross and commanded it to retreat, thus saving his follower's life. As Richard Sharpe points out in his edition, 'This is the oldest story of the Loch Ness Monster'[12] – or at least the first to make its way from oral to textual tradition.

Clearly, much more could be done with research into the impact of Scottish saints' lives on traditional tales, which embody much early lore as well as provide popular vehicles for its transmission. Perhaps the greatest of such legends is that of an angel guiding St Rule to carry the relics of the apostle Andrew to Fife, thus grounding the apostle's status as Scotland's patron saint in native soil, so, arguably, conferring his prestige on the land, its people and their traditions.

CHAPTER SIX

Vernacular Gaelic Tradition

Robert Dunbar

Gaelic's vernacular literary tradition, primarily orally-transmitted, was not significantly recorded before eighteenth-century manuscripts and printed collections appeared, though the oldest specimens may be fifteenth century, while its roots probably go back well into the Middle Ages.[1] Much material continued being collected in the later twentieth century, in Scotland – by Edinburgh University's School of Scottish Studies fieldworkers and independent collectors like John Lorne Campbell of Canna[2] – and elsewhere – most notably Nova Scotia,[3] where the language survives, albeit weakly. That a 1960s Tiree informant could provide otherwise unavailable biographical data about an early eighteenth-century female poet,[4] or Cape Breton fieldworker active between 1960 and 1990 could amass a sizeable body of song,[5] some perhaps dating from the seventeenth century, speaks of the tradition's enduring vigour. Its record, compiled to the nineteenth century's conclusion,[6] is sizeable and impressive in range, depth and quality; we may reasonably surmise that it represents only the tip of a very formidable iceberg that would have circulated when Gaelic-speaking populations were several times greater than today's, and assimilation, though powerful, less all-encompassing.

The *cèilidh*, or neighbourhood house-visit, has been called the 'power-house of eighteenth-century Gaelic culture',[7] a claim surely generally true of the period discussed here, though by the nineteenth century other important cultural transmission media were emerging. Certainly, it was a 'power-house' of Gaelic oral tradition. Alexander Carmichael noted the cèilidh was

> a literary entertainment where stories and tales, poems and ballads, are rehearsed and recited, and songs are sung, conundrums are put, proverbs are quoted, and many other literary matters are related and discussed.[8]

Carmichael described it as he observed it in the second half of the nineteenth century in much of the Hebrides. He noted people of all ages attended, many of those, particularly women, taking care of household tasks like carding, spinning and knitting. Conversation would at first be general – local news, weather, the price of cattle – and proceed to 'higher' themes, like 'the clearing of the glens, the war, the parliament, the effects of the sun on the earth and the moon upon the tides'. Then the man of the house would be asked to tell a story, which would be discussed, its characters' behaviour analysed and so forth. Carmichael noted that, if not too late, proverbs, riddles, conundrums and songs followed.[9]

Although cèilidhs were undoubtedly crucial for oral tradition's transmission, aspects – particularly song – were all-pervasive and ever-present. Shaw notes that well into the twentieth century, 'occasions for singing were so numerous that Gaelic song – and the social and affective content of the verses – has over generations inevitably made up a large part of the inner verbal dialogue among many traditional Gaels'.[10] Song accompanied virtually all work-types: in the fields, at the shieling, at the fishing and most domestic tasks.[11] Other important loci for transmission were social events: betrothals – the *rèiteach* – weddings and wakes (although certain genres could be prescribed).[12]

Generically, poetry and song were central: in practice, generally no sharp distinction was made between them in our period; we might better speak of 'song-poetry'. A diverse range of oral narrative existed. At its heart were hero-tales; particularly valued were those from a Gaelic literary tradition common to Ireland and Gaelic Scotland, including Fenian lore. International tales were also plentiful, including *Märchen* and romantic tales, including many of cleverness. A genre well-represented in Scotland, particularly vis-à-vis Ireland, is clan lore, due partly to clan-based society's much later survival in the Scottish Highlands. Anecdotes, particularly humorous, often involving 'wise fools' like 'Gilleasbuig Aotrom', were staples of cèilidhs and daily exchanges. Any account of oral tradition must also encompass other lore, including the supernatural, charms, incantations, proverbial expressions and riddles. Indeed, genealogy, weather lore, astronomy, plant-lore, folk medicine, place-name lore and local lore could also appear, though this chapter focuses on other genres. Though, as noted, manuscripts and books were primary records of oral traditions, by the early nineteenth century, other print media were appearing – newspapers, periodicals and scholarly journals – providing additional modes of preserving oral tradition and initiating new genres.

Before the eighteenth century, very limited collecting of the massive vernacular literature then orally circulating is evident. The 'Fernaig Manuscript'[13] is a notable exception, sitting 'poised somewhat uneasily between classical and vernacular literatures'.[14] Compiled between 1688 and 1693 by Duncan MacRae ('Donnchadh nam Pìos') of Inverinate, Wester Ross, it contains mostly religious verse, some by MacRae and some older, beside some contemporary Jacobite poetry. Around then, Rev. Robert Kirk (1644–92), minister of Aberfoyle, Perthshire, completed *The Secret Commonwealth of Elves, Fauns and Fairies and a Short Treatise of Charms and Spels*.[15] Although in English, it was, and remains, an important work on Highland folklore, where the bilingual Kirk recorded accounts of fairies and second-sight from people of his Highland parish. The role of such clergymen established an enduring pattern for collection of oral tradition: 'Gaelic Scotland [...] owes the survival of a considerable proportion of its vernacular ballads, songs and tales to the Protestant Church.'[16] Edward Lhuyd (1660–1709) was another important early figure in such collection. Between 1697 and 1701, he travelled extensively in Celtic lands to collect material for *Archaeologia Britannica*: ultimately only the first volume was published, in 1707.[17]

The 1700s were profoundly important for vernacular tradition's recording: collectors' interest primarily focused on poetry and song.[18] The manuscript attributed to Alexander Pope, minister of Reay, Caithness, containing significant numbers of heroic ballads, dated to about 1739, was a harbinger. From the 1750s, some of the collection of the minister of Lismore, Rev. Donald MacNicol (1735–1802), has survived,[19] and between about 1750 and 1756, Jerome Stone (1727–56), a Lowland schoolmaster resident in Dunkeld, learned Gaelic and made a collection of Gaelic poetry, including some heroic material and songs circulating locally. Perhaps this period's two most important manuscript collections were made by Rev. Ewen MacDiarmid (d. 1801)[20] and Rev. James MacLagan (1728–1805).[21] MacDiarmid was native to central Perthshire; it appears he began collecting about 1762 and completed his work about 1769 or 1770. The collection comprises primarily songs and poems, including compositions of some of the most important seventeenth- and eighteenth-century poets, like Niall MacMhuirich (c. 1550–c. 1630), John MacDonald ('Iain Lom', c. 1625–post 1707), Cicely MacDonald ('Sìleas na Ceapaich', c. 1660–c. 1729), Alexander MacDonald ('Alasdair mac Mhaighstir Alasdair', c. 1695–c. 1770) and Duncan MacIntyre ('Donnchadh Bàn', 1724–1812), besides several heroic ballads and Ossianic items. It also includes other valuable material: an early collection of proverbs and even some Gaelic toasts. MacLagan was also a Perthshire native – for a time chaplain to the 42nd Regiment, the Black Watch – before finishing his ministry at Blair Atholl. He appears to have begun collecting in the early 1750s, carrying on almost until his death. The surviving manuscript amounts to 1,650 pages, comprising about 630 individual items. Almost half is anonymous verse, much of the rest being verse attributed to particular authors, and there is a significant number of heroic ballads.[22] Again, the work of many of the most important seventeenth- and eighteenth-century poets is included: Iain Lom, Mary Macleod, ('Màiri nighean Alasdair Ruaidh', c. 1615–post 1705), Alasdair mac Mhaighstir Alasdair, Donnchadh Bàn and Robert Mackay ('Rob Donn', 1714–78), although there are also some sixteenth- and early seventeenth-century songs associated with the MacGregors. Many texts were clearly derived from contemporary Highland Perthshire and Argyll oral tradition; however, MacLagan had a wide range of correspondents, including through the Church and Army – there is material from a much wider geographical area.[23] Dr Hector Maclean (1704–83) of Grulin, Mull and Alexander Irvine (1773–1824), minister of Little Dunkeld, Perthshire, compiled two other important manuscript collections. The latter is a large Gaelic poetry collection, completed about 1801. Alexander Maclean Sinclair (1840–1924), into whose possession Dr Maclean's manuscript came, claimed his collection was partly made between 1768 and 1773.[24] Containing some sixty-five poems, the majority not appearing in other collections,[25] the manuscript had a strong representation of poetry associated with Maclean kindreds.[26]

As already noted, much verse in these and later collections was meant for singing, and was composed to pre-existing airs. Although manuscript compilers and printed collection editors sometimes named the air, very rarely was it noted down itself. In 1784, however, Rev. Patrick MacDonald (1729–1824), minister of Kilmore, Argyllshire, published A Collection of Highland Vocal Airs,[27] commenced, apparently, by his brother Joseph in Sutherland, Patrick adding Perthshire, Argyll, Skye and the Western Isles song tunes, beside some dance tunes and bagpipe music specimens.[28] Others followed MacDonald. Elizabeth Jane Ross, later Lady D'Oyly (1789–1875), in about 1812, while in Raasay, collected 150 airs, most meant as songs.[29] In 1816, Captain Simon Fraser of Knockie (1773–1852) published The Airs and Melodies Peculiar to the Highlands of Scotland and the Isles. Although many of the 234 items noted are instrumental – strathspeys and reels – several song airs were included. Unlike Patrick MacDonald, who apparently travelled widely through the Highlands to compile his collection, most of Fraser's song airs were based on his grandfather's repertoire. None of these early collections contained the songs' words, only the airs' names and notations.[30] The first collection to marry words to notated airs appeared also in 1816: Albyn's Anthology, compiled and published by Alexander Campbell (1764–1824), native of Tombea, Loch Lubnaig, of whose ninety-one items fifty-two were Gaelic airs. About 1848, another collection, Orain na h-Albain, was published. Attributed to Finlay Dun, it includes forty-three items, all supplied with English words.[31] William Matheson notes that Patrick MacDonald was in some respects ahead of his time, and of these other early collectors of Gaelic airs, in understanding the complexities and difficulties of recording airs from the Gaelic oral tradition within Western musical notation conventions: he did not feel authorised to alter or improve pieces according to his own ideas.[32] However, even he only partially succeeded in this respect, while most early collectors and publishers 'improved' the items, 'fitting them into a style that was fashionable at the time'.[33]

The printing press allowed material being collected to circulate to wider audiences, and from the mid-eighteenth century, Gaels seized this technology's opportunities. Thanks to the huge social and economic changes sweeping the Highlands after Culloden, ever-increasing numbers of Gaelic-speakers settled in Lowland towns and cities, and overseas which is where most Gaelic printing and publishing took place during the period discussed here. The first secular book published in Gaelic was Alasdair mac Mhaighstir Alasdair's *Ais-eiridh na sean chánoin Albannaich; no, An nuadh oranaiche Gaidhealach* (1751). Perhaps greatest of the eighteenth-century poets, his book contained twenty-six of his poems, two songs by John MacCodrum (1693–1779), another important eighteenth-century poet, and some other items. It was partially reprinted in 1764 and 1802. In 1767, Dugald Buchanan (1716–68), one of the most significant evangelical poets, published a collection of his spiritual songs, *Laoidhe Spioradail*, reprinted on many occasions in both eighteenth and nineteenth centuries. In 1768, a collection of twenty-six poems by yet another of the century's 'greats', Donnchadh Bàn,[34] was published. The unlettered poet was supported in this by Rev. Donald MacNicol, minister of Lismore, who, as noted above, was himself an early collector. Like MacDonald's collection, this one was reprinted, significantly expanded, in 1790, and again in 1804.

Others followed suit. Before the end of the century, notable poets like Kenneth MacKenzie (1758–c. 1837) of Castle Leather, near Inverness,[35] and Allan MacDougall ('Ailean Dall', c. 1750–1828), the blind poet originally from Glencoe, who came under MacDonell of Glengarry's patronage, had published poetry collections.[36] Ailean Dall's collection also included thirteen poems by his friend Ewen MacLachlan (1773–1822), an important Lochaber poet who became librarian at King's College, Aberdeen, and several songs by less well-known poets. Some poets were important collectors in their own right: like MacDougall's 1798 collection, their collections contained significant amounts of work by others, besides their own. Donald MacLeod, 'Dòmhnall nan Òrain' (1787–1873), of Glendale, Skye, father of Neil MacLeod, published such a collection, *Orain Nuadh Ghaeleach*, in 1811. John MacLean, 'Bàrd Thighearna Cholla' (1787–1848), the important Tiree poet, made a significant collection between about 1814 and 1817,[37] including eighteen of his own songs and 119 poems of others, including inner Hebridean poets and some major figures like Iain Lom, 'Eachann Bacach' (c. 1600–post 1651), 'Mairghread nighean Lachlainn' (c. 1660–post 1751) and Alasdair MacKinnon (1770–1814). MacLean brought the manuscript, as well as Dr Hector Maclean's, discussed earlier, with him on emigrating to Nova Scotia in 1819. In the year before his emigration, however, he published twenty-two of his own songs, as well as thirty-three he had collected, as *Orain Nuadh Ghaedhlach*.

The early nineteenth century was a period of spiritual revival in much of the Protestant Highlands. A considerable body of spiritual poetry appeared, including collections of some of the genre's most important poets like Peter Grant (1783–1867), the Speyside poet,[38] Bàrd Thighearna Cholla[39] and John Morison (c. 1796–1852), the Harris blacksmith.[40] Books of other important nineteenth-century poets' work were published, including that of Evan MacColl of Lochfyneside (1808–98), William Livingston of Islay (1808–70), John MacLachlan of Rahoy, Morvern (1804–74) and Mary MacPherson ('Màiri Mhòr nan Òran', 1821–98) of Skye, poet-laureate of 1880s land agitation. Some of these, like *Clàrsach an Doire* (1883), primarily comprising the poems of Neil MacLeod (1843–1913) of Glendale, Isle of Skye and Edinburgh, were highly popular, particularly amongst late-nineteenth-century urban Gaelic communities.

The first Gaelic poetry anthology drawn from the vernacular tradition was *Comh-chruinneachidh Orannaigh Gaidhealach* (1776), the 'Eigg Collection', published by Ranald MacDonald ('Raghnall Dubh', c. 1728–c. 1808), Alasdair mac Mhaighstir Alasdair's son, at that time tacksman of Laig in Eigg. Containing 106 items, it included some of the earliest vernacular tradition poetry, like the 'Brosnachadh Catha' ('Encitement to Battle') attributed to Lachlan MacMhuirich, composed for the 1411 Battle of Harlaw, and the sixteenth-century 'Òran na Comhachaig', attributed to the Lochaber poet Dòmhnall mac Fhionnlaigh, as well as six poems of Màiri nighean Alasdair Ruaidh, ten by Ranald's father, three by John MacCodrum and a wide variety of other material, including two poems which appear to be waulking songs (about which, see below).[41] In 1780, John Gillies, a Perth-based publisher and bookseller, added sixteen poems to his *History of the Feuds and Conflicts among the Clans*, including 'Òran na Comhachaig' and another important pre-1600 vernacular poem, 'An Làir Dhonn', two songs by John MacCodrum and several other poems.[42] Gillies followed this in 1786 with the eighteenth century's largest collection, *Sean Dain, agus Orain Ghaidhealach*, containing 114 items. Drawing heavily on MacLagan's collection, but including material provided to him by Rev. Donald MacNicol, Sir James Foulis of Collington and James Macintyre of Glenoe, it included a significant number of Ossianic ballads. Although containing few poems by important poets, it is notable for its wide variety, with about thirteen songs seeming to be waulking songs, a genre not terribly prevalent in most important early collections.[43]

In the early nineteenth century, several large and fundamentally important anthologies appeared: with the Eigg Collection, Gillies's collection and the important latter eighteenth- and early nineteenth-century manuscript collections already referred to, these provided the foundations on which virtually all important modern collections relating to the eighteenth century and earlier are based. These include *Cochruinneacha Taoghta de Shaothair nam*

Bard Gaëleach ('A Choice Collection of the Works of the Highland Bards, collected in the Highlands and Isles'), published in 1804 by Alexander and Donald Stewart, of North Uist; *Co-chruinneachadh nuadh de dh' Orannibh Gaidhealach* ('A New Collection of Gaelic Songs') of 1806, also known as the 'Inverness Collection', which included some previously unpublished poems; the 1813 collection made by Peter Turner ('Pàruig Mac-an-Tuairneir'), *Comhchruinneacha do dh' Orain Taghta, Ghaidhealach* ('A Collection of Choice Highlnad Songs'), which contained 128 items, including a large number of poems not previously published; *Co'-chruinneachadh de dh' orain agus de luinneagaibh thaghta Ghae'lach* ('A Collection of Choice Highland Songs and Ditties') also published in 1813, by Peter MacFarlane; and an 1821 collection of the Rev. Duncan MacCallum, *Co-chruinneacha Dhan, Orain, &c, &c.* ('A Collection of Poems, Songs &c.'), which again included some previously unpublished songs. Of later collections, three are particularly notable, because of their content and, crucially, their wide circulation in Gaelic communities, not only in Scotland, but overseas, in places like Nova Scotia, where they were prized possessions – often, besides the Gaelic Bible, one of the few books in the household. John MacKenzie's *Sar-Obair nam Bard Gaelach: The Beauties of Gaelic Poetry and the Lives of the Highland Bards*, first published in 1841, but regularly reprinted well into the twentieth century (once, in 1860, in Nova Scotia) contained relatively little poetry not already published, but it provided an overview of many of the vernacular tradition's most important poets, with brief biographical sketches and a selection of other popular songs. This could, until William J. Watson's *Bardachd Ghàidhlig/Specimans of Gaelic Poetry 1550–1900* appeared in 1918 (now itself supplanted), be considered the 'canonical' collection. The second important anthology was *An Duanaire*, published by Donald MacPherson of Bohuntin, Lochaber in 1868, which included many local compositions, none previously published. Perhaps the best and most influential, however, was *An t-Oranaiche*, published by Archibald Sinclair, about which Prof. Donald Meek writes:

> While reflecting the Argyllshire roots of the compiler, An t-Oranaiche is a splendid example of nineteenth-century printing and publishing, containing an extremely valuable selection of songs, many of which were composed before 1860. An t-Oranaiche represents the more robust days of the Lowland Gaelic community before it was infected by the romantic virus and subsequent poetic rigor mortis of the last quarter of the century.[44]

One should also note Rev. Alexander Maclean Sinclair (1840–1923), grandson of Bàrd Thighearna Cholla, who, over a quarter of a century from 1880, brought out several collections of Gaelic poetry and song, drawing heavily on his grandfather's and Dr Hector Maclean's manuscripts, but also his voluminous correspondence with many leading Gaelic publishing and scholarship figures in Scotland. He was, however, an inveterate 'improver' of texts and his collections, though valuable, should be treated with caution.[45]

A particular strength of *An t-Oranaiche* is the breadth of genres represented, including many anonymously-composed songs, particularly waulking songs and other work songs, genres generally under-represented in earlier collections. Other later nineteenth-century collectors and publishers did much to address this gap, including Frances Tolmie of Uiginish, Skye (1840–1926) and Keith Norman MacDonald (1834–1913). Although much of Tolmie's collecting, which began about 1860, has not been published, a valuable collection of 105 work songs, including many waulking songs, was published by the Folklore Society in 1911;[46] it included song notations as well as some song-text, besides valuable descriptions of some of her informants. Morag Macleod notes she was the 'first collector to present the songs as she heard them', and 'appreciated the qualities of the indigenous art that her predecessors as collectors had to varying extents failed to do'.[47] William Lamb notes that '[d]ue to her fine ear, her musical ability and literacy in Gaelic, her transcriptions of Gaelic song set a new standard, and one that would not be matched for almost half a century.'[48] In 1895, Keith Norman MacDonald, native to Sleat, Skye, published *The Gesto Collection of Highland Music*, which, in addition to dance tunes for the fiddle and pipe tunes, included Gaelic songs. Although he included piano scores for the melodies, he did not attempt to 'improve' the songs. In two appendices in 1898 and 1902, MacDonald added other material, including twenty-eight songs provided by Tolmie.[49] In 1901, MacDonald published *Puirt-a-Beul*, still the only substantial collection of this genre, Gaelic mouth-music – essentially dance tunes like strathspeys, reels and jigs set to words and sung. The collection included eighty-five dance tunes, as well as some waulking, children's and rowing songs, and a few other items. Lamb, editor of a modern edition, notes that although the collection

> was compiled hastily, and exhibits certain orthographical and musical inconsistencies, editorial errors, lack of citation and some historical conclusions that we now know are wide of the mark [. . . m]any of the puirt that [he] included in the book are only to be found within it, and without his efforts, our knowledge of Scottish traditional music and culture would be greatly impoverished.[50]

Another major contribution to the body of songs not well represented in early collections was that of Donald MacCormick, of Kilpheder, South Uist, who in about 1893 made a collection of thirty-seven waulking songs, mostly from his district. It was only in 1969 that this collection was edited and published. As the editors of that collection note, 'generally waulking songs, not being felt suitable for literary treatment or for solo singing at concerts, have been neglected by the compilers of Gaelic anthologies and Gaelic song-books'.[51]

As a whole, the body of poetry and song preserved from vernacular tradition is impressive. Praise poetry is central to this tradition: praise of clan chiefs and certain other heroic figures was the core of most seventeenth- and eighteenth-century major poets' known work, much of lesser poets' work and the large body of unattributed poetry. It has been argued panegyric is 'an organised rhetorical system, concentrated in certain metrical forms but certainly not confined to them', and in this sense 'a pervasive style'. It has also been suggested that it is, additionally, 'a mode of communication, expressed in sets of images and formulas, often very precise and detailed'.[52] The subject's appearance would be praised and personal qualities enumerated: hospitality (for example, ample provision of food and drink), generosity to the weak and vulnerable, support of the learned orders and cultural leaders, wise counsel, and, crucially, physical courage, were common themes. Physical attributes and roles were praised, especially ferocity and skill in battle, good seamanship, good horsemanship and skill in the hunt. A range of kennings were typically deployed, with the subject likened to a species of tree – always a 'noble' tree like oak or yew, rather than a 'base' tree – or to an animal associated with nobility, like salmon, eagle or lion. In a classic of the genre, an elegy like 'Alasdair à Gleanna Garadh' ('Alexander from Glengarry'),[53] composed by Sìleas na Ceapaich on Alasdair Dubh, 11th Chief of the MacDonells of Glengarry's death (?1721), one motif piles onto another in densely-packed cataloguing of the subject's heroic attributes. The collapse of the clan system after Culloden in 1746 meant panegyric for the clan elite became less common, but, in the nineteenth century, the style – and even rhetoric – of this 'panegyric code' was redeployed in praise of new community leaders – like clergy, Highland soldiers in the British army and a wide variety of 'culture heroes' – and even important new media, like Gaelic journals.

Other subject matter central to vernacular tradition includes political verse – there is a considerable body of poetry documenting seventeenth-century civil wars, the 1688–9 revolution and its aftermath (including Glencoe) and, of course, the Jacobite risings, especially 1715 and 1745–6. Much poetry and song relates to the Napoleonic wars. From the 1760s right through to 1900, commercialisation of estate practices, clearance and emigration were important subjects. Another staple was satire, as were various sorts of love and nature poetry. As time passed, collectors paid more attention to what has been called 'township verse', songs (mainly) chronicling local events and characters, where the poet, acting as the community's spokesperson, often expressed deeply-felt emotions at times of local tragedy, like a young man's loss at sea or in battle. Moreover, besides greater attention to waulking songs, other forms of work songs were recognised, including milking, churning, spinning and rowing songs, known as 'iorram'. These tend to be highly rhythmical (the refrains of the waulking songs are often composed of vocables of no obvious meaning) and the authors were often women, as waulking was traditionally women's work (though it has come to be associated with male singers in Cape Breton). Given the authorship, the corpus provides an interesting view of women's perceptions and concerns – unrequited love, unfaithful or unattainable lovers (a man of a higher social status is often involved), the death of a lover at sea or in war, and so forth. Imagery is usually sharply drawn. There is great economy and beauty of expression.

As we have seen, until the mid-nineteenth century, songs and poetry fared better than other traditional vernacular genres in terms of collection and publication, with few exceptions. One of these was proverbs. Ewen MacDiarmid's manuscript contained a collection of them,[54] while the two earliest systematic collections appear to be in the National Libary of Scotland in Alasdair mac Mhaighstir Alasdair's hand.[55] The first significant collection, however, was Donald Macintosh's *A Collection of Gaelic Proverbs and Familiar Phrases, with English Translation* (1785; republished 1819), based largely on Lochaber and east Perthshire collecting. In 1881, Sherriff Alexander Nicolson of Skye published *A Collection of Gaelic Proverbs and Familiar Phrases*, a collection still in print and influential. Nicolson drew heavily on Macintosh's work, but he also drew on MacDiarmid and on Dr Alexander Cameron's collection, itself published later,[56] adding comments, explanatory notes and examples from other cultures with some similarity to the Gaelic material. Alexander Campbell's collection is also important, though not published until 1978, edited by Donald Meek.[57]

The first printed Gaelic folk tale was *Eachdraidh Mhic-Cruislig*, published by John Mackenzie in 1836.[58] However, thanks to the work of major figures, John Francis Campbell of Islay ('Iain Òg Ìle', 1821–85),[59] Alexander Carmichael, native to Lismore (1832–1912) and Rev. John Gregorson Campbell (1836–91), Gaelic folk tale and the rich lode of charms, incantations, rhymes and so forth gained unprecedented international acclaim. The work of Campbell of Islay, Carmichael, J. G. Campbell and others in this field is discussed further in Jason Harris's chapter.

Clergy played an important role as collectors of vernacular tradition through the end of the period under discussion. Rev. James MacDougall (1833–1906), a native of Craignish, Aryellshire, and minister of Duror, collected much oral narrative, including Fenian tales, some being published in 1889[60] and 1891,[61] and a collection of wonder tales, fairy lore and lore about supernatural creatures drawn from MacDougall's work appeared in 1910, as *Folk Tales and Fairy Lore in Gaelic and English, Collected from Oral Tradition*.[62] Another significant figure was Fr Allan MacDonald (1859–1905),[63] parish priest in South Uist, then Eriskay, who besides collecting substantial material, crossing most genres discussed here, also composed spiritual verse. Much of his collection, which included seven notebooks, only five being still available, has yet to be published,[64] although others, most notoriously Ada Goodrich-Freer, have drawn liberally on his work.

One final important figure is Lady Evelyn Stewart Murray (1868–1940), youngest daughter of John, 7th Duke of Atholl. Unlike most contemporary members of his class, he encouraged his children to learn Gaelic; Lady Evelyn applied herself assiduously. She also developed a keen interest in oral tradition and, during 1891, collected 241 Gaelic tales and songs in Highland Perthshire. Besides capturing important elements of a now-disappeared dialect, she collected Atholl tales and historical tales from other parts of Perthshire, lore concerning fairies, brownies, witches and wizards, songs, ghost stories and other material. Lady Evelyn's manuscript collections, like many, waited a long time, until 2009, for publication.[65]

The Gaelic periodical press emerged in the nineteenth century. Although a Gaelic periodical briefly appeared as early as 1803, this got properly under way only in the late 1820s. Crucial was Rev. Dr. Norman MacLeod, 'Caraid nan Gàidheal' (1783–1862), both editor and leading contributor to *An Teachdaire Gae'lach* ('The Highland Messenger', 1829–31), and to *Cuairtear nan Gleann* ('Traveller of the Glens', monthly March 1840– June 1843). The 1840s were relatively vibrant, including *Teachdaire nan Gaidheal* ('The Messenger of the Gaels'), *An Fhianuis* ('The Witness'), a Free Church of Scotland publication, and *Fear-Tathaich nam Beann* ('The Mountain Visitor'). After a hiatus, publications like *An Gaidheal* ('The Gael', 1871–7) and the *Celtic Magazine* (1875–88) – which, though primarily in English, had significant Gaelic content – appeared. The *Celtic Monthly* (1892–1917) included some Gaelic material. Fundamentally important was *Mac-Talla* (1892–1904), discussed by Michael Newton, published in Sydney, Cape Breton, by Jonathan MacKinnon, as the only all-Gaelic weekly (and from 1901 bi-weekly) newspaper. Such publications contributed to vernacular literature in two ways.

First, much vernacular literature in oral tradition or unpublished manuscripts was printed in the new periodical press, while material reprinted in some earlier published collections received wider circulation. Also important were mainly English-language newspapers like *The Highlander* (1873–81), the *Northern Chronicle* (1881–1969) and the *Oban Times* (1861–present), publishing Gaelic prose and, especially, verse.[66] The *Transactions of the Gaelic Society of Inverness* (1872–present) are especially significant: particularly in the late nineteenth and early twentieth centuries, these published traditional vernacular literature in all genres discussed, some gathered by, inter alia, J. G. Campbell, Carmichael and other important collectors like Rev. Thomas Sinton and Rev. John MacRury. Although belonging to the twentieth century's earlier years, *The Celtic Review*, another scholarly journal, whose driving forces were Donald MacKinnon, first holder of Edinburgh University's chair of Celtic, and Ella, Alexander Carmichael's daughter, published such material, from late nineteenth-century collectors like Carmichael, J. G. Campbell and Fr Allan MacDonald.

Gaelic periodicals' second major contribution was as a forum for creation of new forms of vernacular prose literature. The earliest periodicals set the tone, including essays – for example, on events in Highland history – sermons, hymns, songs, letters and reportage. Caraid nan Gàidheal's publications featured many accounts of lands whither Gaels were emigrating, and could be considered an early form of Gaelic travel-writing. New forms of fictional writing, especially 'conversations', of which Caraid nan Gàidheal was master, were particularly important.[67] These featured dialogues between stock characters, representing archetypal figures in contemporary Gaelic communities, in rich, colourful, idiomatic Gaelic.[68] They were crucial in the development of Gaelic fiction,[69] really a twentieth-century genre: see Michael Newton's chapter.

Seventeenth- to nineteenth-century Gaelic vernacular literature's evident intrinsic value sustains its legacy as a basis for scholarship and pleasure. Despite a great deal of traditional material now available (thanks to the efforts of publishers like Birlinn, publishing excellent modern Gaelic verse anthologies and reprinting *Popular Tales of the West Highlands* and *More West Highland* Tales, representative samples are now widely accessible), much in important manuscript collections, including Campbell of Islay's, awaits editing and publication. The song tradition continues to form the core repertoires of contemporary popular Gaelic singers like Julie Fowlis, Margaret Stewart and Art Cormack in Scotland and Mary Jane Lamond in Canada, as the tradition is mined for 'new' material. Such songs are staples of the Royal National Mòd. Traditional oral narrative's role in Gaelic fiction's development has been hypothesised,[70] and its cadences and idioms are echoed in some twentieth-century autobiographical literature but more research on such matters is needed. Oral narrative's rich storehouse provides material capable of re-application and exploitation in modern Gaelic fictional writing, and even new media. Fionnlagh Macleòid's *Gormshuil an Rìgh* (2010), a literary folk tale brilliantly drawing on traditional Gaelic oral narrative, provides an outstanding example to other creative writers of this literature's on-going relevance. Macleòid's generation is closer to the cèilidh and its traditions. For this great vernacular tradition to achieve its full potential as a creative wellspring in twenty-first century Gaeldom, it needs deeper integration into pre-school, primary, secondary and tertiary curricula.

CHAPTER SEVEN

The Early Modern Period

Sarah Dunnigan

In 1801, at the age of twenty-six, the Roxburghshire writer, John Leyden, published an edition of *The Complaynt of Scotland*. A long, allegorical prose work in Scots from the middle of the sixteenth century, it was then (as now) relatively unknown. Composed by Robert Wedderburn, dedicated to Mary of Lorraine, and printed in Paris c. 1550, it was a political and religious polemic, an 'attack on tyranny', a 'national document' and a piece of 'social criticism'.[1] It also contained striking evidence of a rich and flourishing store of narrative tales and songs, beguiling Leyden who would contribute local lore and ballad for the *Minstrelsy* collection of his friend, Walter Scott. Here is a brief sample:

> the volfe of the varlis end, Ferrand erl of Flandris that mareit the deuyl, the taiyl of the reyde eyttyn vithit the thre heydis, the tail quhou perseus sauit andromeda fra the cruel monstir, the prophysie of merlyne, the tayl of the giantis that eit quyk men, on fut by fortht as I culd found, vallace, the bruce, ypomedon, the tail of the thre futtit dog of norrouay [. . .][2]

All these are 'pleysand storeis' – in this brief extract alone fable, romance, myth, wonder tale – told to the text's narrator by a gathering of shepherds; in trying to assuage the 'sadnes' inflicted by study and writing (as well as associated 'caterris', 'hede verkis, ande indegestione'), he has sought the 'greene hoilsum feildis'. Along with 'sueit melodius sangis', dances and pipe-playing, these stories belong to the 'ioyus comonyng' urged by one of the shepherd's wives ('fortunately', as Leyden notes). In so being renewed and made 'contentit', the *Complaynt*'s narrator joins a circle of story listeners and tellers that evokes the multiple narrations of Chaucer, Boccaccio and the *Arabian Nights*, and the recreational, 'therapeutic' power of storytelling. Simultaneously, it catches the resurgent flow and ebb of Scottish tradition for a handful of these sixteenth-century oral tales re-appear as 'The Black Bull o Norroway', 'The Wolf at the Warldis End', 'Red Etin', in Robert Chamber's *Popular Rhymes* (1826) – stories inherited from his nurse.

In considering the idea of 'traditional literature', or the relationship between 'tradition' and literature in the early modern period in Scotland, both this excerpt and its context are suggestive. For what we might call the 'early modern' or 'Renaissance' period in Scotland peculiarly magnifies the difficulties that inherently beset any attempt to recover cultural history. Even if arguments about temporal beginnings and ends are brushed aside (how to pinpoint a chronology of the 'Scottish Renaissance'?),[3] there are other fractious points: sixteenth- and seventeenth-century (non-Gaelic) Scottish culture is perhaps not as visible or secure as that of other periods, though seen as a watershed which ushered in a slow but powerful process of cultural and linguistic attrition through the successive, troubled reigns of Stewart/Stuart monarchs. Yet, this rather complex and inchoate picture may help to disclose those cultural fragments which, pieced together, open up fascinating ways in which we might speak of 'traditional literature' at this time, as the pioneering work of Hamish Henderson, Edward Cowan and Emily Lyle has suggested.[4] Debates about orality versus print, 'popular' versus 'high' cultures and so on assume new and interesting shapes in the early modern period when we look at some surviving materials (ballads, songs, lore), as Adam Fox, Alison Shell and Mary Ellen Lamb, for example, have in relation to English culture.[5] Although this chapter will, for the most part, confine itself to a century (c. 1500–c. 1600), and exclude folk drama tradition,[6] it seeks to open up the ways in which literary writers adopt and transmute elements from popular and oral tradition, and how oral and literary channels of transmission are enmeshed. Some of the uses of popular tradition in the period will also be suggested: how it helps to articulate a sense of cultural and social communality; how it becomes the glue by which social, cultural, or religious bonds are stitched together; how it might give 'voice', often in poignant and powerful ways, to varieties of historical experience.

But it is apt to return to the strange, fascinating *Complaynt*, and its scene of traditional orality, for it gives us an interesting starting point: how Scottish Romantic writers, involved in the recovery – and creation – of 'folk' culture were (perhaps surprisingly, given its current reputation) keen to recuperate the early modern period. The relationship between eighteenth- and early nineteenth-century Romanticism and the rediscovery of popular culture across Europe has been well-documented: a wider antiquarian fascination for popular religion, traditional festivals and vernacular cultures, seen to embody regional and national identities, is seeded in the well-known ballad, song and tale collections of Percy, Herder, Arnim and Brentano, Scott and the Grimms. Most collectors (however inaccurate or disingenuous we might now know their practices to be) declare themselves compelled by the sense of a vanishing culture. And in terms of our own desire to 'access' early modern popular and oral traditions, we have ironically, but inevitably, to rely a great deal on many of these printed collections which, in Peter Burke's terms, become 'processes of mediation'.[7] Whilst we know that a significant number of ballads existed in oral transmission prior to the eighteenth century, it is by and large only the later collected, printed versions (with their variants) that we have.[8] As much as this is a provisional, complex, and imperfect 'imprint' of the materials of an earlier living culture, the antiquarian and collecting revival (of which Leyden's work is part) is vital to our material understanding of early modern Scottish culture. Scott, and associated antiquarian circles, 'resurrected' the Bannatyne manuscript, that great edifice of mid-sixteenth-century Scottish culture ascribed to the prodigious energy of one George Bannatyne, collating and transcribing during the reign of Mary, Queen of Scots.[9] This encyclopaedic 'ballat buik' attests Mary Ellen Brown's observation that within this period it is impossible to 'pin down "ballad" with any exactitude: for balladry, that which utilised the ballad style, included a multitude of things'.[10] Within it, however, is a section entitled 'ballettis mirry' which, as we shall see later, contains material which is richly folkloric in content – traditional beliefs become the stuff of comically bizarre 'fantasyis' – whilst folk custom, tradition and ritual fuel the comic bawdry of 'The Wyf of Auchtermuchty' and 'My Guddame Wes ane Gay Wife' as well as 'Sym of Lyntoun', 'The Cursing of Sir Johne Rowlis' and 'Ane Littill Interlud', for example.[11] The Bannatyne manuscript is also one of the sources for the well-known 'Christis Kirk on the Grene'.[12] As Allan H. MacLaine points out, although the poem is 'not of folk origin',[13] it generates its own resilient tradition (especially fertile for Allan Ramsay who had printed it, along with other Bannatyne material, in his collection *The Ever Green*, 1724), and engenders its violent, comic riotousness out of folk-elements associated with feasting, drinking and social licence:

> Was nevir in Scotland hard nor sene
> Sic dancing nor deray,
> Nowthir at Falkland on the grene
> Nor Peblis at the play [. . .][14]

Within this matrix of connections between early modern Scottish tradition and Romantic recuperation lies the *Complaynt of Scotland*; for this little-known, obscure text was known by none other than the brothers Grimm, Jacob and Wilhelm, who, in their antiquarian and philological guise, for a time pursued northern vernacular variants of traditional tales and ballads.[15]

I

> I saw Raf Coilyear with his thrawin brow,
> Craibit Johne the Reif *and* auld Cowkewyis sow

> And how the Wran come out of Ailssay,
> And Peirs plewman that maid his workmen fow,
> Gret Gowmakmorne *and* Fyn Makcoull, *and* how
> Thay suld be Goddis in Ireland, as thay say.
> Thair saw I Maitland vpon auld beird gray,
> Robene Hude and Gilbert with the quhite hand,
> How Hay of Nauchtoun flew in Madin land.

This stanza is from the dream vision poem, *The Palis of Honoure*, by Gavin Douglas, better known for his vernacular translation of Virgil's *Aeneid*.[16] Amongst the many wonders that the narrator glimpses within a magical mirror are these: protagonists from popular Scots and English romance tales, and from early Irish and contemporary (Scottish) Gaelic tradition and legend (Goll mac Morna and Fionn mac Cumhaill),[17] including the pig from the poem, 'Cockelbie's Sow', a composite folk tale, or 'a wyfis taill', in three parts, surviving in the Bannatyne manuscript but presumably in oral circulation much earlier; whilst the apparently odd allusion to the appearance of a wren might draw on this tiny bird's large legendary associations as king of all the birds.[18] These wonderfully compressed, heterogeneous allusions to popular, folkloric and fantastical material occur within Douglas's formal, allegorical, 'high-style' text. We see this pattern of incorporation in other writers associated with the provenance of 'the court'. David Lyndsay's prefatory epistle to his poem, 'The Dreme', for example, dedicated to James IV, tenderly reminds him of 'The prophiseis of Rymour, Beid, and Marling / And of mony uther plesand storye / of the Reid Etin, and the Gyir Carling, / Comfortand the quhen that I saw the sorye'.[19] The poet's songs, ghost and witch stories evidently lulled the young king. Though (as in the *Complaynt*, and the poems by Douglas and Lyndsay), this mode may have ultimate philosophical, ethical, or spiritual import, its revelation of dream states and visionary worlds fittingly accommodates otherworld belief and manifestations. Dunbar's narrators are frequently consumed by demonic visions and visitations whilst the Bannatyne manuscript includes within its category of the 'mirry' and 'blyth' lyric tales of fairy dreams and visions, diabolic conjurations and abductions.

These poems acquired popularity beyond their context, attracting the attention of Scott and Leyden, and earning the sobriquet 'eldritch' poetry.[20] Showing kinship with the mythopoeic, folkloric content of medieval popular culture, they are also highly stylised and crafted.[21] These poems frequently explore the boundaries between dreaming and waking; when the narrator of 'King Berdok' finds himself coming to consciousness 'Down in ane henslaik' [in a hollow depression in the ground] – having fled in the dream world from the jaws of whales – the genre's inherent self-reflective fictionality is further spun out:

> As wyffis co[m]na[n]d[is] this dreme I will conclude
> god and the rude mot turn it all to gud
> Gar fill the cop for thir auld carlingis clames
> That gentill aill is oft the causs of dremes (BM, vol. 2, pp. 270–1, ll. 87–90)

This nonsensical tale, internally set in motion by a dream of a traditionally seven-year fairy abduction, was therefore begun by beer (finely brewed, of course) and at the behest of women, two incitements to excess in the comic tradition.[22] This epilogue, cast in the 'expository' mould of allegorical dream poetry, seems like a tongue-in-cheek apologia. Lichtoun's fairy dream, inspired by the loquacious powers of drink and women, proliferates into different fragmentary episodes, just as the process of narrative telling seems itself self-renewing: 'To see mae farleis [t]at I mycht tell agane' (l. 46), he announces, or perhaps beseeches, at mid-way point. Other fairy lyrics echo this sense of tale-framing and 'tale-sharing'. This is partly derived from a shared motif of orality: the tale of 'the littill ghaist', for example, begins, 'Listis lordis I sall yow tell / off ane verry grit m[ar]vell.' Aptly in a fiction which gestures towards its courtly audience and characterises itself as a 'gentill geist' [a refined, 'well-bred' story] (l. 94), the narrator is steeped in a familiar romance inheritance.

Although we are here dealing with written, textual evidence, such material enables us to understand how provisional and imperfect are our categories of 'oral' and 'literary', 'high' and 'popular' culture at this time; instead, both apparent 'binarisms' or 'opposites' are connected fluidly and interchangeably. In the late medieval and early modern periods, there is two-way traffic; tales and poems are in oral circulation, are then reworked and written, before being returned to oral form until the major late eighteenth- and nineteenth-century collecting movement. There is also another way in which tradition and orality enter into Scottish Renaissance courtly culture, and this is due to the popularity of oral entertainment – the public 'performance' of poetry, entwined with music. At Mary's court, for example, songs and dances were celebrated; as John Purser notes, they 'were part of the oral tradition, passed from voice to voice and player to player'.[23] In the work of the eminent Jacobean court poet, Alexander Montgomerie, we can see what might be called 'the poetics of orality'. Montgomerie's linguistic dexterity is usually interpreted in terms of Renaissance poetic art theories but, as R. D. S. Jack in particular has pointed out, so imaginatively hybrid a writer incorporates proverbial allusions, colloquialisms, the registers of 'informal discourse': 'For I haif hard in adagies of auld, / That tyme dois waist and weir all things away; / Then trow the taill that treu men oft hes tauld – / A turne in tyme is ay worth other tway.'[24] What Amodio calls 'the vitality and presentness of oral poetics' despite the 'textuality of the evidence'[25] is most fully realised in Montgomerie's 'flyting' with Polwarth: that ritualised, combative and vituperative exchange of insults and abuse between poetic opponents which is publicly enacted.[26] A single stanza shows how 'oral poetic experience'[27] rips through the text:

> Vyld, venomous vipper, wanthrievest of thingis,
> Haif ane eph, half an aip, of nature denyit,
> Thow flyttis and [th]ow freittis, [th]ow fartis and [th]ow flingis,
> Bot this bargane, vnbeist, deir sall [th]ow by it.
> 'The kuif is weill warit [th]at twa home bringis',
> This proverb, peild pellet, to [th]e is apply it.
> Sprung speidder, of spyt thow spewis furth springis.
> Wanschaippin wobat, of [th]e Weirdis invyit,
> I can schaw how, quhair and quhat begate the,
>   Quhilk wes nather man nor wyf
>   Nor humane creature on lyf.
>   Fals stinkand steirar vp of stryf,
>   Hurkland howlat, have at the.[28]

Since damnation is the raison d'être of the poetic task, it is not surprising to find that the realm of the occult – of popular belief and lore – is plundered: demonic magic, witchcraft, conjurations, diabolism. Popular beliefs and living tradition are used for defamation, as if to test the boundaries of the imaginable. As the source of comic subversion and scurrility, however violent, the *Flyting* might suggest that tradition is simply the 'stuff' of 'idle stories' or 'fancies'; but we should also remember that accounts of witches, fairies and other spirits appeared in other contemporary contexts such as the testimonies of witchcraft trials; in that respect, popular culture could have a troubling topical currency.[29]

II

'Oral poets strive to make the collective past present once again in their necessarily anonymous acts of poetic making.'[30] This assertion carries resonance in terms of the historical ballad. Freed from authorial imprint and the fixity of print, the mode can serve as a powerful, sometimes polemical, 'witness' to social and political events or as a record of lives and voices that might otherwise remain unarticulated. A corpus of ballads survives tied to incidents and individuals from sixteenth-century Scottish history; as Hamish Henderson observed, '[n]early all of the best known of the Border ballads' belong to this period.[31] Characteristically, the versions that we know almost all stem from post-1700, but this in itself sheds interesting light on the way in which historical memory is transmuted and transformed through the power of oral tradition; and there are extant tunes for a number of these ballads. Many are partisan, brandishing political, national, or regional allegiances through the overt manipulation of tonal and narrative perspectives. The fate of the famous Border reiver, John Armstrong of Gilnockie (d. 1530) – he and his men were tricked by James V, then killed – is related in ballads of both English and Scottish provenance (Child 169). The former has Armstrong's young son vow vengeance on 'treacherous Scots'; the latter asserts that 'Scotlands heart was never sae wae, / To see sae mony brave men die. // Because they savd their country deir / Frae Englishmen'[32] so, like their topography, the Borders ballads divide across 'debateable land'. The English ballad about the murder of Lord Darnley in 1566, Mary, Queen of Scots' second husband and an English Catholic (Child 174), has him pierced by 'Twelue daggers [. . .] all att once' and has the fallen queen 'ffled into merry England [. . .] through the Queene of Englands good grace'.[33] In another ballad of death-commemoration, we see oral tradition become the carrier of political grievance and public mourning. 'The Bonny Earl of Murray' (Child 181) famously laments the murder of James Stewart, the second Earl, by his enemy the Earl of Huntly, in 1592; accusing him of treason against the king, Huntly burnt his castle before killing him at Donibristle in Fife. No matter how complexly orchestrated the politics behind the event,[34] the ballad variants 'transmit' the event in pared, stark style, characteristic of the mode. In Ramsay's version, simplicity of repetitious phrasing and the use of tense make his death a perpetual re-enactment: 'They have slain the Earl of Murray, / And they layd him on the green'; in the later version, the first quatrain ironically imagines Moray's own voice: '"Open the gates, / and let him come in; / He is my brother Huntley [. . .]'.[35] This embodies what Henderson called the 'orally powered artistry' of the 'made-to-order polemical song'.[36]

Frequently, we see how the ballad 'template' moulds documented events into the shape of romance. Underpinning 'The Laird o Logie' (Child 182), for example, is the incident of John Wemyss's (the titular laird) escape from sovereign jurisdiction/imprisonment, having been accused of conspiring with the Earl of Bothwell to kill James VI on 9 August 1592. His deliverance was contrived, according to a memoir, 'by the means of a gentlewoman whom he loved, a Dane' [in Queen Anna's household] who ushered him 'through the queen's chamber, where his Majesty and the queen were lying in their beds, to a window in the backside of the place, where he went down upon a tow [rope], and shot three pistols in token of his onlouping [mounting his horse]'.[37] An escapade which apparently 'ministered great occasion of laughter',[38] it furnishes subsequent balladic reimaginings, such as this taken by Scott from 'a gentleman residing near Biggar', with a redoubtable ballad heroine:

> May Margaret has kilted her green cleiding
> And she has curld back her yellow hair:
> 'If I canna get Young Logie's life,
> Farewell to Scotland for evermair!'[39]

Described in formulaic terms of beauty, this heroine nonetheless delivers the imperilled laird to safety with 'a loud laugh [. . .] / "The egg is chippd, the bird is flown"; she in turn is delivered of his 'bairn', thus forming what another variant terms a 'pretty story'.[40]

The 'distillation' of history through the particular verbal repertoire and narrative structure of the ballad form can therefore be used to powerful effect. 'Mary Hamilton' (Child 173), which survives in many variants, narrates how one of Mary Stewart's four 'Marys' was hanged for killing the child whose father was 'the hichest Stewart of a''.

> She's tyed it in her apron
> And she's thrown it in the sea;
> Says, Sink ye, swim ye, bonny wee babe!
> You'l neer get mair o me.[41]

The indifferent cruelty of both Mary's narrated gestures and words is sharpened by rhythmic simplicity; at other points narrative detail performs a crucial role in manipulating and nurturing our emotional responses – imagining that she is going to a wedding in Edinburgh, not her own execution, Mary wears a dress of 'the glistering gold' (in other variants, white or 'red scarlet');[42] the youngest of a lord's three 'dochters' (a folk and fairy-tale motif), her father would not have thought to 'see me yellow locks / hang on a gallow's tree'.[43] The first-person narration of many variants allows Mary's own narrative to be fleshed out sympathetically as she awaits the 'coming hame' at her death.[44] The ballad, in fact, lacks historical evidence; four Marys indeed attended the sovereign Mary, but none were charged with infanticide. It may have been spun out of a seed-kernel of possible truth for, as noted by Scott, John Knox records that 'a French woman that served in the queen's chamber had played the whore with the queen's own apothecary' and committed infanticide;[45] and given that the ballad 'is not known before 1790',[46] other nineteenth-century ballad editors speculated that it memorialises an entirely different Mary Hamilton punished for the same crime at the court of Peter and Catherine the Great in 1719. Ultimately, however, the question of historical veracity may not matter wholly; for a ballad like 'Mary Hamilton', however criss-crossed by different temporal and transcultural influences, arguably gives voice to the historically dispossessed – the single, fallen female – and this is sensitively explored in the historian Deborah A. Symonds's study of the representation of infanticide in ballad tradition, *Weep Not For Me: Women, Ballads, and Infanticide in Early Modern Scotland* (Philadelphia: Pennsylvania State University Press, 1992). That many early modern ballads envisaged a female audience[47] might in part explain the possibility of sympathetic, if not empathic, space opened up here for the woman protagonist. John Knox's diatribe against 'the whores and whoredom' of the court which 'the ballads of that age did witness, which we, for modestie's sake, omit'[48] might suggest that the mode is associated with, or is intrinsically adapted to, the expression of what might be termed (somewhat anachronistically) 'counter-cultural' expression, but this leads us to another facet of the early modern relationship between popular tradition and literary culture: the uses of ballad, broadside and song for satire and dissent.

III

In exploring popular culture, Tim Harris cautions against 'thinking about [it] "in the singular"' because it 'encourages us to think of the culture of those below the elite as if it were a coherent whole'.[49] In sixteenth-century Scotland, however, there is a vein of popular literature – one might say propagandistic, polemical – which insists on the need for reform: reform which, in the context of establishing a post-Reformation, Protestant church in the 1560s, assumes spiritual and political varieties.[50] This also alerts us to what Mary Ellen Lamb calls the 'social and experiential contexts' of early modern culture.[51] The most effective, immediate means of communicating dissent (whether, in the decade of 1560s, against monarchical rule or religious hierarchy) was through the means of broadside and ballad.[52] Robert Sempill was especially adroit at manipulating public and political sympathies in the context of an increasingly literate urban class; relatively cheap to produce and distribute, the broadside ballad used the medium of print to 'replicate' the illusion of a speaking voice. Sempill also expediently harnesses the long-standing associations between gender and oral tradition when he contrives a female voice to be the 'carrier' or 'tradition bearer' of protest in 'Maddeis Lamentatioun' and 'Maddeis Proclamatioun', except that the 'wyfe with sempill lyfe, / [. . .] ay selling caill' 'indyte[s]', in other words, writes down, her fulmination at the famous murder of the Regent Moray in 1570 by the Catholic Hamilton of Bothwellhaugh, a Marian supporter.[53] In this case, the poem shuns the conventional disdain for women's 'idle' tales, and fuses the conventions of print and orality, popular and literate culture, in order to vent the fury of Sempill and the Protestant, political faction which he represented.

The Sempill broadsides and ballads also exemplify a persistent and interesting relationship between Protestantism (the reformed faith) and popular culture in early modern Scotland. This is most richly illustrated in the case of the collection printed in 1567 known as *The Gude and Godlie Ballatis*, or 'A Compendious Book of Godly and Spiritual Songs'. These were gathered by the Wedderburn brothers, intended to promulgate the newly reformed Word of God. The collection of 'ballatis' and 'carralls' was extraordinarily diverse and heterogeneous. Some songs were German or Scandinavian in origin, or possibly derived from English broadsides;[54] others were set to older tunes that had persisted in oral currency, thereby retaining traditional forms. Many were, in fact, reworkings (or *contrafacta*) of secular courtly songs (their erotic traces occasionally stubbornly ineradicable); commenting on this, Peter Burke notes how these 'pious parodies of the profane' reverse the usual practice whereby 'much traditional popular culture parodies official culture'.[55] These spiritual 'ballatis' thereby exemplify the rather complex relationship between Protestantism and popular culture in early modern Scotland.[56]

Burke's observation that '[r]eform of the church necessarily involved reform of popular culture'[57] is exemplified by the volume's attack on the 'baudrie and unclene sangis' sung 'among young personis'[58] – secular, oral and communal culture – not least the Reformers' more general hostility against other kinds of perceived 'immorality', crypto/pseudo-Catholicism and paganism. The incremental challenges made by this 'new religion of the Word' to traditional Catholicism sets up, in Jonathan Barry's words, the 'makings of a highly polarised cultural confrontation between literary and oral cultures'.[59] The danger of this kind of reading is that, in the context of early modern Scotland, it drives a doctrinal wedge between print and literacy, and oral and non-literate culture and, as we have seen, the actual work of Protestant agitators and evangelists implies that there are no such convenient dividing lines between the two cultures. It perhaps remains the case, though, that our understanding of popular culture and religious devotion in the period is governed by the more visible, dominant heritage of Protestantism, and that the culture of what might be termed indigenous and recusant Catholicism remains far less understood. It would be interesting, for example, to use Alison Shell's work on early modern English Catholic culture and tradition as a way of unearthing other voices; oral tradition can render articulate socially marginalised or politically disenfranchised experience. It may not, as Burke writes, 'provide a reliable narrative of events but they are invaluable as evidence of reactions to those events, for seeing them with "the vision of the vanquished"'[60] – though the changing political and religious fault lines of sixteenth-century Scotland often shift the identities of 'the vanquished'.

This chapter began by pointing out how the *Complaynt*'s allusions to tales of otherworld creatures (a wolf, a giant, a dog) are retold and reframed in Chambers's nineteenth-century volume; they also resurface towards the end of that century in Andrew Lang's famous *Blue Fairy Book*. Once part of early modern living tradition, but now encased within a volume for the 'nursery', these narratives might seem part of a wider process whereby tradition is 'degraded' or 'diminished'. But they might also speak of its adaptive vitality, hybridity and resilience. There is something moving in the knowledge that these early modern wonder tales have more than endured their criss-crossing of genres, cultures and centuries. These 'pleysand storeis', after all, first appeared in a context in which they flourished amidst a diversity of 'sueit melodius sangis', dances and pipe-playing, not least in fields full of 'holisum flouris gyrsis and eirbis maist convenient for medycyn'.[61]

CHAPTER EIGHT

The Heroic Ballads of Gaelic Scotland

Anja Gunderloch

The Genre and its Connections

Gaelic Scotland can look back on a tradition of narrative verse that spans the period at least from the first half of the fifteenth century to the present.[1] These heroic ballads form one of the most recognisable and popular genres of the literary canon of Gaelic Scotland. A host of characters populates this extensive corpus, for example Fionn mac Cumhaill, the leader of a band of warriors (the Fian); his son Oisean, the poet; his grandson Osgar, the warrior; Diarmaid who eloped with the beautiful Gràinne and was killed by a wild boar; or Goll mac Morna who often saves the day, but occasionally appears as Fionn's enemy. A small number of ballads belong to the environment of the Ulster Cycle, and a few have Arthurian protagonists. As was the case for most of Gaelic literature until relatively recently, ballads were transmitted in a predominantly oral environment; fortunately, enough texts were written down to provide a view of the scope of the tradition at different times. Although gaps remain because our record is not continuous and does not cover all of the Gaelic-speaking districts at all times, enough material is extant to show the genre's significance. Prose tales that tell of the deeds of the same protagonists complement this corpus of verse.[2]

The ballads are a genre shared with Gaelic Ireland.[3] The professional poets in both Ireland and Gaelic Scotland, who produced the bulk of the ballads from the twelfth century onwards, composed in Classical Common Gaelic, the high-register literary dialect that was in use in both countries among educated Gaels and survived in Gaelic Scotland until the eighteenth century.[4] Originally composed in a looser form (*ógláchas*) of the strict metres (*dán díreach*) of the classical tradition,[5] the ballads exhibit a set number of syllables per line and follow rules regulating the use of such metrical decoration as assonance, alliteration, end-rhyme and internal rhyme that are slightly different for each metre. The most popular ballad metres are the *ógláchas* forms of the quatrain-based *rannaigheacht mhór* and *rannaigheacht bheag* as well as the couplet-based *deibhidhe*.[6] By the time the ballads are transcribed from reciters in an oral environment in the eighteenth and nineteenth centuries[7] their former metrical intricacy has been worn down (although it is usually possible to identify the original metre), and we are broadly dealing with texts in Scottish Gaelic. It is clear from the range of the extant texts that the ballads were immensely popular among all sectors of Gaelic society, an entertainment form that could also have a didactic element.

The heroic ballads look back on a long literary pedigree: material relating to Fionn mac Cumhaill was classed together under the heading *fianaigecht* ('lore of the *fian* or warrior-band') in the Middle Ages, and includes both prose and verse material.[8] The most significant source of material relating to Fionn and his companions, the twelfth-century *Acallam na Senórach* ('The Colloquy of the Ancients'), is a substantial compilation of prose and some poetry that has as its setting a fictional meeting between St Patrick and the ancient heroes Oisean and Caoilte.[9] They travel together all over Ireland and at each stopping point the old men tell the saint and his retinue what great deeds were performed at these locations.[10] The conceit of casting Oisean in the role of the ancient survivor, who meets St Patrick and imparts much knowledge to him, is maintained or implied in many ballads. Some are set in a full narrative frame of dialogue between saint and hero; others begin with this setting, but do not return to it at the conclusion; and there are texts that consist entirely of dialogue between these two characters. The typical trajectory juxtaposes the saint's Christian perspective and concern for the state of Oisean's soul with the old hero's wistful reminiscence of the days of his youth, filled with hunting, music and heroic deeds. The clash of Christian and heroic values is explored in dialogue form, as in this extract from Peter MacFarlane's collection:[11]

'S olc leam sin uait Oissain	I think this wicked from you, Oisean
Fhir nam briathra boile;	Man of the foolish words;
'S gum b' fhearr DIA ri aon uair	And God were better any time
Na Fionn na Feinne uile.	Than Fionn of all the Fian.
B' fhearr leamsa aon chath laidir	I'd prefer one strong battle
A chuireadh Fionn na Feinne	That Fionn of the Fian would wage
Na TIGHEARN' a chràidh sin	To that Lord of anguish
Agus d' thusa, a Chlèirich.	And to you, o cleric.

The typical ballad audience, certainly from the eighteenth century onwards, would be familiar with the Christian dimension, thanks to the efforts of ministers and catechists, and with the heroic point of view through their knowledge of the ballads and other Gaelic literature.[12]

The ballads, of course, came to play a part in the major literary phenomenon of the 1760s known as the Ossianic controversy mentioned elsewhere in this volume. Macpherson undoubtedly had access to the Gaelic oral tradition of his native Badenoch where he encountered local versions of tales and ballads about Fionn. These provided inspiration, but he soon developed his own distinctive and inventive approach to style, plot and protagonists.[13] Some aspects from tradition he retained: the third-century date that is ascribed to characters and events is in keeping with the dating favoured by Irish and Gaelic scholars since the Middle Ages. Since then, the historicity of protagonists and events had never been in doubt, although modern scholarship recognises that many a literary or originally mythological character was fitted into a historical scheme developed by medieval Irish scholars. These endeavoured to make their own traditions conform to the template of Christian and classical history.[14] Though Fionn is traditionally associated with Ireland, specifically the province of Leinster, some ballads are set in Gaelic Scotland, and by the eighteenth century, several more had localised themselves in various districts.[15] Fionn is consistently portrayed as the leader of the Fian in the ballads, frequently described by 'royal' epithets such as 'rìgh na Fèinne' ('king of the Fian') or 'flath-Fhionn Almhuin' ('lordly Fionn of Allen');[16] 'mo rìgh' ('my king') is another way of referring to Fionn.[17] Such imagery may have helped Macpherson to bestow unwarranted royal status on Fionn. One defining characteristic of the ballads, the relationship between Oisean and St Patrick, has been edited out altogether because it did not fit into Macpherson's scheme of pre-Christian epic.[18] Despite the profusion of material that he encountered when he undertook two trips to the Highlands in the early 1760s,[19] Macpherson did not discover a full-scale epic, but a substantial corpus of self-contained ballads. He proved rather more successful as a collector of manuscripts, including the Book of the Dean of Lismore. This contains the earliest surviving corpus of heroic ballads, alongside a substantial and varied collection of classical bardic verse from Ireland and Gaelic Scotland.[20]

Collectors and Collecting

Compiled between 1512 and 1542 by James MacGregor, the eponymous dean, and his brother Duncan,[21] many of the ballads in this important early collection are also found in the later Scottish Gaelic tradition. While it is impossible to prove that any later text is directly descended from the Dean's version, it is clear that these ballads retained their popularity through time. The collection shows some characteristics that set it apart from what we might expect of a Gaelic document of the time: it is, for example, not written in the Irish hand customarily used for Classical Common Gaelic, but in the secretary hand used by Lowland scribes in legal and official documents.[22] Apart from his clerical role, James MacGregor also held the position of

Notary Public, and must have been educated in Latin and Scots. His brother Duncan, the manuscript's main scribe, also participated in this multilingual and multicultural intellectual environment. The contents reflect the kind of texts that would be found in anthologies of poetry made by trained poets for Irish patrons. Gaelic Scotland, for all its dearth of surviving examples of such collections, can thus be seen as part of a wider literary landscape. Written sources may be assumed for much of the ballad material that the compilers selected for inclusion.[23]

The manuscript record of ballads in Gaelic Scotland is fairly silent until the eighteenth century when the oral dimension takes centre stage. Collecting predominantly took place in the mainland regions of Gaelic Scotland, going back to the 1730s, for example, in the shape of the collection of ballads made by the Rev. Alexander Pope of Reay parish in 1739.[24] Interest in Gaelic literature was growing among the educated classes of Gaelic Scotland; Derick Thomson suggests that this was linked to the Union of Parliaments and the Jacobite Risings of 1715 and 1745.[25] The negative outside view of the Gaels as uncultured and savage, which prevailed particularly after the failure of the last Rising, seems to have motivated many to investigate Gaelic literature with the aim of contradicting such prejudices. High educational standards became increasingly important to the Highland gentry,[26] and thus the collectors that emerge in this period are well educated, often to university level. They generally start their collecting activity young and, once established in a profession (often the ministry), the opportunities for collecting diminished, although some, for example the Rev. James MacLagan of Blair Atholl, continue their literary interests into old age.[27] MacLagan's collection is of particular importance because it contains not only ballads, but a wide-ranging collection of poetry then current in the oral tradition of Gaelic Scotland; it is now housed in Glasgow University Library.[28] Taken as a whole, the McLagan material 'seems to give us an accurate reflection of the cultivated Gaelic literary taste of his times', as Derick Thomson points out.[29] Just under half of the ballad material in the MacLagan collection has been published.[30] McLagan was also significantly involved in the production of one of the early anthologies of Gaelic poetry, the Gillies Collection of 1786, another important source of ballad texts.[31] Alongside the ballads, this volume contains a wide selection of poetry and song by named authors as well as much anonymous material.

The heroic ballads largely disappear from the view of the literate elite in the first half of the nineteenth century, no doubt as a result of the realisation that Macpherson's work was not, after all, the genuine product of a third-century bard. A few texts are collected almost by accident, as in the case of Christina Sutherland's ballads, which were taken down by George MacLeod and James Cumming in 1854. The reciter was born in Forsinard in Sutherland in 1775 and grew up in a family of tradition-bearers with a wide and well-regarded repertoire. By her own testimony, her interest in literature and song began early:

> She heard these and many other old pieces of poetry recited in her father's house, both her parents being remarkable for the quantity which they could say of them, as well as for the precision with which they retained them [. . .] She remembers herself and one *Isbil Bhàn*, or Isabella MacKay, to have sat up for a whole winter night reciting poems of every description, each in turn and sometimes together repeating them. When under twelve years of age she would sooner commit to memory a long Duan than most if not any of her acquaintances who were come to maturity. She would go three miles and more to hear a poem not previously recited in her hearing.[32]

This passage gives an insight into the processes by which a keen reciter would acquire and practise new material; it also highlights the fact that the literary community of reciters and audiences had fairly specific expectations of textual accuracy and quality of performance.

It is only when John Francis Campbell of Islay appeared on the scene and set about the collecting of Gaelic tales in the 1850s that the ballads received attention from collectors again. Campbell's interest in narrative material soon led him to recognise the importance of the heroic ballads, and he provides a sample in the third volume of his influential *Popular Tales of the West Highlands*. Campbell felt that the ballads deserved to be presented to a reading public in their own right, and thus he set about compiling ballad material for publication, with texts from the Book of the Dean of Lismore down to the living tradition of the 1870s. As he had done for the *Popular Tales*, Campbell enlisted a number of collaborators who sought out material for him and himself went on a collecting trip to the Hebrides in 1871.[33] The schoolmaster and Islay native Hector MacLean, who had already been involved in the *Popular Tales*, once again travelled around the Gàidhealtachd to collect material. Another collaborator was the young Alexander Carmichael who is best known for his later *Carmina Gadelica*, discussed in Chapter 12.

The methodology that Campbell and his collaborators used was remarkably modern. The texts were to be written down from reciters as accurately as possible, without normalisation of spelling in order to preserve dialectal features. No editorial 'polishing-up' was to take place. The name of the reciter and any useful background information, such as their age, source and place of residence, were taken down too. In 1861, Donald Torrie, another collaborator, took down a version of 'An Ionmhuinn' ('The Maiden') from the Benbecula reciter Donald Macintyre, who also provided the information that he learned the ballad around half a century before from a John MacInnes. MacInnes had lived at the southern end of South Uist, but emigrated in his old age to America.[34] Six years later, Alexander Carmichael obtained a fragmentary version of the same ballad from Macintyre, whom he describes as a Roman Catholic catechist.[35] Texts that were taken from manuscript sources, and a few contemporary specimens, appeared in Campbell's *Leabhar na Féinne* in 1872. The rest of the material gathered from oral tradition was to follow separately, but because the first volume was not the financial success that Campbell had expected, this plan was abandoned. Most of the texts that were intended for the second volume remain in manuscript form among Campbell's papers in the National Library of Scotland.[36] Only a few of the ballads that were collected by Carmichael were printed in *Leabhar na Féinne* while several more are part of Campbell's unpublished papers. Quite often, these are copies that Carmichael provided when he was still collecting for Campbell. More ballad material collected by Carmichael, part of it after their collaboration, remains unpublished and is scattered throughout his extensive papers in the Carmichael–Watson Collection in Edinburgh University Library.[37]

Although the tradition became progressively attenuated, the ballads continued to be recited into the twentieth century when at last it became possible to record the words and the tunes together. A number of recordings are in the Archives of the School of Scottish Studies.[38]

Themes and Subject Matter

As noted before, the ballads link up to two prestigious literary cycles of the Irish tradition, the Ulster Cycle and the Fionn Cycle, with ballads relating to Fionn mac Cumhaill and his companions in the overwhelming majority. Of the Ulster Cycle material, 'Bàs Chonlaoich' ('The Death of Conlaoch') deserves a closer look. The ballad narrates how the Ulster Cycle hero Cú Chulainn killed his own son. This is the Gaelic manifestation of an international folk tale,[39] and a prose account is known from Early Irish literature.[40] The earliest extant version of this ballad is in the Book of the Dean of Lismore where its composer is identified as Giolla Coluim Mac an Ollaimh, a professional poet who probably belonged to the MacMhuirich bardic family.[41] The ballad follows another poem by the same poet, 'Thánaig Adhbhar mo Thuirse' ('Matter for Grief is Come to Me'), lamenting the murder of Angus Òg, heir to John II, Lord of the Isles, in 1490.[42] The ballad is clearly intended to act as an apologue to the lament, implying that John was implicated in the death of his own son.[43] From its classical beginnings in Gaelic Scotland, the ballad gained widespread currency here as well as in Ireland, although the original connection with a murky episode in the history of the Lordship of the Isles was forgotten.

The subject matter of a small number of ballads is drawn from an Arthurian context. 'Am Bròn Binn' ('The Sweet Sorrow') tells how King Arthur falls in love with a woman he saw in a dream. Gawain is sent to find the girl and has to rescue her from a giant whom he beheads with the giant's own sword.[44] Many different versions have been collected since the last quarter of the eighteenth century, and the plot exists in a number of variants. In addition to the texts we have a substantial amount of information about the reciters, especially from the mid-nineteenth century onwards.[45]

'The Girl with the Mantle' is a humorous ballad which describes how a woman challenges the wives of several leading heroes from the Fionn-context to a chastity contest, with disastrous results as the women take turns to try on a mantle that only fully covers a virtuous woman. Here is an extract from the earliest extant text in the Book of the Dean of Lismore:[46]

Gabhais bean Osgair 'na dhéidh	The wife of Osgar then took the cloak so
An brat comhfhada coimhréidh;	smooth and flowing. Though ample was the
Giodh leabhar sgód an bhruit fhinn,	skirt of the fair cloak, it did not cover her
Nochar fholuigh a h-imlinn.	middle.
Gabhais Maighinis gan fheall	Maighinis, without deceit, took the cloak
An brat is do cuir fá ceann;	and put it over her head. The cloak only
Do chas is do chuar mas soin	rumpled up and curled at once about her
An brat go luath fá cluasaibh.	ears.

The exact nature of the marital lapses of Fionn's wife Maighinis and the other women is left for the audience to extrapolate from the information later provided that a single kiss leaves the wearer's little toe uncovered. Originally, the tale related in the ballad belonged to the Arthurian context, but the change of its protagonists to Fionn and his associates has been effected in a careful and sophisticated manner.[47] Among the ballads that tell of the adventures of Fionn mac Cumhaill and his companions, adventure ballads are particularly popular: Fionn and his companions go on quests or repel invaders. A number of ballads tell of the death of a famous hero; such elegies generally contain passages of praise highlighting achievements and characteristics of the deceased.

In many ballads, the introductory quatrains do not launch the listener straight into the action, but instead seem intended to quieten down the audience. 'Cath Rìgh na Sorcha' ('The Battle of the King of Sorcha'), for example, first advertises the tale as one worth listening to before beginning the story proper:[48]

Tha sgeul beag agam air Fionn,	I have a little tale about Fionn,
Ge bè chuireadh an suim e,	Whoever should hold it in regard,
Air Mac Cuthail bu dhearg drèach,	About the son of Cumhall who was ruddy of face,
'S eibhinn leam re mo ré.	I will think it pleasant all my life.

Latha dhuinn air beagan sluaigh,	One day, when we were with a small company
Aig Eas Ruaidh na n' eighin mall,	At Eas Ruaidh of the slow salmon,
Chunnacas fui sheòl o'n ear	We saw under sail from the west
Curachan oìr is bean ann.	A golden coracle and a woman in it.

Not all surviving versions of the ballad preserve the first quatrain, but the second is present in all extant texts.

The composers of the ballads clearly intended them to be sung or chanted, and this is supported by the presence of a number of structural and stylistic features that are particularly suitable for oral performance and actually aid intact oral transmission over generations. Adventure ballads generally exhibit a plot where events follow each other in a clear and logical fashion. The plot is frequently made livelier by dialogue passages, where each change of speaker is clearly indicated in order to enable the audience to keep track of who is speaking. In other instances, the speaker addresses his or her dialogue partner by name, as in this exchange between Gràinne and Diarmaid in 'Laoidh Dhiarmaid':[49]

A Dhiarmuid na freagair an fhaghaid	Diarmaid, do not answer the chase,
'S na tadhaill am fiadhach breige,	And do not attend the treacherous hunt,
'S na rach teann air Fionn mac Cumhaill,	And do not go near Fionn mac Cumhaill,
O 's cumhadh leis a bhi gun cheile.	Since it grieves him to be without a wife.

A ghradh nam ban a Ghrainne,	Darling of women, Gràinne,
Na toill-se naire do d' cheile,	Do not cause shame to your husband,
Fhreagairinn-se guth na seilge	I would answer the call of the chase
Dh'ain-deoin feirge fir na Feinne.	Despite the fury of the men of the Fian.

Another way of identifying a protagonist is through a narratorial aside, for example in a short monologue in 'Laoidh Fhraoich', a ballad with an Ulster Cycle connection, where the hero is first identified by his patronymic and then by his given name:[50]

Cnuasachd riamh ni 'n drìnneam fein	Berrypicking I never did myself
Thuirt mac Feadhaich nan gruaidh tla;	Spoke Feadhach's son of the tender cheeks;
Gar an drinneam, arsa Fraoch	Though I should do it, said Fraoch
Theid mi bhuain a chaor'nn do Mhai.	I shall go to reap the rowanberries for Mai.

Description is a device that enables the audience to imagine the scene more clearly; it may also help the reciter's own recall of the ballad in the same way that storytellers use descriptive passages as a mnemonic device.[51] Such descriptive passages can provide a great deal of detail, as in this description of a hero and his weaponry in 'Dàn an Deirg mhic Drabhaill' ('The Ballad of the Dearg, Son of Drabhall'):[52]

Leum an Dearg bu mhath dreach	The Dearg, of good appearance, leapt
Air tìr ri crannaibh a chraois	Ashore on the shafts of his spears,
Tharruing a bharc bu ghlain snaighe	He pulled his boat that was well crafted
Air an trai' gheal ghainmhe	Up on the white sandy beach.
Folt fionn bhuigh mar or cearda	Fair yellow hair like smithy's gold
Os cionn mala gruai' an Deirg,	Was above the brow of the Dearg,
A dha dhearc-shuil ghorm mar ghloin	His two blue eyes like glass,
Bu ghlan gnuis a mhìli.	Bright was the face of the warrior.
Bha dha shleagh chrann[53] reamhar catha	Two thick-shafted spears for battle
Ann laimh mic an ard-fhlatha	Were in the hand of the high lord's son,
Sgia òir air a ghualainn chlì	A shield of gold on his left shoulder
Aig Mac uasal an ard-riogh.	Had the noble son of the high king.
Lann nimhe ri leadart chorp	A poisonous blade to rend bodies
Air an laoch gun eagal comhraig	Was on the hero without fear of combat,
Mìn comhdaigh clochara corr	A helmet, set with stones and excellent,
Air a mhìli shochar suil ghorm.	Was on the modest blue-eyed warrior.

This extract comes from an example of an invader ballad: the Dearg, a famous warrior from the Land of the Fair Men, arrives by sea and attempts to defeat first the king of Ireland and then the Fian; he finally finds his match in Goll mac Morna and is killed. This passage introduces him pole-vaulting, for heroic effect, from his boat and combines a description of his good looks and noble descent with a picture of his weaponry. According to a note at the end of this text, 'the vulgar suppose this poem to be one of the best of the ancient poems', indicating both the quality and popularity of this ballad in the view of contemporary audiences.[54]

Dialogue passages are a prominent stylistic feature of the ballads. A conversation between important protagonists can impart a particularly lively feel to the plot, when an exchange creates dramatic tension. This can be done through dialogue that imparts information; for example, when the mysterious lady who arrives on the boat in 'Cath Rìgh na Sorcha' explains that she is fleeing from an unwanted suitor and requests Fionn's protection. There are exchanges between opposing heroes that precede combat, where the tension is heightened by a combination of formal addresses and challenges to combat. Here is an example from 'Dàn an Deirg mhic Drabhaill' where Fionn's son Raighne asks the Dearg why he has come to Ireland and defies his intention to take over:[55]

Tabhair sgeul dhuinn fhir mhoir	Give us your story, great man,
O 's ann oirne tha coimhead a chuain	Since we are charged with watching the sea,
Dithis mac righ gu sar bhuaigh sinn'	Two kings' sons of excellent virtue are we
Do Fhianaibh lan uasal na Eirin	Of the truly noble Fian of Ireland.

A chrioch as an d' thainig mi a nis'	The land from which I have come now
'S tearc innte neach do m' ainfhios	Rare there are those to whom I am unknown,
'S mi an Dearg mac righ nam fionn	I am the Dearg, son of the King of Fair men,
Air teachd a dh' iarrai' riachd na Eirin	Come to ask for the sovereignty of Ireland.
Labhair Roidni an aigne mhir	Raighne of the keen spirit spoke
Gu dian ris an Dearg Mac-drabhaill,	Swiftly to the Dearg son of Drabhaill,
Ni 'm faigh thusa a laoich lain	You will not get, complete hero,
Urram no gèil fear Fodhla	Honour nor submission from the men of Ireland.

Combat swiftly follows this exchange, and the Dearg ties up Raighne and proceeds to meet the king of Ireland. After another challenge he defeats the king's troops and Fionn and his companions are sent for. In the end, Goll mac Morna kills the invader after a fierce fight:[56]

Cith tine, cith cailce cruaidh	A shower of fire, a shower of hard chalk
Do 'n armaibh s do'n sgiathaibh nuaigh	From their weapons and their shields
Agus cith fola da nimh	And a shower of blood to heaven
Bhiodh do lannaibh na mili	Would come from the heroes' blades.
Bhitheadar a' comhrac tri laeth	They would battle for three days –
Bu tuirseach mic agus mnaibh	Boys and women were weary –
Gus na chlaoi an Dearg ann	Until the Dearg was slain there
Le Goll mor air cheart eigin	By great Goll in proper hardship.

Death was an occupational hazard for heroes; this is recognised in ballads that double as elegies. 'Laoidh Fhraoich' narrates how Fraoch met his end thanks to the machinations of his prospective mother-in-law Mai who, out of jealousy, sent the hero to pick rowanberries for her on an island that was guarded by a monster. Fraoch woke up the monster and both were killed in the ensuing combat. A formal lament praising his beauty and accomplishments is put in the mouth of Mai's daughter:[57]

Truadh nach an còmhrag laoch,	Pity that it was not in the combat of heroes
A thuit Fraoch le 'm pronntadh òr,	That Fraoch fell by whom gold was bestowed,
'S tursach do thuitim le beist,	Woeful is your fall by a monster,
Aon mhic de! nach mairtheann thu beo.	One son of God! that you do not remain alive.

Going by the evidence of place-names in the oldest extant version of the ballad, in the Book of the Dean of Lismore, its original place of composition appears to have been in Ireland, in County Roscommon, where the place-names Cluain Fhraoich (Clonfree) and Carn Fhraoich (Carnfree) attest to its localisation there.[58]

In Gaelic Scotland, a number of places compete for the honour of being the scene of Fraoch's encounter with the monster. Bodies of water with islands, on which rowan trees grow, are not in short supply throughout the Gàidhealtachd. Coincidence lends a hand as well, because the hero's name, Fraoch, corresponds to the Gaelic word for 'heather', a not uncommon element in place-names. Fraoch Eilean is near the northern end of Loch Awe in Argyll, and, accordingly, several sources claim that the events narrated in the ballad took place there. Thomas Pennant, who toured in the Highlands in 1769, notes this in somewhat romanticised fashion:[59]

> On Fraoch-Elan, the Hesperides of the Highlands, are the ruins of a castle. The fair Mego longed for the delicious fruit of the isle, guarded by a dreadful serpent: the hero Fraoch goes to gather it, and is destroyed by the monster. This tale is sung in the Erse ballads, and is translated and published in the manner of Fingal.

Loch Awe was not the only place where the ballad was localised. Loch Freuchie near Amulree was given as the place where Fraoch met his end in the Gillies Collection.[60] A fragmentary version of the ballad recorded by Alexander Carmichael in 1862 from Kate Lawrie of Port Appin localises the ballad in Rannoch.[61] John Francis Campbell met a man on Mull in 1870 who pointed out the places where the ballad played out around Bunessan.[62]

No surviving texts of 'Laoidh Fhraoich' are in evidence in Gaelic Ireland. The ballad, like the others, is a product of the once strong cultural and literary connections between both countries. At the same time, a version was recorded in the mid-twentieth century,[63] a late example of a long line of many individual texts which demonstrate the strength and independence of the heroic ballad tradition in Gaelic Scotland.

CHAPTER NINE

Eighteenth-Century Antiquarianism

Valentina Bold

This chapter considers the significance of eighteenth-century literary antiquarianism for Scottish traditional literatures. It is impossible to mention every person, or publication, of significance, but it includes some of the most interesting in a century of constant activity. The discussion begins in 1703, with Martin Martin, and ends in 1802 with Scott's *Minstrelsy of the Scottish Border*.[1] The cut-off point responds to a nineteenth-century shift, when antiquarianism become increasingly separated from natural sciences (although many intellectuals were involved in both) but it is, of course, relatively arbitrary. Antiquarians born in the mid-1700s, such as George Chalmers (1742–1824), continued to publish in the next century and sustained their approaches in the process; Chalmers's lexicographer opponent, John Jamieson (1759–1838), too, published his major work *The Etymological Dictionary of Scotland* in 1808.[2]

A number of general points need to be made. Firstly, the term 'antiquarianism', in use from the sixteenth century onwards, is multifaceted. It covers a wide range of activities, from the recording of 'tours' to observations of the local, regional and nationally significant. It involves the documentation of physical as well as intangible 'reliques' of the past – stories, songs and poetry, in language, names, custom and beliefs – and the identification of areas of loss and progress. It was at once voyeuristic and participatory; while antiquarians observed at a distance, personal attachments to region and nation often informed their work. Antiquarians pioneered techniques that would become common in cultural studies: the amassing of parallel examples of specific texts for comparison, for instance (albeit with less textual apparatus than modern scholars prefer, and more in the way of collation and polish). Eighteenth-century antiquarians drew on strong precedents, starting with John Leland (c. 1503–53), the self-styled *Antiquarius* and the antiquary to the king of England from 1533. The holistic approach of William Camden (1551–1623) in *Britannia* (1586, expanded by Edmund Gibson in 1695 and Richard Gough in 1789) – including a review of British antiquities and topography alongside an account of beliefs relating to horses in Ireland – also set precedents for later antiquarians. John Aubrey (1626–97) is another influential English figure: *Miscellanies* (1696) includes pioneering accounts of the supernatural.[3] In Scotland, writers like Sir John Scot of Scotstarvit (1585–1610), Sir Robert Sibbald (1641–1722) (see further below) and Sir John Clerk, 2nd Baronet of Penicuik (1676–1755) who patronised Allan Ramsay, continued the tradition of working around topography and archaeology, among other interests. The Earl of Buchan, at the founding meeting of the Society of Antiquaries of Scotland in 1780, noted a discrete tradition of antiquarianism in Scotland, traced back to Hector Boece, John Major and George Buchanan and more recent luminaries like Sir David Dalrymple, Lord Hailes (1726–92), David Crawford, Historiographer Royal for Scotland and Thomas Ruddiman.[4] The Society's aims were to celebrate the 'ancient' in a comprehensive way, covering the material past, as well as language and constitutional matters. In fact, most antiquarians were interested in a range of activities including, as indicated above, exploring archaeological remains. Carluke-born General William Roy (1726–90), for instance, was an active member of the English Royal Society (proposed as a fellow by members who included the Edinburgh-born mathematician and surveyor, James Short) as well as of the Society of Antiquaries of London. His professional competence, as a pioneer of surveying and cartographic techniques, combined with a fascination for traces of the Roman occupation within the landscape – his *Military Antiquities of the Romans in North Britain* (1793) is still highly regarded.[5]

Antiquarianism was, predominantly, for men; as Rosemary Sweet has observed, it was 'a "manly" pursuit, encouraging masculine qualities, whether it was through identification with the political virtue and patriotism of ancient Rome or the military glory and contempt for death evidenced by the Goths'.[6] This is certainly true of the published record although, as Sweet goes on to acknowledge, British women were involved in disseminating knowledge as editors, translators, biographers and, in the latter part of the eighteenth century, in the growth of Celtic revivalism. In Scotland, the contribution of women to the process of antiquarian collection and documentation should not be overlooked, from the songs of Isobel Pagan (1741–1821), which made their way into the *Scots Musical Museum*, to those, at the tail-end of the century, of Anna Gordon, Mrs Brown of Falkland.[7] This is an under-researched topic deserving future exploration.

In eighteenth-century Scotland, significantly, antiquarianism was integrally related to a contemporary desire to understand the nation, and its meaning within the newly British context. After the Union of the Parliaments, antiquarianism offered a means to understand Scotland's past and, in that past, the present's foundations.[8] Similarly, perhaps paralleling this impulse, in England the first minuted meeting of the Society of Antiquaries of London was in 1707, although its roots are earlier, and its charter is dated 1751. In its literary context, antiquarianism for Scots often involved seeking alternative forms of expression to the polite idioms then in vogue – the anglicisation processes many scholars have noted; the work of Allan Ramsay, mentioned below, can be perceived in this way.[9] Paradoxically, as well as its potential to define the discrete elements of Scotland – in language, song and story – antiquarianism could be used to discern what was shared and British. It was a pursuit, then, that combined the satisfaction of fresh discovery, and the validation that came with ancient pedigree.

It is impossible, however, to separate Scottish antiquarianism's growth from its English counterpart. The Society of Antiquaries of London included members of the Scottish aristocracy, such as Sir John Clerk and Alexander Gordon (both elected in 1724), along with the founder of the Scottish Society, the Earl of Buchan (then Lord Cardross), who was a fellow from 1764. Equally, significant English antiquarian books were informed by Scottish contributions. To take one example, Thomas Percy was assisted in compiling his *Reliques* by prominent Scots like Sir David Dalrymple, Lord Hailes (1726–92) and the Edinburgh antiquarian John McGowan.[10] It included substantial Scottish material, from 'Sir Patrick Spens' in Book I to the 'The Bonny Earl of Murray' in Book V. The English antiquary, Joseph Ritson (1752–1803) made an impact on Scottish antiquarianism, from the *Select Collection of English Songs* (1783) to *Scotish Songs* [sic] (1794) which was in Burns's collection of books.[11] Nor did British antiquarians limit their interests to their point of origin within the United Kingdom or, indeed, to the British Isles. Thomas Pennant, for instance, as well as making two influential tours of Scotland in 1769 and 1772, travelled in continental Europe (1765), the northern counties (1773), Northamptonshire (1774), Kent (1777) and, only lastly, his native Wales (1778). His insatiable curiosity was inspirational to – if at times disparaged by – Johnson in his own Scottish tours accompanied by James Boswell, which produced the *Journey to the Western Isles of Scotland* in 1775 and Boswell's own *Journal of a Tour to the Hebrides with Samuel Johnson LLD*.[12] There are antiquarian elements, too, to Boswell's own *Account of Corsica* (1768), particularly in the first chapter, which surveys historical and archaeological elements, as well as topography and climate.

While being aware of the ambitious range of the antiquarian, it is worth remembering the word itself had disparaging associations. John Earle's *Micro-Cosmographie* (1628), for instance, dismisses the antiquarian as 'a great admirer [. . .] of the rust of old Monuments [. . .] [who] reades onely those characters, where time hath eaten out the letters [. . .]'.[13] In *The Antiquary* (1816), Scott's Jonathan Oldbuck is both unscholarly and gullible (although Scott's attitude was somewhat ambivalent in itself – the preface to *Ivanhoe*, for instance, acknowledges a debt to 'antiquarian stores').[14] In a more positive vein, Sweet has eloquently argued that antiquaries did not deserve to be disparaged as backward-looking and, instead, should be seen as key Enlightenment figures: 'antiquarianism had as much to contribute to the Whiggish project of charting the rise of a polite and commercial society as it had to give to the consolidation of a Tory ideology based upon nostalgic conservatism'.[15] Yoo Sun Lee, similarly, draws attention to the ways in which antiquarianism highlighted change: 'the very egregiousness of [. . .] antiquarian foraging drew attention to the troubling processes of loss and extinction that made the retrieval necessary'.[16] Both these observations are useful to the understanding of antiquarianism in eighteenth-century Scotland.

To turn to specifics, probably the first major antiquarian work of eighteenth-century Scotland is the *Description of the Western Isles of Scotland* (1703) by Martin Martin (d. 1718). The *Description*, with its mixture of accounts of traditional cures (animal and human), diets, lifestyles – fishing, fowling, husbandry and crops – archaeological remains, language, folk sayings such as those relating to weather, poetry, allegiances to clan chiefs, religious lives and beliefs, set a high benchmark for later antiquarians, indicating a breadth of interest and holistic approach that has rarely been equalled. Born in Bealach, Skye, and educated at Edinburgh University, Martin's survey of his native Gàidhealtachd was groundbreaking, because it included personal observations of a range of traditional cultural activities, gathered in his native Gaelic. Having spent a period of time in the Netherlands, Martin settled in London where, through the patronage of scholars like David Gregory, Walter Curleton and Hans Sloane, along with Sir Robert Sibbald (1641–1722), Martin was encouraged to collect in the Western Isles. (Sibbald was a prominent Edinburgh-based antiquarian, first Professor of Medicine at Edinburgh in 1685, earlier (1682) appointed Geographer Royal. His work shows the typical range of the eighteenth-century antiquarian. He was key in founding Edinburgh's Royal Botanical Gardens and Royal College of Physicians, and also published *An Account of the Scottish Atlas* (1683), *Scotia Illustrata* (1684) and, subsequent to Martin's tours, a *History Ancient and Modern of the Sheriffdoms of Fife and Kinross* (1710) and *Descriptions of the Isles of Orkney and Shetland* (1711).) Martin presented his findings to the Royal Society in 1696, which financed his further forays. 'Several Observations in the Western Islands of Scotland' was published in *Philosophical Transactions* (1697), and was followed by the *Late Journey to St Kilda* (1698). In addition to collecting, the Episcopalian divinity student Martin assisted Rev. James Campbell in the island of Harris in 1697, and participated in an ill-fated Hebridean surveying expedition, under John Adair (c. 1655–1722).[17] Sloane's efforts to raise a subscription for Martin, along with a Treasury grant, allowed him to complete the field journeys for his *Description*, although delays in payment led to his taking work again as tutor to Donald MacDonald. Despite ambitions for government work, he accompanied George Mackenzie to Leiden

University, studying medicine himself there, and subsequently practised as a doctor in Middlesex, publishing a second edition of the *Description* in 1716, and graduating MD at Rheims. Described as 'collector of curiosities, natural historian, and ethnographer', there is an element of paradox to his mission to capture accounts of contemporary customs and beliefs, alongside his desire to see the Western Isles as British; to his audience in London, his belief in some of the traditions he documented, for instance relating to second sight, meant that he was sometimes dismissed as 'little more than a curiosity'.[18]

Further milestones in Scottish antiquarianism include the work of Allan Ramsay (1684–1758). The publication of early and edited material in *Scots Songs* in 1718, closely followed by the *Ever Green* in 1724 and *Tea Table Miscellany* (1724–7), presented important models to the literary antiquarian: respectful, polemically-framed and creative. As a founding member of the Easy Club, Ramsay actively engaged in the discussion of Scottish culture and politics (his interest in Jacobitism, at a period when it was still a living cause, is well-known). Ramsay's *Collection of Scots Proverbs* (1737) and *Fables and Tales* (1722) were also important in fostering understanding of, and sympathetic approach to, vernacular culture in an antiquarian audience and beyond. Unapologetically prejudiced towards the language identified with his nation, his explicit commitment to the Scots 'native' language presented a manifesto to later writers, although, of course, he was equally adept in his own work with polished English-based forms. William Thomson's influential collection of 1725, *Orpheus Caledonius*, for instance, drew texts directly from *Tea Table Miscellany*, with the innovation of including performance settings.

In terms of Gaelic culture, the manuscript collection of James Maclagan (1728–1805), minister of Blair Atholl discussed in earlier chapters is significant,[19] while the 1751 publication of *Ais-eiridh na sean chanoin Albannaich* (1751) by Alasdair mac Mhaighstir Alasdair (Alexander MacDonald) laid important foundations for the century's arguably most significant, and certainly most visible, celebration of Gaelic culture. More poetic than antiquarian in its approach, although using collecting and assembling techniques associated with antiquarianism, James Macpherson's 1760 *Fragments of Ancient Poetry*, followed by *Fingal* (1761/2) and *Temora* (1765), set a controversial benchmark for the study and treatment of Gaelic texts which would have a (disputed) impact for the rest of the century, and beyond. Macpherson's use of first-hand collection techniques, combined with materials gathered from manuscript, combine antiquarian thoroughness with creativity. His decisions about editing for publication were, of course, controversial but, as has been argued recently, anticipated many issues faced by the modern field collector.[20] Even if his methodology was disputed, he drew attention to a rich vein of Gaelic poetry and song, inspiring later collectors – into the present century – to engage with this material directly, although his reception made it clear that assertion, without a clear textual paper-trail, was no longer in vogue. The second half of the eighteenth century, too, was a crucial period in establishing many of the images of Scotland that would persist well into the twentieth, through text and through illustration. Pennant's *Tour in Scotland and Voyage to the Hebrides* (1774–76), for instance, as Amy Gazin-Schwartz has shown, contributed to the process of visualising the Highlands as 'picturesque and remote, yet tamed by English control'.[21]

The conceptualisation of Scotland and its past in song reinforced visual images. Bishop Percy's publication in 1765 of *Reliques of Ancient Poetry* has been mentioned above and, in the Scottish context, an equally influential text is David Herd's *Ancient and Modern Scottish Songs* (1769, revised in 1776). Herd, a Kincardineshire farmer's son, conducted his antiquarian collecting activities while working as an accountant in Edinburgh, noting down many of his texts from recitation. Herd was a pioneer in collecting terms. Unlike Percy – who was encouraged to go against his impulse and to edit in an arguably interventionist way – he decided to leave texts relatively intact and even included incomplete items, hoping to inspire readers to contribute elements which might have been missing. Like Ramsay, he was a sentimental patriot, asserting:

> The merit both of the poetry and the music of the Scots songs is undoubtedly great [...] the characteristic excellence of both [...] is [...] a forcible and pathetic simplicity, which at once lays strong hold on the affections; so that the heart itself may be considered as an instrument, touching all its strings in the most delicate and masterly manner [...] which may in truth be termed, *the poetry and the music of the heart*. There is another species, to wit, the humorous and comic, no less admirable for genuine humour, sprightly naivete, picturesque language, and striking paintings of low life and comic characters; the music whereof is so well adapted to the sentiment, that any person of a tolerable ear [...] feels a difficulty in restraining a strong propensity to dance.[22]

Such characterisation of Scots songs had a long and lasting impact, encouraging later antiquarians and folksong collectors of the future to seek out the 'typically' tragic and sentimental in addition to the comic; it also prejudiced them to look primarily at ballad and lyric traditions alongside that of humorous Scots songs. This affected James Johnson's *Scots Musical Museum* (1787–1803), as did the influential appearance of European contributions, such as Johann Gottfried Herder's *Von Deutscher Art und Kunst* (1773). Born in Ettrick and apprenticed to an Edinburgh music-seller, Johnson was a pioneer printer of sheet music in his shop in Bell's Wynd. The *Museum* contained about six hundred songs; its comprehensiveness is typically antiquarian, and hugely influential on later collectors and writers. It was particularly valuable, as Donald Low noted, because of its inclusion of unornamented music.[23] Most famously, from 1787 onwards, it involved Robert Burns as the major collector and reframer of folk songs, many drawn from his native Ayrshire, as well as his adopted Dumfriesshire and further afield. Burns was the ideal antiquarian: knowledgeable, engaging no doubt as a collector, though with the capacity to 'polish' in a way which has, unusually, not detracted from his literary reputation. His interests ranged over lyric, ballad and narrative songs, into the bawdy – a clandestine collecting pastime for more than one antiquarian.[24] His antiquarian interests, too, informed his writing, from the Ayrshire traditions celebrated in 'Halloween' (alluding to Fergusson's earlier Edinburgh-based 'Hallow-Fair') to the historical interests reflected in the Jacobite 'Charlie, He's My Darling' and the reflections on 'The Solemn League and Covenant' (both historical areas which would prove of particular interest to nineteenth-century writers).[25]

Antiquarianism was, in itself, often a sociable act – Charles Withers has written about this, for instance, in the context of contemporary map-makers – and Burns's enthusiasm for oral traditions brought him into contact with a range of other antiquarians. These include, most famously, the Middlesex-born Francis Grose (c. 1731–91), described by Richard Dorson as 'the complete antiquary of the eighteenth century'.[26] Founder and editor of *The Antiquarian Repertory* from 1775, Grose's interests ranged from customs to language and regional traditions, with publications including *A Classical Dictionary of the Vulgar Tongue* (1785) to *The Antiquities of Scotland* (1789–91), alongside those of *England and Wales* (1773–87) and *Ireland* (1791–5), the last mentioned published posthumously and completed by Edward Ledwick. Burns commemorated Grose as 'a fine, fat, fodgel wight / O' stature short, but genius bright' who followed the '_____ Antiquarian trade' and, famously, sent him the tale of 'Tam o' Shanter' as an epistolary enclosure.[27] The 1780s and 1790s saw, however, in many ways, the formalisation of antiquarianism into something close to a recognised discipline in Scotland. A. S. Bell's edited collection,[28] as well as discussing its roots, profiles the Society of Antiquaries from its foundation in 1780, largely as the brainchild of its polymathic, Whig founder, David Steuart Erskine, the 11th Earl of Buchan (1742–1829), ambivalently described by Scott as a man '"whose immense vanity, bordering on insanity, obscured, or rather eclipsed, very considerable talents"'.[29]

The Society's charter, like Buchan, expressed ambition 'to investigate both antiquities and civil history in general, with the intention that the talents of mankind should be cultivated and that the study of natural and useful sciences should be promoted'.[30] Buchan took a pragmatic decision in 1780 to invite John Stuart, 3rd Earl of Bute, to be president (Buchan remained vice-president and involved until 1790); the next president (1792–1813) was James Graham, 4th Duke of Montrose. Other contemporary societies included the Literary and Antiquarian Society of Perth, founded in 1784 (Buchan was an honorary president from 1785) and Scottish antiquarians also had Scandinavian links, to the Royal Danish Society (founded 1785) and its Icelandic equivalent (from 1791). There were personal connections to scholars like Grímur Jónsson Thorkelin, assistant keeper of the Royal Archives in Copenhagen, who was interested in locating Danish, Norwegian and Icelandic antiquities in Britain and was based in London from 1786 to 1791 in this capacity. Buchan and others were equally interested in locating Scottish material outwith the nation.

The Society was influential in several ways: through its active publication schedule, for instance, in its *Transactions*, published from 1792 by William Creech; and through its meetings, membership and officers. At the first meeting, fourteen people attended, including Alexander Tytler (later Lord Woodhouselee), the bookseller William Creech and the *Encyclopaedia Britannica* (1771) printer and editor William Smellie, with the blessing of influential non-attenders including Lord Kames, Hugh Blair and Gilbert Stuart. The Charter of 6 May 1783 defined the Society as intended 'for investigating antiquities, as well as natural and civil history in general'. Its legitimisation was controversial; Edinburgh University had opposed the charter on the grounds that one Royal Society of Scotland would be preferable, to concentrate resources; the Faculty of Advocates also disapproved, on the grounds it might lose access to future donations, as did the Philosophical Society of Edinburgh. In the event, on the same date as the Society's charter was granted, another was given to create the Royal Society of Edinburgh, incorporating the scientifically interested Philosophical Society (Buchan resigned from the latter at this time). Initial ideas included Buchan's desire to create a parochial survey of Scotland, drawing on ministers' local knowledge (and feeding Sir John Sinclair's 1790 scheme for the *Statistical Accounts of Scotland*). Although a library collection was not its main impulse, manuscripts, books and printed materials were donated, including a first folio Shakespeare and thirteen volumes of papers by, and associated with, William Drummond of Hawthornden, loaned in 1934 to the National Library of Scotland. Items of visual interest included prints and drawings, now held in the National Portrait Gallery. The Society amassed other collections: of natural history, for instance, curated from 1781 by Smellie, curiosities, miscellaneous antiquities and artistic works, from the Covenanters' Flag carried at Bothwell Brig, and again in Edinburgh in 1745, to ethnographic items from Captain Cook's last expedition, donated by Sir John Pringle (Cook's father was from Ednam, Roxburghshire). Coins,[31] natural history materials, Bronze Age, Roman, Viking and medieval items were all represented. Walter Scott, significantly, first attended the Society meetings to see the donation of the Edinburgh guillotine, the Maiden (built in 1564, used till 1697) in 1797;

Scott referenced the Society's sporran-top, with four hidden pistols (given by MacNab of MacNab) in *Rob Roy*.[32]

In this eclectic approach, the Society followed in the development of museums in London (the London antiquaries, for instance, and the British Museum, founded twenty years beforehand). Equally, it paralleled the development of museum collections in other parts of Scotland – William Hunter's, for instance, which was bequeathed to the University of Glasgow in 1783, and the museum at Aberdeen University, founded in 1786, as well as specialist collections like Surgeon's Hall Museum in Edinburgh, which grew rapidly after 1699, seeking out 'natural and artificial curiosities'.[33] Antiquarianism in eighteenth-century Scotland, therefore, covered a broad range of activities: eclectic, comprehensive and nationally relevant. It was part of an impetus to find the rare, the distinctive and the significant, in literature and song, just as in physical collection and archaeology, and in understanding customs and beliefs through observation. In the process, it provided materials and approaches that would be used (and disputed) by later writers in their construction of narratives of Scottish identity.

CHAPTER TEN

Lowland Song Culture in the Eighteenth Century

Katherine Campbell and Kirsteen McCue

During the long eighteenth century it was common for poets and writers to compose songs in the native idiom. These were often based on songs or tunes already present in the tradition. This chapter will explore the work of three of the most important songwriters of the eighteenth century – Allan Ramsay (1686–1758), Robert Burns (1759–96) and John Skinner (1721–1807) – and examine the major role the native melodies of Scotland played in inspiring new sets of words. The fascination for publishing collections of songs and tunes was shared across Europe during this period, but it is commonly acknowledged that such activity was notable in Scotland, and her collections influenced editors and writers elsewhere on the Continent.[1] Following antiquarian principles, editors initially set out to preserve elements of the tradition, but the songs and tunes they printed were frequently amended and expanded from the material they collected (both oral and sometimes written). This chapter shows how complex the process of movement from oral tradition to published tradition could be, by concentrating on a number of Lowland Scots songs of the lyric tradition, the ballad tradition being explored elsewhere in this volume.

In the seventeenth century, songs and ballads were disseminated both orally and in popular cheap printed format: either in single-sheet broadsides, or in chapbooks commonly of eight or twelve pages.[2] The material in them reflected old songs (e.g. commonly recognised ballads) as well as newly-composed songs, often referring to topical public and political events. Printed music was not usually included, though often a tune title was given, illustrating that these tunes were in the popular domain, clearly known orally rather than through print; sometimes the same tune was used for several different sets of lyrics. The tradition of ephemeral printing was joined in the eighteenth century by many formally published songbooks. Thomas Crawford's seminal work *Society and the Lyric* (1979) illustrates that before 1786, around seventy-four songbooks were published in Scotland, amounting to 'approximately 3000 separate songs'.[3] These books typically ranged in length from around 100 to 400 pages, and many more were printed without music than with.[4]

Various key collections of poetry appeared at the beginning of the eighteenth century, and the inclusion of lyric poetry (often with tune titles alongside) illustrates the overlap with oral and popular prints of such songs. Allan Ramsay's *Scots Songs* (1718–19) comprised new lyrics set to specified traditional tunes.[5] Clearly inspired by its success, Ramsay followed it with one of the most influential collections of Scots songs of the period, namely the *Tea-Table Miscellany*. It appeared initially in 1724 as one volume including over eighty songs by Ramsay and others, allied to traditional tunes.[6] Both this collection and Ramsay's pastoral comedy *The Gentle Shepherd* (1725), including twenty-two songs within the form of the ballad opera, were to remain hugely popular throughout the eighteenth century, running quickly to numerous editions. Audiences would have clearly been familiar with the tunes Ramsay chose for inclusion. Such titles as 'Polwart on the Green', 'Cauld Kail in Aberdeen', 'Leith Wynd' and 'O'er Bogie', are frequently found in popular chapbooks and broadsides, suggesting that they were regularly heard.[7] Ramsay's dedication for the *Miscellany* makes it clear that he is concerned as much with 'Ladys Charlotte, Anne and Jean' as he is with 'ilk bonny singing Bess / Who dances barefoot on the Green': he is keen to encompass the interests and the sounds of the rural singing maid, while, at the same time, sharing her songs around the tea-tables of the urban upper classes. In Steve Newman's opinion Ramsay's Scots songs, so widely circulated at this time, played a key role in founding and disseminating 'some of the Enlightenment's central ideas'.[8]

One of the songs included in the *Miscellany* was Ramsay's 'Nanny O', set to the tune of the same title, and opening with the line 'While some for Pleasure pawn their Health' (1724, pp. 81–2). This is Ramsay's lyric as it appears in William Thomson's *Orpheus Caledonius*, vol. 1, no. 38 in 1725 (thought to be the first publication of the tune) (Fig. 1).[9]

The use of this particular tune transports the song both forward and back in time and helps trace the song's popular provenance. It was used in the seventeenth century for a broadside called the 'Scotch Wooing of Willy and Nanny', printed in London between 1685 and 1688,[10] a common song of wooing with the chorus:

It's Nanny, Nanny, Nanny O,
The love I bear to Nanny O,
All the world shall never know,
The love I bear to Nanny O.

Here Nanny is of lowly status, but, notwithstanding, the narrator would rather have her than court 'Betty with five thousand marks'. The setting is Tinmouth Castle and the ballad has much riding and chivalrous imagery,

Figure 1 My Nanny o

but we are also invited to visualise Nanny in her smock (with her 'lily white cheeks') and a 'bonny boy' is called to remove the narrator's boots so that he can 'go to bed to Nanny O'. Ramsay's version, some forty years later, keeps the same tune, but he turns the earlier broadside ballad of ten quatrains (abab) with chorus into two octaves (ababcbcb) with an amended chorus:

My bonny, bonny Nanny – O,
My lovely charming Nanny – O,
I care not though the World know
How dearly I love Nanny – O.

Ramsay's reworked version is more decorous and his decision to expand the quatrain to an octave elevates the simplicity of the popular sing-along broadside. Moreover his inclusion of European references ('Lais' and 'Bagnio', meaning courtesan and brothel), not to mention classical allusions (Jove, Leda and Danae) and a nod to portrait painting in the first octave, illustrate that the song is being lifted from the street to the parlour. Ramsay's second stanza, like the broadside, celebrates Nanny's finer physical attributes, but there is even a reference to Britannia here, clearly stressing Ramsay's awareness of his clientele.

Some sixty years after this Robert Burns turned his hand to the same tune. It is found first in his *Commonplace Book* for April 1784 where he is posing as the eighteenth-century songwriter, influenced as much by nature and love as he is by delusions of literary grandeur.[11] The tune he mentions is 'As I Came in by London O', but no one has yet found a tune with this title. Burns keeps the quatrain (abab) and includes eight verses with a chorus:

> And O my bonny Nannie O,
> My young, my handsome Nannie O,
> Tho' I had the world all at my will,
> I would give it all for Nanie O.[12]

His lyric thus resonates more closely with the broadside than with Ramsay's version. Burns's hero singer is a ploughman lad who recognises that his love for Nannie is vastly superior to the ownership of worldly goods. As in the original broadside he celebrates Nannie's beauty and simplicity and retains the sensuality of the original song by referring euphemistically to sheltering her under his plaid (in stanza 2). His lowly social status is celebrated when compared directly to that of the 'Guidman', much as the original narrator compares Nanny's simplicity to Betty's complex wealth. Such resemblance to the original would suggest that Burns knew 'The Scotch Wooing' or had heard it somewhere. But as his editors James Dick and subsequently James Kinsley note, another collector had since added a layer of complexity to the circulation of the song. David Herd (1732–1810) published his *Ancient and Modern Scottish Songs* in 1776, and there are notable links between materials included by Herd, and the contents of a separate manuscript collection of his, and several of Burns's lyrics and those of other songwriters of the period.[13] Herd's published collection included Ramsay's lyric, but his manuscript collection included the following extract:

> As I came in by Edinburgh toun,
> And in by the banks of the city, O,
> And there I heard a young man cry,
> And was na that great pity, O?
>
> [Chorus:]
> And still he cried his Nanie, O,
> His weel far'd, comely Nanie, O,
> And a' the warld shall never ken
> The love that I bear Nanie, O.[14]

Retaining the reference to bearing love for Nanie from the early broadside, this lyric also refers back to the tune title Burns gives in his *Commonplace Book*, except here 'Edinburgh' replaces 'London'. The use of 'Nanie O' in the lyric would strongly suggest that the tune title Burns refers to in 1784 is one and the same as that used for the earlier versions of the song. Burns's lyric first appeared with the tune 'My Nanie O' in 1793 in the first set of George Thomson's *Original Scotish Airs* (no. 4) with a setting by the composer Ignace Pleyel. There was no chorus and Stinchar had become Lugar, as Thomson did not like the former.[15] When his song appeared after his death in 1803 in the final volume of James Johnson's *Scots Musical Museum* (SMM, no. 580) it had no chorus and Stinchar had become 'rivers', but it also appeared with an altogether different melody. Ramsay's tea-table verses appeared with 'My Nanie O' in the first volume of the *Museum* in 1787, but the lack of the original tune (and missing chorus) with Burns's song breaks the magical chain back to that inspirational broadside.

The musical context is thus often of crucial importance in maintaining the links between old and new, ancient and modern, oral and printed song. Ramsay's *Tea-Table Miscellany* did not appear with musical notation in 1724.[16] Instead it was a London Scot, William Thomson (c. 1684–c. 1752), who picked up Ramsay's song texts, clearly seeing an opportunity for musical sales.[17] Thomson's *Orpheus Caledonius*, with an impressive subscription list of over 300 individuals, appeared in 1725 and published fifty Scots songs including several of Ramsay's tea-table songs without his permission, a theft to which the poet angrily referred in the Introduction to later editions of the *Miscellany*. Thomson's collection (expanded in 1733) is a major source of information and materials for later songwriters and collectors, and references to the tunes and texts in his *Orpheus Caledonius* are commonplace in the context of Burns's songs and the major illustrative compendia of both William Stenhouse and John Glen later in the nineteenth century.[18] A key fiddle collection of the 1740s was to be equally influential, especially in the case of Burns. James Oswald (1710–69), who was originally from Crail in Fife, also spent a considerable period of his life in London. Between c. 1745 and c. 1760 Oswald published his *Caledonian Pocket Companion*, containing some 550 tunes and including Scottish, Irish and English material as well as his own compositions.[19] He added many of his own variations to the traditional tunes, expanding some of them considerably.

Burns left a total output of some 373 songs across various sources,[20] and although these were later seen as products of Romantic impetus – emerging from nature with little skill required on the part of the poet – this view does not take account of Burns's great skill in fusing poetry and music together to make a successful song.[21] Burns based many of his songs on those he heard and experienced from the tradition, and he then amended and expanded lyrics as he felt best suited the projects on which he was working.[22] Moreover, by his own admission, the melody was always his starting point, influencing not just the mood or theme of his muse, but the form and rhythms of the lyric itself.[23] His most important song work, on which he collaborated with the Edinburgh engraver James Johnson, was the *Scots Musical Museum* (1787–1803), containing 600 songs spread over six volumes. This collection is highly significant for our understanding of Scots song during the period, especially since the tunes were often absent from other contemporary publications. The *Museum* brought together a group of like-minded individuals who set out to preserve national melodies (by providing new words for them) and to capture existing songs from around Scotland including Oswald's north-east and Burns's south-west. Much of the music for the *Museum* was supplied by Stephen Clarke (c. 1744–97), an Episcopal organist in Edinburgh, originally from Durham. He supplied bass lines for volumes 1–5 of the *Museum* and his son William supplied them for volume 6; this bass line included figured bass for some of the tunes, thus offering a trained musician the opportunity to improvise a more elaborate accompaniment.[24] Clarke composed some of the melodies himself, took down airs from live singing (e.g. SMM 264 'Ca' the Yowes' or SMM 454 'Our Goodman Came Hame at E'en'), advised Burns on the musical settings and sometimes adapted instrumental airs to make them more suitable for the voice. As Hamish Mathison has noted, the borrowing, collecting and amending of tunes somewhat confused their origin.[25] This was helpful in the process of creating a 'national repository' where the involvement of the individual needed to be downplayed and the project was to be seen as part of a bigger, communal or collective process. But not all of the musical sources came from 'the field'. Some of the tunes Clarke used were drawn from printed collections like Oswald's *Companion* (e.g. 'Address to the Blackbird' (SMM 190) set to 'The Scots Queen', and 'When I upon thy Bosom Lean' (SMM 205) set to the tune of the 'Scots Recluse' – one of Oswald's own compositions).[26] Having often notated songs from actual performance Clarke understood how tunes should sound in a traditional context. This is expressed in the way he presented the music for the *Museum*. His work thus contrasted with the arrangements of the contemporary European composers whom some editors and publishers commissioned.

Burns could play the fiddle and had a deep understanding of traditional tunes both old and new.[27] His lyric 'Of a' the Airts', dedicated to his wife, Jean Armour, and initially published in the *Museum* as 'I love my Jean' (SMM 235), used William Marshall's recently-composed fiddle tune, 'Miss Admiral Gordon's Strathspey' as its lyrical inspiration. Fiddle composers in the eighteenth century were experimenting with the capabilities of the violin that had come into Scotland around 1680, replacing more primitive instruments within the tradition.[28] This meant that tunes in more complex keys, with greater ranges, and with more technical requirements were written. Some of these were chosen as the basis for new song lyrics and can be difficult to sing. Whereas seventeenth-century fiddle tunes were often song airs, eighteenth-century song airs were often fiddle tunes. This development in fiddle composition styles expanded the range and type of melodies on which lyricists could draw. The 'strathspey' is a slow reel characterised 'by its dotted quaver-semiquaver rhythm and the inversion of this, the Scotch snap'.[29] It is a form that does not appear in print until the mid-eighteenth century where it is frequently found in the collections of Oswald and Robert Bremner, and, in this example, William Marshall (1748–1833). Some of Burns's finest love songs were written to match strathspeys, including his famous 'O My Love's Like a Red, Red Rose' ('Major Graham's Strathspey', SMM 402). This stylised melodic form enhanced Burns's natural skill for sentimental emotional expression in his lyrics, which was very much enjoyed in the salons of Enlightened Scotland. With 'Of a' the Airts', it is the expansive quality of the opening of Marshall's melody which Burns uses to link to the western winds, which in turn (as the melody almost repeats itself) connects to Jean and the local landscape. The second part of the tune then has a new sense of movement about it which likens Jean to the birds and the flowers – the smaller, living elements of the natural landscape – and that leaves the final melodic phrase, rising upwards and expanding again, to express the natural and boundless love he feels for her.

While this particular example (Fig. 2) epitomises the highly personal

Figure 2 Of a' the airts

Figure 3 Tullochgorum

lyric, Burns was also a master of the social song, as illustrated by his collection of bawdy songs, *The Merry Muses of Caledonia*, not to mention many drinking songs in which his cronies are named. Writing songs for specific social occasions was one of the key stimuli for songwriters of the period. The Reverend John Skinner (1721–1807), Episcopalian minister at Longside, not far from Peterhead in Aberdeenshire, composed eighteen songs, four of which appeared in Johnson's *Museum*; namely 'Tullochgorum', 'Ewie wi' the Crooked Horn', 'Tune your Fiddles', and 'John o' Badenyon'. Although Skinner wrote poetry in Latin and Scots and often on ecclesiastical themes, his songs appeared as a result of his teenage daughters badgering him to write words for their favourite tunes, several of which were by local musician William Marshall – clearly many of these songwriters and fiddle composers knew one another or used one another's work.[30] Burns was particularly taken with Skinner's abilities and wrote something of a fan letter to him from Edinburgh on 25 October 1787 in which he clearly stated: 'I assure you, Sir, as a poet, you have conjured up an airy demon of vanity in my fancy, which the best abilities in your *other* capacity would be ill able to lay' and in which he referred to Skinner as 'the Author of the best Scotch song ever Scotland saw, – "Tullochgorum's my Delight!"' (Fig. 3).[31]

Skinner's 'Tullochgorum' was written at the request of a Mrs Montgomerie, to ease a tense situation at a diocesan meeting in Ellon, as referred to in the first verse of the song.[32] The tune was well known in tradition and appears in a manuscript dating from 1734. Skinner uses a twelve-line stanza to match it. The successful fusion of poetry and music is notable at certain points in the song: in line 5 Skinner introduces a phrase and then repeats that in lines 6 and 7 corresponding with the octave leaps and repetitions in the music. He ends each verse with the word 'Tullochgorum', reminding us of the tune he is using, and he rhymes this with an impressive set of classical or mock-classical words, which are particularly amusing because the song is very much written in the vernacular. The sentiment contained in 'Tullochgorum' is chiefly about the need for unity rather than conflict, and some of the lyrics are also found in a Masonic song of the period containing the line 'We have no idle prating, of either Whig or Tory'.[33] Indeed, Masonic song was a key eighteenth-century genre, with songs published in general collections, and with specific collections of Masonic song also available. Many poets and musicians – like Burns and Oswald – were connected to the Craft. In verse 3 Skinner comments on the influx of Italian music, describing it as 'dowf and dowie' and unsatisfying to a Scottish ear. This theme was very topical, having been publicly circulated before Skinner's song in 1772 when on 5 March Robert Fergusson published his 'Elegy on the Death of Scots Music' in Ruddiman's *Weekly Magazine*. This is an issue discussed in a number of contemporary essays and dissertations on Scottish music.[34] As Bertie rightly notes, the Skinner family was moved to publish the lyric with Skinner's name, because 'Tullochgorum' had already been widely circulated orally, after the event itself, and then printed in both broadside format and in the *Weekly Scots Magazine* in 1776 with no reference to Skinner at all. Again this proves that such songs were often circulated orally before making their way into popular print. Bertie also states that by the late 1770s several of Skinner's most popular songs had appeared in little song volumes with no attribution to Skinner's authorship, and this is a process understood by all contemporary songwriters, even up to the early lyrics of Burns's key successor, James Hogg (1770–1835), who recounts a similar situation with his first song 'Donald McDonald'.[35]

Such a process was commonplace and has continued to be normal practice in the genre of Scots song, as exemplified by another of Skinner's lyrics. 'Widow Greylocks', with its farmer hero John Penny, was also based on a traditional tune and has been frequently linked with one of the other popular songs of the period, 'Auld Robin Gray' by Lady Ann Lindsay, one of a group of lady songwriters of the later eighteenth century.[36] Jane Millgate's recent work on Lindsay's song shows just how complex the issue of attribution could be (the song was initially published anonymously), and she traces the song's many variants across a fifty-year period. Lindsay claims that she was setting out to give an alternative acceptable lyric for the bawdy song known to the traditional tune 'The Bridegroom Greets when the Sun Gaes Doun'. But it is possible that the lyrics of both Lindsay's and Skinner's songs are based on another traditional north-east song, 'Johnnie Lad'. Here are the opening lines of the three songs:

Skinner:
Fin the lads are in their beds, an' the lasses sleepin' soon',
An' ilka thing fu' silent and calm aboot the toon [. . .]

Lindsay:
When the sheep are in the fauld & the ky at hame,
And a' the warld to sleep are gane [. . .]

Johnnie Lad:
The sheep are in the fauld,
And the kye are in the byre
And a' the rest are sittin' roon'
A braw rantin' fire.

'Johnnie Lad' (Greig–Duncan no. 756) was collected in Aberdeenshire in the early twentieth century from a Mrs Halley who learned it c. 1860 from her mother in Glenbervie, but it is likely to stem back in the oral tradition beyond this. Some similarities can also be found in Lindsay's original choice of tune, believed to be the same as 'The Bridegroom Greets when the Sun Gaes Tee' (Fig. 4),[37] in the tune of 'Johnnie Lad', and in the melody published to Skinner's 'Widow Greylocks' in Greig–Duncan (no. 1365).[38] These comparisons offer further evidence that both Skinner's and Lindsay's creations

Figure 4 The Bridegroom Greets[39]

have their roots in tradition, and that they worked their way, by a mixture of oral transmission and popular printed dissemination across the next century.

What becomes clear when looking at these eighteenth-century Scottish lyrics is that tradition is ever-changing. What is performed in 'the field' is passed around orally, but is also harnessed in many variant forms by popular print and transformed by writers, collectors and editors. Editorial policies are marked by time and place, by the cultural politics of their moment, but intrinsically these songs are linked to tradition by melody. Indeed, as shown by the *Museum*, lyrics were often written to protect such melodies for future generations. The continuity of mixing oral dissemination with popular song sheets and more formal collections of songs has continued. Gratifyingly for songwriters of the period, many of today's performers are looking again to these sources for their own renditions of Scotland's songs and tunes.

CHAPTER ELEVEN

Tradition and Scottish Romanticism

Suzanne Gilbert

Romantic writers of all nationalities acknowledged debts to traditional sources, and many found inspiration in Scotland's ballads, songs and tales. Most literary accounts of Romanticism, however, refer to these sources only in footnotes, if at all. This chapter addresses this imbalance. When eighteenth-century agrarian reform and industrial change were still transforming Scottish society, literary culture engaged with new ideas about traditional heritage. Influential collectors and editors sought, with culturally-nationalistic urgency, despite radically different political agendas, to preserve Scottish culture. Some writers' work of the period was irrevocably shaped by personal encounters with tradition.

Any survey of traditional practices in the decades around 1800 must be derived from sketchy information. Glimpses are seen in the *Statistical Accounts of Scotland* (1791–9, 1834–5), parish ministers' memoirs, writers' accounts of rural childhood and margins of ballad collectors' notebooks or finished volumes' paratexts. With increasing literacy, local memoirs detailing life in local communities suggest 'patterns of behaviour which fostered the perpetuation' of tradition.[1] These probably offer the most accurate picture. In 1818, a self-described Selkirkshire 'Old Farmer' attests to traditional expression's function in rural culture: '[W]e beguiled the long evenings with story-telling, ballad-singing, tales of bogles and witches' and 'the wandering beggar and the pedlar, always welcome guests, added other varieties of entertainment'.[2] Janet Hamilton recalls,

> [O]n song-singing, story-telling, and 'speering guesses', there was laid no restriction; and round the fire, heaped with peats and sticks, peals of song and laughter rang through the sooty rafters, and round the clay brace, and up the 'muckle lum' of the Scottish farmer's kitchen at the 'haudin' the kirn', as well as all merry-makings of the kind enjoyed by the peasantry of Scotland in the olden times.[3]

Duncan Anderson remembers in 1895 local figures contributing to a winter evening's entertainment: the miller telling stories about 'the water kelpie', the blacksmith who 'dealt chiefly with feats of manly strength that he had witnessed', the tailor who 'retailed the gossip that they had gathered during their wanderings', the cobbler whose stories 'very graphically brought out the pawky character of Scottish humour'.[4] But, he says, one performer stood out: 'Jean Barden was pre-eminently the story-teller of Sillerton'. Compared to the others she

> operated in another field altogether – the horrible in what was human, and the blood-curdling in what was supernatural, being the commodities in which she dealt. Nor was her stock of these by any means limited, as kelpies, goblins, fairies, brownies, elves, ghosts, wizards, witches, and sundry others of a kindred nature, were to her household words [. . .] Then, in addition to melancholy songs and ballads, all invariably of a lugubrious character, and covering a wide field of weird literature, her vivid imagination, and her peculiar faculty of finding suitable words to express her meaning, would make her remarkable in any community.[5]

Contrary to the notion of a communal mass culture subsuming nameless traditional storytellers or singers, influential performers were known and respected during this period.

While Barden's reputation was limited in extent, some tradition-bearers became far more widely-known. The most celebrated source for Walter Scott and Robert Jamieson was Anna Gordon (Mrs Brown of Falkland) (1747–1810), a professor's daughter and minister's wife who eschewed the limelight and was angry her ballads were published. Like Margaret Laidlaw Hogg, she learned her impressive range of ballads through hearing them sung by her aunt, her mother and 'an old maidservant'. She claimed never to have seen them in print or manuscript. In a note to 'Willie and May Margaret' in *Minstrelsy: Ancient and Modern*, William Motherwell referred to Brown as 'a lady to whom much of the traditionary poetry of Scotland is mainly indebted for preservation'.[6] Margaret Laidlaw Hogg (1730–1813), daughter of an influential storyteller and wife of an unsuccessful Ettrick farmer, famously scolded Walter Scott when he visited to transcribe the ballad of 'Auld Maitland'. As reported by her son James, she rapped Scott on the knee, telling him he had spoiled the ballads altogether: 'They were made for singing an' no for reading; but ye hae broken the charm now, an' they'll never be sung mair. An' the worst thing of a', they're nouther right spell'd nor right setten down.'[7] Others recount her 'vivid imagination and retentive memory: she eagerly heard, and scrupulously retained, the legendary ballads that were floating about the border district';[8] notable here is commentators' tendency to detach song from singer. Margaret's son William Hogg brings traditional expression back to the source: '[O]ur mother to keep us boys quiet would often tell us tales of kings, giants, knights, fairies, kelpies, brownies [. . .] These tales arrested our attention, and filled our minds with the most dreadful apprehensions', thereby serving to 'keep the bairns out of mischief'.[9]

Diverse, less-known voices perpetuated traditional expression. James Nicol of Strichen received only a basic education, but David Buchan notes he was 'a well read and intelligent man', 'a bit of a character' who championed Tom Paine's egalitarian views, visited America and, returning, worked as cooper and bookseller in Aberdeenshire, authored pamphlets 'which set forth views quite advanced for his time' on topics such as child education, crime and punishment and deism, and left money in his will to found a school for poor children.[10] Nicol was a major contributor to Peter Buchan's collection and, though Buchan's editorial methods were much maligned (some claim unjustly), seven of Nicol's ballads later earned Francis J. Child's approval for inclusion in *The English and Scottish Popular Ballads*. Weaver's daughter Agnes Lyle of Kilbarchan provided twenty-six songs for William Motherwell's collection, being recognised as his chief contributor. Many more were tapped for that project, among them weavers, servants, coal-heavers and various 'singing women'.[11]

The period witnessed a vibrant living tradition, but agricultural 'Improvement', through which traditional farming methods were replaced by the modern agrarian system – and industrial change – also shook it. T. M. Devine observes, '[between 1760 and 1830] the face of the Scottish countryside was radically altered and the way of life of the people fundamentally changed'.[12] Introduction of turnips and sown grasses, for example, allowed more control over cattle-feeding. This contributed to widespread land enclosure, thus ending the run-rig system of cultivation – and the communal culture that it fostered – changing farm labourers' lives dramatically.[13] Cultural practices were most likely to survive in areas less exposed to the improvement agenda's homogenising, mechanising effects. In some circumstances, nonetheless, people adapted. Even as communally-structured 'fermtouns' were lost, certain factors in rural districts encouraged some practices' continuation – for example in north-east textile industries: 'The country women engaged in these congregated most nights at one house in the neighbourhood where they knitted or span their "stents" together, and enlivened the evening by singing songs and ballads.'[14] But a sense of loss was widespread. Witnesses to economic change's dramatic effects on rural life include James Hogg, the Ettrick Shepherd:

> On looking back, the first great falling off is in SONG. This, to me, is not only astonishing, but unaccountable. They have ten times more opportunities of learning songs, yet song-singing is at an end, or only kept up by a few migratory tailors. In my young days, we had singing matches almost every night, and, if no other chance or opportunity offered, the young men attended at the ewe-bught

or the cows milking, and listened and joined the girls in their melting lays [...]
Where are those melting strains now? Gone, and for ever![15]

The belief that what had been common in Scottish life was verging on oblivion drove ballad, song and tale collection.

Enlightenment philosophy shaped eighteenth-century antiquarianism. This employed an 'objective', scientific approach to analysing and classifying cultural antiquities: from Iron Age architecture to the ballads of Scotland. Certainly antiquarian initiatives played a substantial role in traditional expression's preservation, even if – witness Hogg's fears – they conspired with social changes to hasten its demise. Following the great eighteenth-century antiquarian projects, a new, dual emphasis emerged; on a culturally-nationalistic drive to reclaim and highlight Scotland's cultural richness and on personal connections to traditions being collected. The distance eighteenth-century critics deemed necessary from a perceived lower form of expression was replaced by subjective appreciation, in line with Romantic trends more broadly. Scottish collectors engaged in reclaiming their own, undertaking the task of documenting what was felt to be an endangered traditional culture, among them David Herd, Robert Burns, Walter Scott, William Motherwell, Robert Jamieson and Charles Kirkpatrick Sharpe – often with the assistance of informants such as John Leyden and James Hogg.

Most prominent of these collectors, Scott engaged ballads in lifelong dialogue as enthusiast, translator, imitator and editor. His *Minstrelsy of the Scottish Border* (1802–3) rivals Percy's *Reliques of Ancient English Poetry* in importance for the history of ballad-collecting. Though Percy's ballads enthralled the young Scott, his own collection repossesses the substantial number of Scottish ballads (not only from the Borders) Percy had gathered under his rubric, 'English poetry'. Scott's presentation of 'Sir Patrick Spens', for example, is fifteen stanzas longer than the eleven-stanza version in the *Reliques*, identifies an imagined 'cause of Sir Patrick Spens' voyage' and shows 'the song has claim to high antiquity, as referring to a very remote period in Scottish history'.[16] On one level, Scott foregrounded Scotland's cultural contributions to an emerging British culture; his engagement was also intensely personal, conjoining genealogical and historical. 'Every Scottishman has a pedigree,' he announces early in his 1808 autobiographical memoir: 'It is a national prerogative, as unalienable as his pride and his poverty.'[17] Fascinated by kinship, he liked to trace ancestral connections in the narratives, as in his variant of 'Jamie Telfer of the Fair Dodhead': 'The Scotts they rade, the Scotts they ran, / Sae starkly and sae steadily!'[18]

Scott was involved firsthand in ballads' movement from singer to page; and Border country, which during Scott's life overran with 'ballad notes',[19] proved an ideal hunting ground for the zealous ballad-collector. In the

Introduction to the *Minstrelsy*, Scott remarks that, lacking precedents, he 'has been obliged to draw his materials chiefly from oral tradition',[20] particularly from 'the shepherds [. . .] and aged persons, in the recesses of the Border mountains, [who] frequently remember and repeat the warlike songs of their fathers'.[21] J. E. Shortreed records an 1824 conversation with his father Robert S. Shortreed, the Sheriff of Roxburghshire, who between 1792 and 1799 accompanied Scott on excursions into the countryside:

> we rade about visiting the scenes o' remarkable occurrences, and *roved away amang the fouk* haill days at a time, for Sir Walter was very fond o' mixing wi' them, and by that means he became perfectly familiar wi' their character and the manners o' the Country [. . .][22]

Scott's attraction to ballads had much to do with preserving historical elements that could be reconstructed into narratives of an idealised past. As described by W. F. H. Nicolaisen, Scott's conception of 'tradition in the folk-cultural register' provided 'windows on the past, illuminating, in some refracted manner, the way of life of ages gone by'. For him, these 'windows' exist as 'fragile fragments and corrupted texts whose authenticity has suffered greatly in the long and unpredictable process of oral transmission'.[23] Entertaining Washington Irving at Abbotsford in 1817, Scott reportedly declares, 'A real old Scottish song is a cairngorm [. . .] a precious relic of old times, that bears the national character stamped on it, – like a cameo, that shows what the national visage was in former days, before the breed was crossed.'[24] Borrowing a metaphor from Joseph Ritson, Scott proclaims tradition 'a sort of perverted alchemy which converts gold into lead'.[25] In 1830 Scott maintains the same belief:

> [U]ndergoing from age to age a gradual process of alteration and recomposition, our popular and oral minstrelsy has lost, in a great measure, its original appearance; and the strong touches by which it had been formerly characterised, have been generally smoothed down and destroyed by a process similar to that by which a coin, passing from hand to hand, loses in circulation all the finer marks of the impress.[26]

The 'original' ballad, according to Scott, suffered irrevocably from 'passing through the mouths of many reciters', which produced the 'impertinent interpolations from the conceit of one rehearser, unintelligible blunders from the stupidity of another, and omissions equally to be regretted, from the want of memory in a third'.[27] To Scott, ballads represent fragments of Scottish poetry in its earliest, least-developed form: 'it cannot be uninteresting to have a glimpse of the National Muse in her cradle'.[28] The work that such a muse inspires, 'however rude, was a gift of Nature's first-fruits'; therefore, 'even a reader of refined taste will find his patience rewarded, by passages in which the rude minstrel rises into sublimity or melts into pathos'.[29] In order to present the best possible version of texts, Scott combines variants of ballads and fills in what he deems narrative information missing. In this, his approach perpetuates Enlightenment-based grand narratives that locate traditional material firmly in an aristocratic past and is concerned with retrieval, preservation and ultimately containment of antiquity's 'reliques'. The narratives are distinctly Scottish rather than British, however: his work's influence on compiling a Scottish national minstrelsy cannot be overstated.

James Hogg (1770–1835) was closer than Scott to oral tradition and became caught up in Scott's search for ballads in Ettrick and Yarrow. His perspective, however, was less antiquarian or genealogical; he considered ballads part of living tradition and later in life became highly sceptical of antiquarian projects. In 'On the Changes in the Habits, Amusements, and Condition of the Scottish Peasantry', published in the *Quarterly Journal of Agriculture* in the early 1830s, Hogg laments cultural loss in Ettrick, blaming it on the *Minstrelsy*:

> The publication of the Border Minstrelsy had a singular and unexpected effect in this respect. These songs had floated down on the stream of oral tradition, from generation to generation, and were regarded as a precious treasure belonging to the country; but when Mr Scott's work appeared their areanum was laid open, and a deadening blow was inflicted on our rural literature and principal enjoyment by the very means adopted for their preservation.[30]

Between assisting Scott with the *Minstrelsy* and this elegiac comment nearly thirty years later, Hogg had become profoundly disturbed, not only by lost songs, but by the effect on rural life. For Hogg, traditional expression was integral to community: his engagement was personal. He perceived himself writing from within tradition, but also trying to project it to a wider world. Hogg occasionally cites evidence from print histories, but authority primarily rests with testimony from oral voices, actual people anchored in genuine places. His work is peppered with accounts of popular tales of Ettrick such as 'the Bogle of Bell's Lakes' and 'Mr Boston and the pedlar',[31] and he repeatedly signals the importance of storytelling as performance.

While coming from a scholarly perspective, William Motherwell (1797–1835) tried to mediate between both Scott's and Hogg's models. In *Minstrelsy: Ancient and Modern* (1827), he maintains scholarly tone and distance, but is careful to credit oral sources. The ballad of 'Fair Annie', he comments, has 'two copies, both obtained from the recitation of old people'; they differ, but are 'both worth preserving'.[32] Regarding 'The Weary Coble o Cargill' he writes that he has taken the 'recitation of an old woman, residing in the neighbourhood of Cambus Michael, Perthshire'.[33] In the meticulously-prepared manuscript notes he records names, ages, often professions and familial connections, and sometimes how sources learned the ballads.[34] In contrast to Scott's distrust of oral sources, Motherwell asserts, 'The reciters of old ballads frequently supply the best commentary upon them, when any obscurity or want of connection appears in the poetical narrative.'[35] Regarding ballads as constituting a national literature, he writes,

> The almost total absence of written monuments to support the claims of Scotland to an inheritance of Ancient National Minstrelsy enforces the stern necessity of not wantonly tampering with the fleeting and precarious memorials tradition has bequeathed to these latter times. Hence it has become of the first importance to collect these songs with scrupulous and unshrinking fidelity. If they are at all worth preserving [. . .] it assuredly must be in the very garb in which they are remembered and known, and can be proved to exist amongst us.[36]

Contrary to views that ballads are fragments and must be dressed up for the reading public, Motherwell insists they be transcribed faithfully, and allowed to speak for themselves.

Motherwell sets out approaches to tradition that presage those relevant in current ethnology. He discerns the differences between literary and oral traditions, addressing ballads' features in a sympathetic manner. The 'Romantick ballad', he asserts, compels attention almost immediately because of the 'almost uniform dramatick cast of its structure':

> The action of the piece commences at once [. . .] The characters and the destinies of those who form the subject of such tales are learned from their actions, not by the description of the poet. They generally open with some striking and natural picture, pregnant with life and motion. The story runs on in an arrow-like stream, with all the straightforwardness of unfeigned and earnest passion [. . .] The charm of the composition lies in the story which it evolves. Strained and artificial feeling has no place in it, and rhetorical embellishments are equally unknown. Descriptions of natural scenery are never attempted, and sentiment is almost unheard of. Much is always left for imagination to fancy, and for the feelings of the auditors, to supply, roused as they cannot fail to be, by the scenic picture rapidly and distinctly traced before the mind's eye.[37]

Further, Motherwell grasps the concept of variation in ballads on the same subject. He reproduces variants of 'Johnie Scot' 'as they occur in the three different copies of the ballad recovered by the Editor, so that the reader may have it in his power to choose the reading which hits his fancy'.[38] He recognises the importance of ballad structure to memory, its crucial significance for oral transmission. Repetitious 'common places' in lines and stanzas – judged a fault in ballads by many of his contemporaries – he describes as 'ingenious devices, no doubt suggested by the wisdom and experience of many ages, whereby oral poetry is more firmly imprinted on the memory' and 'in the absence of letters, the only efficacious means of preserving and transmitting it to after times'.[39]

Even as collecting ballads and songs rose to a national priority, during the 1820s short fiction became a staple of periodicals, and collections of tales also appeared as books. Introducing Allan Cunningham's tales, Tim Killick observes, 'Many of the authors and publishers of this new wave of stories and collections sought to tap into the contemporary vogue for traditional or folkloric material'; the term 'folklore' not being coined until the 1840s, such material appeared in publications as 'popular antiquities, superstitions or simply as traditions'.[40] Robert Chambers is notable for gathering such antiquities in the long-lived *Popular Rhymes of Scotland* (1826), which contained material ranging from nursery rhymes to tales to proverbs, nostalgically associated with 'the production of rustic wits', and 'the whimsies of mere children', whose original purpose was 'to convey the wisdom or the humours of the cottage, to soothe the murmurs of the cradle, or enliven the sports of the village green'.[41] But if the editorial tone contributes to the nineteenth-century trend of infantilising traditional expression, the collection is notable for its 'acute perception of what was authentic' and his 'preservation of local speech patterns.[42] Another major contribution was his making available 'fireside nursery stories' that had originally appeared in the 1548 *Complaynt of Scotland*: 'The Red Etin', 'The Black Bull of Norroway' and 'The Wal at the Warld's End'; as well as 'a few of the simplest narratives of the Scottish nursery, in prose as well as verse'.[43] Among these are the tales 'The Milk-White Doo', 'Whuppity Stoorie' and 'Rashie-Coat' (a Scottish variant of 'Cinderella'), mentioned elsewhere in this volume. Here too readers would have encountered the compelling storytelling of 'Nurse Jenny' Blackadder of Annandale, identified at the conclusion of several pieces as coming 'from the memory of the late Charles K. Sharpe, Esq., who would be sitting at the knee of Nurse Jenny, at his father's house of Hoddam in Dumfriesshire, about the year 1784'.[44]

Scottish writing owes much to traditional expression that emerged during the period of literary Romanticism. Writers like Scott and Hogg borrowed liberally from ballads and tales, repurposing folkloric material in profoundly influential ways. In Scott's work, evidence of ballad-collecting days resurfaces in the metrical romances and novels long after these genres replaced the ballad as his preferred medium, prompting Thomas Carlyle to call the *Minstrelsy* 'a well from which flowed one of the broadest rivers'.[45] Hogg recycled narratives across genre and time; many of his strategies are grounded in the characteristic features of traditional ballads and tales: circular structures, incremental repetition, abrupt introduction of perspectives through dialogue, folkloric motifs, intertextuality through traditional formulae. These centuries-old techniques, intrinsic to the ways in which oral traditions operate, provided Scottish Romantic writers and their successors with tools that prefigured modern – and postmodern – techniques.

CHAPTER TWELVE

Nineteenth-Century Highland and Island Folklore

Jason Marc Harris

The wealth of Scottish folklore collected in the nineteenth century is rivalled by the passion and industry of the collectors and informants who performed, gathered and analysed the materials, especially in the Highlands and Islands where geographical isolation fostered cultural preservation. This folklore includes multiple genres: folk 'fairy tale' (fictional episodic narrative involving a protagonist encountering magical helpers and challenges), hero tale (legendary tales of regional warriors), folk belief legend (confrontations with the supernatural that are alleged to have occurred locally), riddle, hymn, charm and animal fable. Among the heroic tales, the Fenian tales are most valued: legendary stories of the heroic leader Fionn and his band of warriors. Besides these genres, there are popular tales of historical events and religious figures. Within each genre, there are many subjects: from harrowing encounters with ghosts, witches and the devil to practical advice on defence against the fairies, the acquisition of wealth, divination of one's future and fortification of one's health.

Some of the narratives encompass plot structures recognised as international tale-types and motifs of migratory folklore (lore that moves from one region to another). The legend of how a brave tailor escapes a voracious ghost in 'The Grey Paw', is 'perhaps the most widely known and most popular story in the Highlands' and thus qualifies as a migratory legend: '[there is] hardly an old church in the Highlands where the event has not been said to have occurred'.[1] The collective body of nineteenth-century Scottish folklore is a hybrid of Christian and pagan elements and local and international narrative structures. Understanding the features of nineteenth-century Scottish folklore and its cultural significance requires exposure to the tales themselves, the tradition bearers who performed them and the collectors who determined their printed form.

Three collectors stand out because of their works' range and insight: for folktales, John Francis Campbell (1822–85); for folk legends, Rev. John Gregorson Campbell (1836–91); and for folk verse and charms, Alexander Carmichael (1832–1912). However, Rev. Walter Gregor (1825–97), Hugh

Miller (1802–56), Andrew Lang (1844–1912), Rev. Alexander Stewart (1828–1901), Rev. James MacDougall (1833–1906), James Napier (1810–84) and Anne MacVicar Grant (1755–1838) all helped to develop standards for folklore scholarship. The collectors' perspectives, outlined below, ranged from sceptical or elitist disapproval and religious anxiety to enthusiasm and advocacy for the preservation of Scottish traditional culture.

Collectors: Cultural Agendas and Methodologies

Conflicting attitudes towards folklore arose in part from the period's archaeological and anthropological debates about human origins. Andrew Lang was not primarily a collector of oral lore, despite his twelve-volume compilation of fairy tales (the 'coloured' *Fairy Books*). His work was anthropological and book-oriented, as was that of James Frazer, the grand comparativist, though it reshaped the borders of folklore as a discipline: 'Lang led the English folklorists away from the prevailing interest in customs and antiquities and into narrative scholarship via his debates on solar mythology and the proper relationship between myth, legend, and Märchen.'[2] Lang promoted the importance of investigating contemporary folk beliefs despite the lack of respect he received from the Folk-Lore Society (founded in 1878). Many scholars dismissed folk beliefs as the 'superstitions' of uneducated peasants: 'faltering steps on the way to rationality'.[3] Lang decries social condescension as an obstacle in his defence of studying ghostly narratives. In *The Book of Dreams and Ghosts*, Lang clarifies that 'superstitions' contain aesthetic, psychological and cultural elements that are far more than irrational curiosities on the stepladder of civilisation from primitive magic to enlightened science.

Religious and scholarly ambivalence characterised attitudes to folklore collection in the nineteenth century. Although some ministers 'suppressed Gaelic recital, others now sympathetically set about recording them' when Alfred Nutt, the president and publisher of the Folk-lore Society, directed the five-volume project *Waifs and Strays of Celtic Tradition* (1889–95). The series was a prodigious achievement of collaboration among folklorists (including Rev. J. G. Gregorson and Rev. James MacDougall), inspired by the previous model of scholarship set by J. F. Campbell with his collection.[4] Religious guilt and cultural oppression, however, took their toll. Alexander Carmichael, tax-collector and folklorist, insists that 'Ignorant school-teaching and clerical narrowness' explain why 'Gaelic oral literature has been disappearing'. 'Better is the small fire' – so said the minister to the fiddler who watched his violin burn after obeying the religious injunction to purge instruments and dancing on the Isle of Lewis. A young woman described to Carmichael the beatings she and other girls had received by the schoolmaster for singing Gaelic songs after school '"He punished us till the blood trickled from our fingers."'[5]

J. F. Campbell suggested that that nature of school education and the proliferation of print culture eroded folklore.[6] He also attributed folklore's decline to the rise of technology, the railroad in particular. Rev. Walter Gregor, who collected Lowland lore in the north-east counties of Scotland (ranging over land from Aberdeen to Banffshire), characterises industrialism as antithetical to tradition: 'The scream of the railway whistle is scaring away the witch, and the fairy, and the waterkelpie, and the ghost.'[7] J. F. Campbell declares that folk belief, at least what qualifies as 'superstition', will remain, but that the particulars of fairy beliefs will perish along with the intricate Gaelic narratives. The 'people who must work' were ceasing to be tradition-bearers; the industrial revolution was disrupting communal work in which storytelling often took place: the chatter of communal labour was being drowned out by the hum of machinery.[8]

J. F. Campbell's approach became the gold standard of collectors. Following his example, James MacDougall provided Gaelic texts along with the English translations. Carmichael gathered lore with J. F. Campbell on trips, and in his own publication announced that his method aimed to follow that of 'Campbell of Islay [. . .] in giving the words and in recording the names of the reciters' as well as asserting that he 'tried to translate literally but satisfactorily'.[9]

Yet before the surge of enthusiasm for gathering Gaelic folklore in Scotland, Anne MacVicar Grant published her *Essays on the Superstitions of the Highlanders of Scotland* (1811). She performed fieldwork in the Inverness-shire region (she makes specific reference to the parishes of Laggan and Kingussie) and communicates psychologically acute observations, as well as commentary lamenting oppressive religious attitudes towards folk narratives: 'These were all declared to be, "visitings of Satan".'[10] Grant presents the range of attitudes the pious may have towards folklore: 'As a devout and rigid Presbyterian, he [one of Grant's informants] thought it his duty to war against superstition in all its forms. Yet he still kept a corner in his mind for one darling idol [. . .] the second sight'.[11]

James Napier collected Lowland folklore in the south-west of Scotland from Glasgow to Killin. The tonal range of attitudes towards folk beliefs in his work indicates that an encounter with folk narratives and beliefs often involves a tension between ideological assumptions about what is rational and direct personal experiences with credible informants whose claims defy rationalism. Reluctantly, Napier credits intelligence to an informant whose lore he would prefer to dismiss: 'an ordinarily intelligent person on this subject [. . .] gave it as his opinion that dumb [mute] persons had their loss of the faculties of hearing and speech recompensed to them in the gift of supernatural knowledge'.[12] Napier also mentions the failure of both medical and clerical aid for a woman who had 'mental derangement', but her case improved after a remedy against the evil eye was used.[13] Despite his derision, Napier's work explores the range of attitudes that informants exhibit: 'My informant believed himself above superstition, yet he related this as evidence for the black airt.'[14] Napier implies that readers should marvel more at the inconsistencies of human nature displayed by the informants than gape at the wonders claimed in their tales.

Rev. Alexander Stewart was a minister in the 'parish of Ballachulish and Ardgour' and fluent in English and Gaelic.[15] His books *Twixt Ben Nevis and Glencoe: The Natural History, Legends, and Folk-Lore of the West Highlands* are collections of letters, which were enjoyed by his parish over forty years and praised in his 1901 obituary in *The Celtic Monthly* as 'a source of pleasure to Highlands in every clime' and 'marvels of versatility' because of their literary merit and wide-ranging knowledge.[16] Rev. Stewart's jubilant greeting to the reader in the beginning of Chapter 30 captures his memoir-like style: 'Such a splendid wild-bird season this has been!'[17] His aesthetic ebullience is not only for the folklore and fauna of Scotland but the landscape and meteorological beauty as well: 'a sight, the magnificence and splendour of which must haunt us till our dying day. It was a double rainbow, both perfect arches of glory [. . .] spanning the dark gorge of Glencoe!'[18]

J. F. Campbell's status as the chief collector of folk narratives in Scotland in the nineteenth century remains unchallenged. Although his family were land-owners, social status did not obstruct his traditional education: he learned Gaelic from a piper and stories from a blind fiddler.[19] His emphasis on comparisons anticipates the historical-geographical method (or Finnish School of folklore research) advanced later by Kaarle Krohn and exemplified in the work of Antti Aarne's and Stith Thompson's tale-type and motif-indexes. Campbell asserts the value of folklore collection is analogous to that done by paleontologists: 'it seemed to me as barbarous to "polish" a genuine popular tale, as it would be to adorn the bones of a Megatherium with tinsel, or gild a rare old copper coin [. . .] stories orally collected can only be valuable if given unaltered [. . .]',[20] insisting that his translations of Gaelic informants – and that of his deputised collectors – were literal.

J. F. Campbell's approach influenced his namesake, John Gregorson Campbell, who grew up bilingual and used his first-hand knowledge of Gaelic and his position as a minister to mix with his informants when gathering legends. A passionate Highlander, J. G. Campbell's fervour showed in his commentary such as when he makes an editorial interjection in 'The Big Lad of Dervaig'. Having come to blows with schoolmates over his Highland heritage, J. G. Campbell sympathised with the Big Lad who defends a Highland colonel from the harassment of an Englishman.[21] After discovering their shared identity through conversing in Gaelic, the colonel agrees to write a 'discharge' for the Big Lad who in turn offers to teach the English officer a lesson: 'giving him a blow he had cause to remember all his life, if he ever recovered from it. The soldier [the Big Lad] was sentenced to be severely punished, but on arriving in England, he deserted – though desertion of the army is not a custom of Highland soldiers – and became a fugitive'.[22] His interjection here amounts to a defence of Highland culture; J. G. Campbell is not a disinterested collector.

Informants

Most collectors did not elaborate on the identity of their informants, but J. F. Campbell was a notable exception: '[They were] men with clear heads and wonderful memories, generally very poor and old, living in remote corners of remote islands, and speaking only Gaelic [. . .].'[23] Hugh Miller, a tradition-bearer as well as folklore collector, agreed: 'greyheaded men, and especially old women, became my books'.[24] Campbell provides the most detail, including a table of contents that lists the name of the tale, collector, informant, date and location. He also offers specific examples. In his introduction, he presents the interplay between storyteller and collector, including the context of family, the visitors, the role of food, and the household animals – not least is Campbell himself who has waded across the ford to get there:

> The owner of the house [. . .] is seventy-nine. He told me nine stories, and like all the others, declared that there was no man in the islands who knew them so well [. . .] he told me plainly that my versions were good for nothing. 'Huch! Thou hast not got them right at all' [. . .] he chuckled at the interesting parts, and laid his withered finger on my knee as he gave out the terrible bits with due solemnity. A small boy in a kilt, with large round glittering eyes, was standing mute at his knee [. . .] three wayfarers dropped in and listened for a spell, and passed their remarks till the ford was shallow [. . .] There we sat, and smoked and talked for hours, till the tide ebbed; and then I crossed the ford by wading up to the waist, and dried my clothes in the wind in Benbecula.[25]

J. F. Campbell's interactions with his informants are entertaining, educational and moving, although some of his generalisations about his folkloric expeditions may seem condescending: 'My next step was to go at Easter to a Highland district, near the lowlands, where a gamekeeper had marked down a lot of tale-tellers, and I was soon convinced that there was plenty of game, though hard to get.'[26] The use of the hunting metaphor 'plenty of game' resonates with the rhetoric of other Scottish folklorists, such as Rev. Stewart:

> the successful angling, so to speak – is a very different matter when you come to try it [. . .] to discover the individual in whom the hidden treasure you are in

search of lies hid, and then you have to extract it, and extract it as much as may be in the completest and most perfect form [. . .]²⁷

Here the Rev. Stewart invokes treasure-hunting, fishing and dissection all in a single paragraph describing the process of gathering folklore. This language of acquisition and extraction exemplifies what Valentina Bold refers to as an attitude of 'collection as colonization'.²⁸ Not all collectors were so quick to offer their perspective or intrude into the territory of their informants; the Rev. Walter Gregor stresses that his editorial restraint is part of what distinguishes his folklore collection, An Echo of the Olden Time from the North of Scotland, as descriptive rather than subjective.²⁹

The Materials

Hero tales

J. F. Campbell asserts that the rarest of the tales he collected were 'the tradition or old history of the Feene', most common in the islands of 'Barra and South Uist' and seldom found 'in any printed book'.³⁰ J. G. Campbell describes sixteenth-century ecclesiastical difficulties with the popularity of the Fenian tradition: 'the Bishop complains that his countrymen were fonder of listening to idle tales about the Féinne or heroes of the time of Fionn mac Cumhaill, than of taking any interest in the Word of God'.³¹ He explains that storytellers would spend several days sharing tales of the Fianna during communal work 'until very recent times'.³² This decline made collection urgent.

Fionn was not always the gentleman that J. G. Campbell suggests. The young warrior takes indiscriminate revenge against the clan of those who killed his father in one tale of his upbringing:

> They came to a loch where a number of children were swimming. Fionn went out among them, and every one he caught he kept his head under water and drowned him. A woman who was looking out at a window said: 'Who is the Fair White one who is ever drowning the children?' ('Co Fionn bàn tha sio bhathadh nam mac?'
> Los Lurgann [Fionn's aunt on his father's side] said: 'May you enjoy your name; you will be called Fionn always after this, and you were without a name till now.'³³

The 'Fair White one' wreaks his vengeance against a fisherman as well; in some versions he 'tore him asunder'; in other variants he was more inventive: 'taking Arky's fishing-rod, broke it against his knee, with this piece of the rod he knocked down Arky, and then killed him'.³⁴ Fleeing the scene of his vengeance against the Lochlinners, Fionn succeeds in escaping, but not without a grisly price:

> He caught his aunt by the feet, threw her on his back, and fled through a thick wood, never looking behind him. Feeling his burden getting light, and looking round, he found he had only the two legs left. He threw them out on a loch, which ever since has borne the name of Loch Lurgann.[35]

This morbid humour is a common Fenian feature, as well as the blunt physicality. In MacDougall's *Folk and Hero Tales* the hero of 'The Son of the Strong Man of the Wood, Who was Twenty-One Years on His Mother's Breast' (after the twenty-one years of suckling) tears a tree out of the ground that grew from a walnut in his lifespan, an amusing metaphor for a protracted upbringing.[36]

Folk beliefs

Besides local legends, traditional practices, holiday festivals, riddles and rhymes, Rev. Gregor provides folk beliefs involving domestic details of everyday rural life in *Notes on the Folk-Lore of the North-East of Scotland*: 'In cooking, all the stirring must be done from left to right. Stirring food "the vrang wye" brought on bowel complaint.'[37] Gregor even details the different types of lamps and describes the foundation of the house having openings for the dog and hens.[38] He reports some of the most striking folk cures in Chapter 20, 'Animal and Plant Superstitions': 'If one take a mole and rub it between the hands till it dies, the power of healing a woman's festered breast lies ever after in the hands. All that has to be done is to rub the breast between the hands'. Among other remarkable cures that Gregor offers 'without comment' is the power to be gained from the frog: 'If a frog is caught alive and its eyes licked with the tongue, the power of curing any eye-disease lie in that tongue. The cure is effected by licking the diseased eyes.'[39] Like Gregor, Rev. Stewart presents a range of folk beliefs: from supernatural lore on weather forecasting to the folklore of rats: 'the incantation was forthwith composed in excellent Gaelic [. . .] not only did the rats shortly afterwards totally disappear, but they actually reappeared in great numbers in the opposite district of Sunart'.[40]

Charms and folk verse: Alexander Carmichael's Carmina Gadelica

To produce the *Carmina Gadelica* Alexander Carmichael gathered his material – charms, love songs, prayers, blessings, riddles and various working songs – chiefly from the 'Western islands', but he covered the Highlands as well: 'Arran to Caithness, from Perth to St. Kilda'.[41] Aside from the religious guilt of some of his informants, he also contended against physical obstacles like walking great distances or facing the noise of an active community. At the north-west island of St Kilda while transcribing from a cottar, aged eighty-four years, who had many old songs, stories and traditions of the island. I would have gotten more of these had there been peace and quiet to take them down, but this was not to be had among a crowd of naval officers and seamen and St Kilda men, women and children, and, even noisier than these, St Kilda dogs, mad with excitement and all barking at once.[42]

There is sadness among some of his informants. On the Isle of Lewis he is told 'old things are passed away, all things are become new', and on St Kilda this idea of transience even carries over to physical extinction: '"We have no marriages or baptisms, rather we are dying out. How shall we marry and baptise, did not the *bramach-innilt* [midwife] die? And we cannot have children, and we are, my dear, like to die out."'[43]

Many of the prayers, blessings, curses and charms include what Carmichael refers to as the 'grafting' of Christian elements onto 'pagan stock', presenting the opportunity to study survivals of an ancient culture, a 'blending' that Carmichael suggests characterises 'Gaelic lore'.[44] Mary keeps company with Gaelic heroes such as Fionn. For example, in a 'Charm for the Face of a Maiden', the speaker appeals first in a conventionally Christian mode to God, the 'Son of God' and then continues the spell by integrating the pagan Celtic tradition with the Catholic: 'The beauty of Mary of the deep love, / A tongue mannerly, mild, modest, / Fair hair between thy two eyebrows – / Fionn son of Cumhall between these'.[45] In some cases, the Christian layer is absent, such as in 'Prayer', which appeals to the ancient Gaelic hero Cuchullin as well as Fionn: 'Power of king Cù Chulainn be thine, / Power of the king of the world be thine, / Power of the king of the Fiann'.[46]

Carmichael's collection offers a wide scope of emotions: ecstatic celebrations of beauty and spiritual joy to malicious vengeance, misogynistic rage and regretful love. In the poem 'The Vixen', the speaker's vehemence against a certain Catherine inspires a series of curses against her body, her community and her livestock:

Shortened be the life
Of herself and her people,
Her goats and her sheep,
   Her stock and her kine
Be they stolen and plundered,
   Be they blasted and burned![47]

This venomous diatribe against Catherine aims for piety as well, for it includes numerous appeals to the Christian saints, angels and other powers to assist and protect the speaker from this 'vixenish wench / In yonder town'.[48]

Whether opposing or mixing with vengeance, the *Carmina Gadelica* offers beauty, love and tenderness, such as the song of the fairy woman in 'The

Hunter and the Fairy Woman': 'There was a time when thy promise / Was as the life of the sun to me, / And when to me thy kiss was sweeter / Than to drink in the sunbeam.'[49] This song is embedded in a narrative where the fairy seeks to destroy the hunter's wife; thus, as is the case in much of Scottish folklore, there is an awareness of the dangers of amorous passions. Consider the great passion voiced by the 'wife of brown-haired Seathan, the wanderer' in 'Seathan Son of the King of Ireland'. Her grief defies religious salvation after her husband is captured and killed:

> O Seathan dear! O Seathan dear! [. . .] I would not give thee to Jesus Christ. I would not for fear I would not get thee myself [. . .] and if all the Clerics say is true [. . .] My share of Heaven [. . .] For a night with my darling.[50]

'Seathan Son of the King of Ireland' crystallises what the work of these Scottish folklorists achieved: they preserved and analysed beliefs and tales that are distinctive, beautiful and disturbing. Sharing a sense of urgency to preserve the legacy of extant Scottish and Gaelic materials, these scholars offered a wealth of Märchen, legends and memorats, hero and Fenian tales, curses, charms, prayers, riddles and fables. The diverse materials display a world-view that integrated local history, Gaelic heroism, Christian piety, worldly wit and creativity into a shared vision to inspire, entertain and educate the community. Stressing the importance of literal translation from orally-collected Gaelic informants, these folklorists advanced a set of principles that helped to guide the next generation of folklore studies, and unlocked the past and present of the Scottish traditional imagination.

CHAPTER THIRTEEN

Tradition and Innovation in Twentieth-Century Scottish Gaelic Literature

Michael Newton

Gaeldom was geographically and culturally fractured across Britain and North America during the eighteenth century. Publications, migrants and travellers continued to transmit and cross-pollinate literary developments between communities, and new texts in traditional genres continued to be composed in several parts of North America until the period between the World Wars. This chapter outlines the continuity of oral literature and the development of twentieth-century prose fiction and poetry, inclusive of immigrant communities in North America, highlighting some of the dominant factors, trends and milestones, and the negotiation over the parameters of literary tradition. The fragments of the older tradition that Gaels inherited were primarily oral in transmission, vernacular in linguistic register and folkloric in style. It continued to be transmitted in informal contexts, especially the cèilidh house, into the mid-twentieth century in some communities, even if the number and integrity of social settings was in constant retreat as the institutions and forces of the anglophone state encroached upon Gaelic life.

Literacy, Audience and Patronage

Oral tradition was arguably the primary channel through which a specifically Gaelic sense of identity and history was transmitted. That tradition was valued not just as entertainment: it was understood to be a means of explaining the past, of reinforcing cultural solidarity and a potentially subversive means of resistance. Orality influenced the stylistics of popular written Gaelic literature: nineteenth-century Gaelic writers adapted dialogue as a textual form for social commentary and criticism, a genre that remained productive well into the twentieth century,[1] even in Canada. Most periodicals catering to a Gaelic-speaking readership offered extremely limited space to the language and literary tradition. Gaelic columns usually were devoted to older song-poems and narratives as people became aware of the increasing frailty of oral transmission. The reverence and deference afforded to older oral tradition, and the priority given to older compositions, was one factor in delaying the emergence of modern genres.[2]

Religious schools successfully fostered Gaelic literacy in the nineteenth-century Highlands before the 1872 Education Act effectively established compulsory secular education through the medium of English. By the opening of the twentieth century literacy in Gaelic had declined significantly in Scotland.[3] North American Gaels were even more disadvantaged by the exclusion of Gaelic from educational institutions.[4] Schools were simultaneously normalising anglophone literature before the Gaelic equivalents had the chance to mature. The shortage of an audience literate in Gaelic dampened demand and hence the economy of scale in Gaelic publishing. Low levels of literacy in Gaelic did not preclude all possibilities for audiences, however: literature of all genres was read aloud from printed sources for audiences, literate and non-literate, at cèilidhs organised informally by neighbours in rural settings and formally by Highland associations in urban settings. Some authors composed texts specifically for such occasions;[5] competitions in Scotland and North America awarded prizes for Gaelic readings. While these practices facilitated sharing texts across the bounds of literacy, they may have been detrimental to the economic viability of Gaelic literature. Publishers and authors reported difficulties in turning a profit, as Dòmhnall MacEacharn (Donald MacKechnie) remarked in his 1904 miscellany:

> 'S e mar a tha nach 'eil tuilleadh 's a' chòir de leabhraichean 'sa Ghàidhlig, 's iadsan a tha deònach agus comasach air cur ris a' bheagan a th'ann, air am bacadh o sin a dheanamh leis cho beag iarraidh 's a th'aig Gàidheil air leabhraichean 'nan cànain fhéin.[6]
> (As it is, there are not too many books in Gaelic, and those who are willing and able to augment the small number that exist are hampered from that activity given that there is so little demand for books in their own language.)

The inability to earn a reasonable income thwarted the emergence of professional writers who could make sustained efforts to create a new literary tradition; writing was a pastime accomplished with limited means and ambitions. John MacCormick (1860–1947), one of the most popular Gaelic authors of his day, attempted briefly to live as a writer; the weekly *People's Journal* offered him a mere £3 3s to serialise his novel *Dùn Àluinn*, compared to the £100 it paid for English-medium serials.[7]

An Comunn Gàidhealach (ACG) was founded in 1891 to encourage and support the teaching, learning and use of Gaelic. It began in 1892 to organise annual Mòds (cultural festivals) throughout Scotland, offering prizes for the best original poetry and prose fiction. Although assailed by critics for its political impotence and Celtic Twilight sentimentalism, it helped to stimulate literary activity and produced a number of substantial publications. These included anthologies of prose and poetry, ranging in complexity from primary school readers (the series *Leabhraichean Sgoile-Gàidhlig* in the 1920s) to editions of classic literature (such as *Rosg Gàidhlig* [1915] and *Bàrdachd Ghàidhlig* [1918]), as well as a journal (named in succession *An Deò-Gréine*, *An Gàidheal* and *Sruth*). At ACG's thirty-fifth anniversary celebration, an anonymous contributor paid tribute to its achievements:

> The isolated and unsettled state of Gaeldom in the olden days was not conducive to a large or varied output of general literature [. . .] We still believe in, and work and hope for, the development of Gaelic literature, as well as for the spread of Gaelic ideals of thought and life [. . .] Many of the best of the Gaelic writers who have come into prominence during recent years, have been Mòd competitors, and they are ready to acknowledge gratefully what they owe to the encouragement derived by them from the success of their Mòd efforts.[8]

Not only does this commentary reveal contemporary assumptions about modernity and literature which underestimated Gaeldom's past attainments, but the defensive tone is striking.

Many critics of ACG gathered under the banner of Ruaraidh Erskine of Mar (1869–1960). A singular figure in twentieth-century Gaeldom, Erskine was born the second son of the fifth Lord Erskine and raised in Edinburgh with a Hebridean nursemaid who taught him Gaelic. He took to both literature and politics. He founded and funded a series of journals containing original prose, poetry and journalism about contemporary issues, promoting the cause of Gaelic as the national language of an independent Scotland and a modern literary tradition that did more than merely mimic that of English. He was patron and editor for *Am Bàrd* (1901–2), *Guth na Bliadhna* (1904–25), *Alba* (1908–9), *An Sgeulaiche* (1909–11) and *An Ròsarnach* (1917–30), and composed and translated texts as needed.[9]

Scottish Gaels were aware that efforts to create modern literature in Irish had the financial backing of the Irish government and other formal institutions that were lacking in Scotland.[10] Comhairle nan Leabhraichean (the Gaelic Books Council) was established in 1968 as an adjunct to the Celtic department of the University of Glasgow to stimulate, co-ordinate and subsidise new Gaelic publications. Club Leabhar of Inverness published paperback books for a popular market in Gaelic from 1970 to 1977, a role taken up by Acair of Stornoway in 1977. North American Gàidhealtachds did not benefit from any system of patronage from individuals or associations on a large scale, although local Gaelic societies sometimes provided social settings stimulating composition in traditional styles.[11]

Narrative

By the opening of the twentieth century, literature from other languages was already being translated into Gaelic. John MacRury's translations of the *Arabian Nights*, which had been serialised in the *Northern Chronicle* in Scotland and *Mac-Talla* in Cape Breton, were printed in book form in 1897 with a second edition following in 1906.[12] Other classic tales appeared in early twentieth-century collections by Katherine W. Grant and the Whyte brothers. Developing a native prose tradition, however, presented greater challenges. Nineteenth-century Gaels were painfully aware that anglophones perceived their literature as deficient and lacking counterparts to modern English literature. Literature signified not just entertainment, but a cornerstone for a new intellectual tradition, a means for Gaels to represent themselves and their history, as well as to reinvigorate their language itself.[13] Malcolm MacFarlane urged his Glasgow audience in 1911 to back these efforts:

Tha sgeulaichean ag éirigh 'nar measg, agus 'se dleas gach comuinn air am bheil leas na Gàidhlig 'na chùram, gach còmhnadh a tha 'nan comas a thoirt dhaibh; na sgeòil a leughadh aig na Céilidh a bhios aca; agus gu h-àraidh na paipearannaidheachd, na mìosachain agus na leabhraichean anns am bi na sgeòil, a cheannachadh.[14]
(Storytellers are emerging amongst us, and it is the duty of every association who has the development of Gaelic in its remit to give them all the help that they can: to read the tales at the céilidhs that they hold; and especially to purchase the newspapers, magazines, and books in which they appear.)

Gaelic oral narrative consists of distinct genres with their own functions and characteristics: wonder tales, local legends, clan sagas, parables and so on. Texts across these genres, nonetheless, tend to share many conventions: characters embody certain qualities or archetypes and do not develop appreciably during the course of the plot, sometimes reappearing essentially unchanged across multiple narratives; the feelings, thoughts and motives of characters are implicit and not explained; tales are told in third-person with minimal descriptive passages; dialogue occupies a large proportion of the text and is chiefly responsible for progressing the plot; the text style is measured, familiar, poetic and formulaic. Although this can only be fully appreciated by reading and comparing a large number of narratives in their original Gaelic forms, a sense of this can be conveyed even by a short excerpt from the translation of 'The Three Who Went to Discover What Hardship Meant':

There were once three princesses whose father and mother were dead and who lived in a house by themselves. The eldest said to the others, 'I will never rest nor remain quiet until I get to know what Hardship is.'

'Well, then,' said the next sister, 'I will do the same myself, for neither will I rest until I find out what Hardship is.'

The youngest sister said, 'I will not stay here by myself after you have gone, but despite that, it isn't to find out what Hardship is that makes me go.'

They set off, and kept travelling until the soles of their feet began to get black and their shoes were full of holes. Then night fell, and they saw a light far away from them; but far away though it was, they were not long in reaching it. They entered the place where the light was, and there was an old man by himself, with a little, smouldering, conical fire.[15]

It should not be inferred that traditional Gaelic oral narratives cannot be sophisticated art forms fulfilling many of the same functions of modern literature: Gearóid Ó Crualaoich has argued that they offer listeners, amongst other things, the means for personal reflection and transformation. The audience must be familiar with a wider body of other narratives, symbols, motifs, archetypes and characters in order for the narrative to convey its full potential. Oral tradition is by nature a shared, communal experience relying upon knowledge distributed across genres and texts, informing and reinforcing common values, beliefs and concerns.[16]

Active transmission of the most archaic and conservative genres (wonder tales, hero tales, etc.) had largely ceased in the inter-war period, but twentieth-century folklore collectors found a surprising wealth of oral narratives preserved in the memories of those who had told them in previous decades. John Lorne Campbell began to use electric recording devices for fieldwork in Scotland and Nova Scotia in 1937. In 1945 the Irish Folklore Commission sent Calum MacLean (1915–60, brother of Sorley MacLean) to record Gaelic materials in Scotland. The narratives that MacLean transcribed from the first major storyteller he recorded, Angus 'Barrach' MacMillan of Griminish, take up nearly 5,000 pages in the archives in Dublin, and MacLean recorded further materials from him once he was transferred to the newly created School of Scottish Studies in 1951. MacLean spent a total of fourteen years collecting folklore in Scotland and recorded enough Gaelic material to occupy a hundred miles of audio tape.[17] His successors at the School of Scottish Studies continued this work of recovery, as did other collectors and scholars.[18]

The Nova Scotian periodical *Mac-Talla* published many folkloric narratives, some relating to events and characters in North America and others containing much older material set in Scotland. Folklorists such as Charles Dunn, Kenneth Jackson, MacEdward Leach, C. I. N. MacLeod, Sister Margaret MacDonell, John Shaw, Ken Nilsen and Jim Watson have recorded high quality narratives and storytellers in Nova Scotia after active transmission ceased at a community level.[19] Narratives from numerous bearers of oral narrative have been published, the most celebrated of which is Joe Neil MacNeil of Big Pond, Cape Breton (1908–96). Fifty-two distinct narratives were transcribed from him and published in *Sgeul gu Latha/Tales until Dawn* (1987), along with information about the persons from whom MacNeil had heard them. Although many of these are international wonder tales found in other folk traditions, others (such as tales about the Cliar Sheanchain, Cú Chulainn and the Fian) are survivals from the medieval Gaelic world.

The development of a written modern literature was another matter, especially because there was a strong correlation between literacy, formal institutions, non-Gaelic communities and the dominance of English. Unlike orality, literacy removes the individual from the group and connects the author directly with the reader, enabling fiction to become a personal expression experienced privately. Some Gaels argued that traditional genres had become obsolete as literary models for describing the new world in which they lived.[20] Regardless of stated intentions to adopt the conventions of modern literature, early fiction still bears the influence of its folk antecedents in oral tradition. The work of two of the most prolific pioneers, John MacFadyen (1850–1935) and John MacCormick (c. 1870–1947), both residing latterly in Glasgow, exemplifies these vestiges. Their tales are generally set in the Highlands and feature archaic customs and songs; their characters lack unique personalities or chronological development; there are recurring plot devices and motifs; there is little detailed description; plot movement relies heavily upon dialogue; echoes of orality linger.[21] Similar compositions appeared in Canadian periodicals.

Early short stories and novels remained close to the precedents set by traditional oral narratives: they do not, for example, act as a vehicle for probing the psyches of characters or for social criticism (of Gaelic or anglophone society) as we would expect of the modern novel in English. This may in part be because the concerns and style of modern literature did not yet have a wide enough currency amongst Gaels. Furthermore, Gaelic communities, still scarred by Clearances, disempowered by formal institutions, and facing continuing anglophone prejudice may have been too vulnerable to contemplate introspection in a public forum at this stage. Early Gaelic fiction provided a literary means for urban authors and audiences to find solidarity and reassurance in an idealised, but inaccessible homeland, avoiding the reopening of fresh wounds and exposure of shortcomings.[22] The Gaelic novel took longer to emerge than the short story, at least in part due to the sustained commitment required by the genre from both author and reader. John MacCormick's 1908 novelette *Gun Tug Mi Spéis do'n Àrmuinn* is set during the Napoleonic Wars and is folkloric in style and content; it opens with a quatrain from a song (from which the book's title comes) and a proverb, and frequently depicts the interfaces between orality and literacy. The *People's Journal* newspaper serialised MacCormick's novel *Dùn Àluinn* in 1910 and printed it in book form in 1912.[23] Its style still bears the influence of traditional oral narrative but its theme of mythic regeneration resonates with contemporary Lowland novels.[24] Although original narratives were composed in twentieth-century Nova Scotia,[25] there seems to be only one example of a lengthy text cast in a modern genre: Angus MacLellan's twenty-six-page novella *Raonull Bàn Mac Eoghain Òig* was published in 1931, the story of a Cape Breton man who fought in the First World War and married a Lewis woman he met in Montreal.

Poetry

There is no distinction in older vernacular Gaelic tradition between poetry and song: all poetry was meant to be sung. The primary characteristic of the tradition has been described as being

> in the main one of celebration and participation. The poet produced an artefact which enabled his audience to participate in their culture; to act out culturally reinforcing roles. The poetry was largely oral-based; much of it was meant to be sung. In such circumstances innovation was not at a very high premium. The verse had to make an immediate impact, and skill in versification and verbal wit culminating in the well-wrought, memorable phrase was therefore the basic requirement.[26]

At the opening of the twentieth century, hundreds of Gaels were still engaged with the tradition across the traditional Gàidhealtachd, from St Kilda to Perthshire, as well as in diasporic communities (in the Scottish Lowlands, England, Canada, Australia, New Zealand, South Africa and so on).[27] The poet could extend the conventions of the Gaelic 'panegyric code'[28] as needed to describe, praise, or critique contemporary events and innovations. This practice is illustrated in a satire of *Mac-Talla* composed by Alexander 'the Ridge' MacDonald (in Antigonish, Nova Scotia) which personifies that newspaper and another, the *Casket*. Alexander castigates the editor of *Mac-Talla* for contradicting Gaelic ideals of generosity and unselfishness:

> Faic an *Casket*, e cho bàigheil,
> Tha e modhail 's tha e sàmhach;
> Cha chluinn thu e 'g éigheach pàigheadh –
> Cleas a' gharlaoich ud *Mac-Talla*.[29]

> (Look at the *Casket*, he is so friendly,
> He is mannerly and quiet;
> You don't hear him crying for payment
> Like that rascal *Mac-Talla*.)

Oral tradition was in fact resilient enough in some rural communities to produce poets employing traditional metres and styles on modern subjects and themes into the late twentieth century. The poet Donald Macintyre (1889–1964), for example, born in South Uist but resident in Paisley, composed song-poems on issues from fascism to the threat of nuclear annihilation using tunes and literary devices that would have been familiar to a seventeenth-century audience.[30]

As the century progressed and literary experimentation intensified, Gaelic poets and audiences became engaged in a vigorous debate about the development of Gaelic poetry: what constitutes 'tradition' and how much can Gaelic poetry absorb external poetic models and conventions and still remain 'Gaelic'? Reactions to poetic developments have tended to be framed in rather broad terms; it may be more productive to consider the numerous literary dimensions of a poem, each of which may be assessed independently regarding innovation or conservatism: language (Gaelic neologisms vs English loanwords), cultural allusions and reference points, intertextuality, metrical structures and forms (oral song-poetry in traditional metres vs free-verse or visually-specific textual representations) and so on.

Ronald Black suggests that each of the four quarters of the twentieth century (in approximate terms) saw distinctive transformations of Gaelic poetry and of attitudes about tradition.[31] The first quarter was dominated by the sentimental and archaistic interests of the exile, a carry-over of Gaelic 'pop songs' heavy on sentiment and nostalgia which had emerged in the last quarter of the nineteenth century, especially by and for Gaels in urban areas. These songs spread across Scotland and North America, occupying a lightweight literary register but co-existing with older 'conservative' strains as well as newer, more innovative and politically radical verse.[32] Gaels did not perceive their poetry as substandard at the beginning of the century. *Modern Gaelic Bards* (1908), comprising articles from the *People's Journal* and entries awarded in ACG competitions, presents ninety-nine Gaelic songs by eleven different poets. Almost all of the entries are light fare: love songs, military paeans, homages to homeland, humorous sketches and accolades to the Gaelic language. There is no hint of inadequacy or need to 'modernise' Gaelic poetry. Early notes of optimism, however, were crushed by the social and economic collapse of Gaelic communities in the wake of World War One and an accompanying crisis of confidence that loomed over the second quarter of the century and which still lingers over Gaeldom.[33]

Sorley MacLean (1911–96) launched his first published poetry (1943) into this bleak environment. His verse was fuelled by romantic passion and political conviction, but a solid grounding in both Gaelic and anglophone literature guided his craft. *Dàin do Eimhir* struck some readers as a revelation of Gaelic poetry's latent expressive power; others adhering more strictly to traditional precedents, however, were bewildered and vexed by his departures, such as the lack of a musical element. MacLean rejected the stultifying effects of the Celtic Twilight and recontextualised Gaelic history and icons within a broader Marxist discourse about social and political justice on a global scale. Although innovative in his scope and analysis, his success rested on his ability to deploy established high registers of Gaelic and rich, multivalent cultural reference points.[34]

George Campbell Hay (1915–84) set himself to the reclamation of tradition, rejuvenating moribund metres to great effect, delighting in the music and aurality of Gaelic song-poetry, and rewriting or extending a number of traditional song-poems. He bound the assertion of Scotland's nationhood and Gaelic's role within it into both the medium and message of his work, reanimating landscapes in verse, especially those of Argyll. His was no narrow nationalism: he was fluent in several languages and his experiences in Arabic North Africa during World War Two engendered a post-colonial literary consciousness explored in several exceptional poems.[35]

The third quarter of the twentieth century saw an unexpected flowering of Gaelic verse, not least due to the quarterly *Gairm* under the supervision of Derick Thomson (1921–2012). A native of Lewis who spent most of his life in Glasgow, Thomson played many vital roles in the development of twentieth-century Gaelic literature as literary scholar, co-founder and editor of *Gairm*, founder of the Gaelic Books Council and a poet productive over the course of some seven decades. Like many of his peers, themes of exile, loss and hard-won wisdom recur in his work in constantly evolving insights and expressions. His use of free verse was a break with tradition, but his symbolism is firmly rooted in the material culture, landscape and traditions of Gaeldom, particularly Lewis.[36]

Iain Crichton Smith (1928–98) was a frequent contributor to *Gairm*. His poetry delves into the human psyche and epistemological dilemmas with deceptively simple symbols from mundane life. It reflects literary modernism's 'crisis of representation', the self-consciousness of traditional literary conventions and the inherited modes of thought which collide, often irresoluably, with the conditions of modernity. His poetic formulae and motifs highlight incongruities in the life of the urban exile and give Gaelic verse irrefutable credentials in literary modernism.[37]

The new directions spearheaded by the aforementioned poets and others in the third quarter were not without critics: Ronald Black has gone so far as to characterise the ensuing clash as 'a holy war [. . .] fought between tradition and innovation for the soul of Gaelic poetry'.[38] These tensions were not just over poetry per se, but coincided with other social and ideological factors. To simplify a complex picture, traditionalists tended to be based in their native rural communities, to compose song-poetry using communally inherited aesthetics for local audiences, to be religiously and socially conservative and to have limited experience of anglophone institutions of higher learning. The innovators, on the other hand, tended to be exiled in urban communities, to write non-musical poetry using erudite literary devices disseminated in print, to be critical of their home communities and to be strongly influenced by the literature that they had encountered in anglophone higher education.[39] The conflict was essentially over the proprietorship and utilisation of what had been an ancestral tradition closely tied to the social functions of rural townships and the Gaelic historical experience itself.[40] With the further decline of traditional communities, it is not surprising that a defensive reaction was provoked by the possibility that an intellectual elite could hijack one of the few cultural assets left to Gaeldom and use it to express anything other than reverence.

Innovation and creative reinterpretation of tradition were largely accepted during the course of the final quarter of the twentieth century to the degree that poets have explored all manner of metrical forms, subjects, themes and literary devices without automatically inciting wary and wry responses. This liberation of the poetic voice and Gaelic imagination was facilitated by social factors not directly related to literature itself: a growing esteem for multilingualism and multiculturalism, the loosening of anglocentric hegemony, the slackening grip of religious dogmatism, the expanding role of Gaelic learners. Gaelic poets of the last quarter of the century composed *haiku* (notably for the performance circuit, so involving an oral/performative dimension even here, albeit for a different community with different demands), recovered mythic symbolism, critiqued matters internal and external to Gaeldom and portrayed people, places, artefacts and events far removed from the Highlands of old – all at the same time that traditional song-poetry has continued to be composed and performed. New material of both traditional and innovative strains is still sung (or declaimed) in informal settings (particularly cèilidhs), the annual Mòd and a few local, national and international events, such as the annual tour of the Gaelic poets of Scotland and Ireland.[41] In short, Gaelic poetry has become as expressive and expansive a modern art form as that of any other language.

Regardless of such advances, poets may be deterred from engaging meaningfully with Gaelic literary tradition on its own terms in their work if they compose for a readership (and critics they hope to impress) who do not necessarily understand that tradition, let alone the Gaelic language. The resulting pressures on Gaelic poets are such that composition has often been between languages as much as in any particular language, with a shift away from cultural reference points, intertextuality and literary devices specific to Gaelic literary tradition. Similarly, the dominance of English as a written language detracts even Gaelic readers from the original poem in bilingual publications.

Such a combination poses a threat to the very willingness to make sense on the part of the Gaelic reader[,] preparing the path for Gaelic natives to condemn what is presented as Gaelic as not Gaelic in nature at all. Such an attitude, in turn, succeeds in denying the development of Gaelic literature as natural in light of cultural exchange both in the particular contact zone occupied by Gaelic verse and in a world wide context of urbanisation and globalisation.[42]

Although some of the innovations of the first quarter of the twentieth century can be traced in Nova Scotia and some oral poets were active into the third quarter of the twentieth century, Gaelic communities were too frail, fragmented and disconnected from wider developments to benefit from literary activity in Scotland by the second half of the century.[43] Some new efforts to revive Gaelic in Nova Scotia and restore connections with Scotland are currently in progress, and a group of Gaelic learners across North America have been producing new Gaelic poetry reflecting both conservative and innovative impulses.[44]

Acknowledgements

Thanks to Wilson McLeod for use of his bibliography on Gaelic literature; to Michael D'Arcy, Wilson McLeod and Máire Ní Annracháin for comments on earlier drafts of this chapter. This research was funded in part by the University Council for Research grant of St Francis Xavier University.

CHAPTER FOURTEEN

The Politics of the Modern Scottish Folk Revival

Corey Gibson

The folk revival in Scotland was not a concerted or homogeneous movement: it had no governing manifesto and it had no definitive beginning or end. In general terms, the 'revival' simply describes the popularisation of folk music in the immediate post-war era, particularly the 1960s, and, arguably, through to the present. It can also be understood as the work of a vast network of organisations, events and institutions of various kinds, such as the Workers' Music Association (WMA), the Traditional Music and Song Association of Scotland (TMSA, est. 1965), the School of Scottish Studies (University of Edinburgh, est. 1951), Topic Records (est. 1939) and the Edinburgh People's Festival (1951–4). In addition, there was a great number of individuals singing, performing, attending folk clubs, concerts and ceilidhs, and buying records, who all had stakes in this expansive enterprise. Those who sought to direct the revival and define its role in society offer us a useful interpretative framework by which to understand its aims and practice. As Dave Harker noted, the ideas underpinning the folk project were rarely set out explicitly; rather they can be inferred through the variety of prefaces, introductions, footnotes and editorial decisions by which the revivalists presented their work. The figures who publicised the revival are, for Harker, the 'mediators' through whom our understanding of 'folk' has developed.[1]

The modern folk revival was not peculiar to Scotland. Traditional forms of music and song were becoming popular across Western Europe and North America in the post-war period. This widely-spread revivalism achieved a degree of political impact, as the cultural capital of the song-voices of communities: regional, class-based, ethnic and national identities were confidently asserted and celebrated. For instance, the Irish Folklore Commission, established by the young republic in 1935, sought to recover and revitalise the traditional arts, and the heritage of the Irish language, as a 'public act of homage to our own people'.[2] Alan Lomax, who became perhaps the most celebrated twentieth-century folklorist and song collector, recorded and lectured on the musical cultures of the African-American South under the tutelage of his father John Lomax in this period up to and including World

War Two. Working in association with the Library of Congress, they began to map this enormous body of folk culture that had developed through generations of suppression and marginalisation and thrived even in the middle of the twentieth century.[3]

The modern Scottish revivalists also had domestic precedents on which they could draw, such as the collecting, editing and publishing work of figures like David Herd (1732–1810), Peter Buchan (1790–1854), Gavin Greig (1856–1914) and John Lorne Campbell (1906–96), and the popular folk-literary forms of Burns, Scott and Hogg. Michael Brocken identifies the commencement of the modern British revival with the work of Cecil Sharp (1859–1924), who is generally associated with the 'first revival' of the early twentieth century and credited with (or accused of, depending on perspective) inventing 'English folk song' and aligning it with rural, agrarian populations rather than industrialised, urban communities.[4] In contrast, Ailie Munro conceives of the Scottish revival's 'beginnings in the USA'.[5] This modern revivalist movement is distinguished in part by the commercial forces, technological advancements in recording and broadcasting, and general developments in mass popular culture that made it possible. Neil V. Rosenberg refers to this in its American context as 'the great boom'.[6] However, this 'boom' was also underpinned by a set of theories about the place of folk culture in society that were, through various writings and broadcasts, the subject of constantly shifting debates.

Like those who preceded them, the proponents of the new movement were ostensibly concerned with restoring the folk music of Scotland to public life, by unearthing and disseminating a song culture that seemed to have been forgotten. In the 1950s, after the establishment of Edinburgh University's School of Scottish Studies, it was discovered that the songs, tunes and folktales that were sought after were in fact more readily available than some had expected. Hamish Henderson (1919–2002), a prolific collector and principal strategist of the revival, wrote in 1956 that the classical ballads, 'condemned to death by successive generations of collectors, continue to be sung up and down Scotland by folk-singers of all ages':

> Travelling with a tape-recorder, I have collected 'The Dowie Dens of Yarrow' from a girl of nineteen, and 'The False Knight upon the Road', from a boy of the same age. In Aberdeenshire [. . .] the vigorous balladry about farm life [. . .] has gone on reproducing itself up to the present day; in Fife and Lanarkshire the miners have a folk-song of their own [. . .] Edinburgh itself, whose adult citizens do not always look as if they regard life as a singing matter, has a children's folk-song rich and strange beyond measure [. . .][7]

It seemed that folksongs and ballads of considerable heritage could still be found in various forms, even set amongst more recently conceived material, and all of it 'living on the lips of the people'.[8] This fact convinced Henderson and others that the historical convention of folk collectors – to regard their songs as the last remnants of a moribund art form – was based on a flawed conception of the nature of folksong. The bleak forecast that informed collection titles, from Burns and James Johnson's *The Scots Musical Museum* (1787) to Gavin Greig's celebrated *Last Leaves of Traditional Ballads and Ballad Airs* (1925), was rejected; the modern revival was to break with this tradition by insisting on the budding of 'fresh leaves on the old branches'.[9]

The belief that the music had retreated in the face of modernity's industrialisation was pervasive, and that it awaited re-collection into a new context that could restore its appeal. Adam McNaughtan, an accomplished revival songwriter, posits that the circumstances that made the revival possible in the 1950s had come out of the ashes of the preceding long period of urbanisation.[10] In this understanding, the old songs sung by families that had at one time lived in the country could not survive the changed environment; as generations passed, they lost their relevance and struggled to compete with music hall and other commercial forces targeted at the new city-dwelling classes. This was in keeping with the idea that popular folk culture had been through periods of suppression and revival throughout the nation's history, first in Reformation Scotland, then resurfacing in the climate of European Romantic nationalism. Accordingly, folksong was due a revival, though the precise reasons for the success of the movement in Scotland are difficult to isolate.

The conception of folk music as a 'living tradition' no doubt helped in its promotion. As material was 'discovered' among the people, the process gained an urgency from the fact that the songs were alive in inherited forms, and had not been simply excavated from library archives, or Georgian and Victorian ballad collections. The portable tape-recorder allowed folklorists to collect songs on site. The setting of the songs, in the lives of 'tradition-bearers', and the route by which they had been inherited, became factors as important as the song-versions themselves. Henderson recognised the role of the collector as a 'deeply humanistic one',[11] and as such, the social, geographical, historical and, above all, personal contexts of songs, were explored in conversation in the recording sessions.[12] The resultant tapes documented folk-memory and the cultural heritage of communities; they explored working and living conditions, mapped the migrations of people, and threaded all of this on the transmission of particular songs and tales. Though this sensitivity to the human agents of the 'folk process' was customary and not necessarily set out in methodological accounts, the collectors were engaging in an interdisciplinary practice that would perhaps now be described as that between folkloristics and ethnomusicology.

The recordings also meant that enthusiasts could study 'native' singing styles. The new revivalists learned to value the intonation, pronunciation and vocal qualities of performances. This development stood in opposition to popularly sanctioned ideas of 'good singing', as aligned with art song and classical training. Henderson dismissed the portrayals of traditional music broadcast by the BBC in the 1930s as an example of art-singers simply prepared to do a bit of 'slumming - "mucking the byre in white tie and tails"'.[13] Great value was subsequently bestowed on the 'authenticity' of singers and the delivery of their songs, and this inspired a resistance to the bowdlerising and sanitisation of songs for the popular market. Ewan MacColl (1915–89) created a 'Critic's Group' whose remit was, in part, to impose discipline and faithfulness onto folksong renditions. The policies that they proposed addressed common controversies in folk clubs, dictating singers 'should limit themselves to songs which were in a language the singer spoke or understood',[14] and pursuing the much debated 'correct way' of singing traditional pieces.[15] These measures were ostensibly put in place to defend against the contaminative threat of popular American influences, commercialism and the tendency toward translating songs into a so-called 'contemporary' style.[16] However, these guidelines also reveal a set of assumptions about who is entitled to perform what, and in what style, and they thereby privilege inherited or 'traditional' forms and restrict the kind of creative adaptability that many were now attributing to the concept of 'folk' itself.

MacColl's was a difficult position to maintain as young singers and musicians began to pore over recordings and reproduce songs in reworked versions, or else create new work entirely, inspired by the 'tradition-bearers'. Henderson described folksong as 'a permanent aspect of human culture, which will go on persisting whatever social and technological changes take place, and will certainly adapt itself, as it has always done, to changing circumstances'.[17] This inherent malleability – exercised by countless participants and through innumerable interpretative performance decisions – seems to undermine the concept of 'authenticity'. It was conceived as a self-regulating system: '[the folk process] is a [. . .] phrase for what happens to folksongs when they begin to take on a life of their own – start shedding some things, accruing others – generally taking on a new and changing form'.[18] Thus the mode of transmission and the consequent adaptability of folk were thought to be its defining characteristics. This distanced the term 'folk' from its traditional association with the pastoral and the unlettered by abstracting it from the sum of its constitutive songs. In its place was a model of folk culture as a natural and indomitable reflex of human society. According to this view, folk culture does not belong to any particular phase of human history, or to any singular set of circumstances, it is simply part of people's response to the experience of living together. As such, it is in a constant state of flux.

Indeed this conception seems to validate the intervention of revivalists who sought to reintroduce folk music to those who had been estranged from it, as figures like Norman Buchan and Morris Blythman held folksong workshops in Glasgow schools, and the People's Festival Ceilidhs astounded city audiences with the songs of rural Scotland. However, if folksong is an ineluctable phenomenon, then the need for the mediation of revivalists can be questioned. Their imposition suggests a degree of concern for the survival of the lore they collected, unless the project of revivalism can be explained according to other ideas about the value of folksong. Henderson wrote that, when he and Calum MacLean began their work for the School of Scottish Studies, 'we rapidly came to realise that by embarking on the study of folk material we were engaged willy-nilly in a political act'.[19] In the same piece Henderson also makes reference to the aphorism accredited to Andrew Fletcher of Saltoun (1655–1716), which is now inscribed on the Canongate Wall of the Scottish Parliament: '(I knew a very wise man who believed that) if a man were permitted to make all the ballads, he need not care who should make the laws of a nation.' The politics of the revival ought to be understood, both in terms of the explicit agendas of some songs, but, perhaps more importantly, in relation to concepts of folksong and its place in twentieth-century Scotland.

The Politics of Folk Revivalism

Alan Lomax was an international influence among modern folk revivalists, and in 1951 he collected songs in Scotland with Henderson and MacLean as his guides. At a conference in 1950 Lomax had staked out the folklorist's vision: 'we have become [. . .] the champions of the ordinary people of the world who aren't backed up by printing presses, radio chains and B29's [. . .] we have to work in [sic] behalf of the folk, the people'.[20] Henderson shared this confidence in the value of folksong as part of the cultural presence of the dispossessed:

> The truth is that the world of authentic traditional art – and particularly the world of folk-song and story – forms a kind of underground [. . .] It is a sort of 'anti-culture' and embodies ideas, predilections and values which are not those of learned culture.[21]

Throughout the 1950s and 1960s Henderson set out his position on the status of folksong in these terms. He attacked 'enemies of folksong': the elite who 'have a vested interest in keeping the songs of the damned well battened down', and those who 'wish to coat it [folksong] with rouge and greasepaint [but] find inevitably that they must first turn it into a cadaver'.[22] The polemical flair of these writings suggested that a national revival, in giving folksong 'back to the people', would achieve a kind of liberation of communal self-expression. Henderson was informed in part by the works of the Italian Marxist philosopher Antonio Gramsci (1891–1937), and identified the following as his most valuable comment on folksong:

> That which distinguishes folksong in the framework of a nation and its culture is neither the artistic fact nor the historic origin; it is a separate and distinct way of perceiving life and the world, as opposed to that of 'official society'.[23]

This statement politicises folksong of any form, from any period. It is not to say that there is no variety among folksongs, or that they present a fixed worldview, but that in the national context, folksongs are defined by their dissent towards dominant ideological structures.[24]

The aims of the Edinburgh People's Festival ceilidhs, which were instrumental in the development of the folk revival, were articulated in terms entirely compatible with these political constructions of folk culture. Supported by trade unions, various Labour Party organisations and the Communist Party, the Festival's defining slogan was 'By Working People For Working People'.[25] The ceilidhs set out to 'restore Scottish folksong to the ordinary people, not merely as a bobby-soxer vogue, but deeply and integrally'.[26] Beneath these pronouncements, 'working class culture', 'popular culture' and 'folk culture' seem to be assimilated in the interest of pursuing the political potential of folksong. The dissident element of this culture was promoted in the widely circulated *Rebels' Ceilidh Song Book* produced by the Bo'ness Rebels Literary Society throughout the 1950s and 1960s. In the Preface for the first songbook William Kellock describes the types of songs that would be presented in the collection:

> songs of the Popular Hero [. . .] of the drama of resistance against impossible odds, Songs of Land-hungry Scots and Alien land-owners, Songs of revulsion against the hypocrites and rogues in our midst, Songs for the Glasgow Irish – both Orange and Green –, Songs of World War II, Songs echoing the heart-cry of farm and city workers for better conditions, Songs of joy, of sorrow, of Scotland's pride [. . .] Sangs o' the Stane that's awa, and Songs on the popular reaction to the fact that London Officialdom just can't count [. . .] Songs of defiance and rebellion, of heilans and Lallans all with a beauty of their own. Through it all runs the magic of the Gaeltacht. (1951: 1–2)

Kellock wanted to appeal to 'all the varieties of Scottish Rebels', and there is an implied unity among the various songs that relies on the idea that these lyrics are consistent with the 'song tradition' that preceded them. While many songs are attributed to their writers, others are transcribed from the versions of individual singers, such as Jimmy MacBeath and Kitty MacLeod. Some are left unattributed, and therefore appear to have come directly from the anonymous rebel tradition, thereby achieving a timeless relevance. The content of these songs also describes a renewed and extended tradition, which frequently turns to satire to express its political position. For example, 'Coronation Coronach' (page 16) by Thurso Berwick (pseudonym of Morris Blythman) envisages a republican Scotland to the tune of the unionist song 'The Sash': 'Nae Liz will ever dae, / We'll mak oor land republican / In a Scottish breakaway'. Henderson's 'Ballad of the Men of Knoydart' (pages 23–4) is accredited to 'Seamus Mor', Henderson's Gaelic moniker, and represents a modern equivalent of the songs of the late nineteenth-century Highland Land Wars, lampooning Lord Brocket who publicly quelled crofters' land seizures on his estate in 1948. The 'White Cockade', a romantic song of the Jacobite cause, has its tune recast in a disillusioned political satire, 'The Labour Provost' (page 15), whose eponymous councillor sings: 'the principles of socialism are a' very well / Bit ye mustnae forget tae look after yersel'.

The politics of the revival in its early years was often even more explicitly asserted. At the John Maclean Memorial Rally in Glasgow in 1948, which Blythman called 'the first swallow of the Revival',[27] poems and folksongs were performed together in celebration of the life and legacy of the Clydeside socialist (1879–1923). Many of these pieces were published with later songs and poems on the subject in a collection called *Homage to John Maclean* (1973).[28] As with the *Rebels' Ceilidh Song Book*, the lyrics seem to speak with the broad and anonymous authority of 'folk culture'. There are numerous examples of songbooks that laid claim to the folk tradition in one form or another, including Henderson's own *Ballads of World War II* (1947), comprising songs from the 'rebellious house' of the 'Army balladeers' on both sides of the conflict.[29] Set in the soldier's perspective, the songs are almost entirely unaccredited except to the regiment or particular arena of war from which they originated.[30] In his Introduction, Henderson emphasised the fact that these songs 'grew up under the shadow of – and often in virtual conflict with – the official or commercial radio of the combatant nations', and expressed the human reaction to soldiering. *Sangs o' the Stane* (1952) gathered some of the songs and folk-poems of the Scottish republican cause, and featured sardonic responses to the 'reiving' of the Stone of Scone in 1950, and the 1952 coronation of Elizabeth II (despite there never having been an Elizabeth I of Scotland).[31]

Ding Dong Dollar: Anti-Polaris and Scottish Republican Songs (Folkways, 1962) was a recorded collection of songs that combined the republican issue with the anti-nuclear movement directed at American submarines docked at Holy Loch. The liner notes read almost like a manifesto, in which the songs and their political stances are explained, and an inherited tradition of Scottish satire is outlined, culminating in the contemporary 'metropolitan', 'folk-rebel corpus' (pp. 1–2). In the notes for both the *Rebels'*

Ceilidh Song Book and *Ding Dong Dollar* a peculiar 'vein of satirical humour', able to puncture the hypocritical, the authoritative and the domineering, is traced in Scottish literary and folksong traditions. Kellock writes that humour is the 'only bloodless weapon against Authority' (p. 2), while *Ding Dong Dollar* explores the 'political corrective' of the early Celtic bard's *aoir* (satire); the fifteenth- and sixteenth-century literary practice of 'flyting'; and a '"sub-literary" tradition of partisan and often scurrilous satirical verse and song' (p. 1). The 'literary' and 'sub-literary' traditions are said to have met in the work of Burns and Hugh MacDiarmid, and the contemporary 'line of advance' that emanates from these figures is identified as the 'Scottish folk-song renaissance' (p. 1).

Since the high watermark of modern folk revivalism in the 1960s, the mediatory role of the revivalists has increasingly attracted the attention of cultural historians and folklorists.[32] While popular ideas of 'folksong' should be recognised as intellectual constructs, this fact cannot necessarily be used to undermine politically framed representations of the folk tradition. If Gramsci's conception of folk as a worldview is accepted, then folk culture is always political in some sense, though not definitively aligned with any particular political philosophy: it is as flexible and mutable in its politics as in its transmission.

Folksong and Literature

Lomax noted that Scottish folk tradition was the liveliest, but, paradoxically, the most 'bookish' of the British Isles, showing 'every degree and kind of literary influence'.[33] This observation was not unusual, and indeed the reputations of Burns, Scott, Hogg, Fergusson and Ramsay have helped to maintain the impression that Scottish literature and folk culture have often inhabited common ground. The ballads are amongst the most celebrated texts in Scottish literary history: anthologies of Scottish poetry frequently include the 'muckle sangs' as well as folksongs and vernacular verse.[34] Scotland's proclaimed literary modernists recognised the relevance of folk culture. In *Living with Ballads* (1965), Willa Muir analysed children's singing games, oral poetry, ballads and corn-kisters, with the interpretative tools of the literary critic. Edwin Muir argued in *Scott and Scotland* (1936) that 'Scotsmen feel in one language and think in another', and that this debilitated their writing, '[shrinking] it to the level of anonymous folk-song'.[35] Whether it was to be valued or regretted, the presence of folk culture in national literary history was undeniable. There were also those who insisted on its presence in contemporary literature; John Speirs for example asserted that far from getting 'back to Dunbar', MacDiarmid had begun with the folk-ballad in his early Scots lyrics.[36] Henderson furthermore found the 'sinewy strength' and 'passionate intensity' of 'anonymous Gaelic song-poetry' in Sorley MacLean's work,[37] and recognised Sydney Goodsir Smith as the 'most successful writer of poems in the folk idiom'.[38] Folksong and literature had shared stages at the John Maclean Memorial of 1948, and the Edinburgh People's Festivals of 1951–4; and in 1955 Henderson declared that 'the national consciousness is stirring; if we act promptly and boldly, we can make the folk-song revival a powerful component part of the Scottish Renaissance'.[39]

MacDiarmid resisted Henderson's aspiration, and in 1964 the two were engaged in an extended public debate over the value of folksong. Published in the opinion columns of the *Scotsman*, these exchanges were characterised by an element of rhetorical flair and invective. Nevertheless, they represent perhaps the only thorough contemporary investigation of the place of folk revivalism in relation to literary culture. MacDiarmid dismissed folksong as inherently antithetical to the demands of modern progressive literature, and spurned the revival as 're-emersion in illiterate doggerel'. The only concession he made came with a poignant qualification: 'the arts grow, like apples, from the periphery, not from the core [. . .] Folksong may be the root from which all else has sprung, but the root is best taken for granted, if the tree or plant is flourishing'. MacDiarmid also attacked folk-song on the basis that it appealed to popular taste, chastising revivalists as a patronising 'interpreting class', and asserting that 'the demand everywhere today is for higher and higher intellectual levels'.

In their contributions, Henderson and the literary critic David Craig celebrated the 'fruitful interaction of folk and art-poetry' in the Scottish literary tradition. They also drew upon the figure of the simultaneously popular and literary poet, citing Burns, Dante, and Mayakovsky. MacDiarmid's own verse was even summoned in their ripostes:

> *Are my poems spoken in the factories and fields,*
> *In the streets o' the toon?*
> *Gin they're no', then I'm failin' to dae*
> *What I ocht to ha' dune.*
> (From 'Second Hymn to Lenin')[40]

MacDiarmid and Henderson accused one another of opposing forms of philistinism. While both aimed for a politically-engaged literary culture, their proposals for the best way to achieve this stood in stark contrast. Where MacDiarmid asked why we should be concerned 'with songs which reflect the educational limitations, the narrow lives, the poor literary abilities, of a peasantry we have happily outgrown', Henderson responded with an assurance that the inherent power of folk culture could be harnessed, and that, when synthesised with the progressive elements of literary practice in

Scotland, popular culture could be effectively politicised.[41] The dispute at the heart of the 'flytings' has still not been resolved. Despite their partisan agendas, Henderson and MacDiarmid had demonstrated that the folk revival had cultural and political implications that effectively explored the role of art in society. When the anonymous masses that act as folksong's carriers are set against the model of the individual literary poet, different conceptions of authorship clash: the 'communal' and the 'individual'. While the relationship between the two can be mutually supportive, as shown in the history of 'fruitful interaction', they are always in dialogue with one another: one speaking from the singular to the many, and the other singing with the voice of countless anonymous 'carriers'.

The modern folk revival gave folksong collectors, folk poets and songwriters the opportunity to connect their work with an existing tradition. While this inevitably involved some manipulation, it is impossible to tell when these 'mediators' were knowingly constructing a tradition to give their work plausibility and when they were making a sincere attempt to present a folk tradition with its contemporary inheritors, without bias. Indeed, both scenarios were probably accurate in most cases. In the terms of modern revivalism, the claim of 'folksong' is, by definition, an assertion on behalf of the collective of the 'folk'. While highly contextualised political songs might not survive beyond their immediate circumstances, as with many of the antinuclear songs of the 1960s, they still have the opportunity to be picked up by the 'carrying stream' of the 'folk process'.[42] The idea of the self-regulating 'process' is the reason for the disappearance of some songs and the survival of others. It is a passive 'process' refusing to impose interpretations or values on songs and lyrics. The survival of a song is, therefore, always hard-won, and the ability to speak with the authority of folk tradition is always desirable. It is perhaps in this sense that folksong is democratic. The modern Scottish folk revival constituted the widespread recognition of this fact. As Henderson wrote: '[if] the people have taken it, possessed themselves of it, gloried in it, recreated it, loved it. That is the only test worth a docken.'[43]

CHAPTER FIFTEEN

Continuing the Living Tradition

Margaret Bennett

The worldwide interest in Scotland's living tradition has generated centuries of correspondence between enthusiasts and collectors. Over the years, information has been shared and sought via letters or articles sent to popular magazines such as *The Scots Magazine* (founded in 1739) and *The Athenaeum* (published in London from 1828 to 1921). Topics described and discussed under general headings such as 'local curiosities', 'popular antiquities' and 'bygones' often drew attention to the fact that what seemed 'curious' in one place was 'ordinary' in another. Moreover, something regarded by one group as 'bygone' might be practised elsewhere, while a curiosity regarded as 'ancient' or 'antiquarian' by some discussants might be found to be 'part of everyday life' among folk outwith their ken. There seemed to be boundless fascination with the multi-faceted lore that was (and is) the living tradition of folk from every walk of life. Thus, in 1846, when a letter appeared in the *Athaneum* proposing that the compound 'folk-lore' would aptly describe the common interest, the newly coined word caught on and was soon adopted in several languages around the world.

The foundation of the Folklore Society in 1878, followed by the American Folklore Society in 1888, not only offered a centre for shared interests, but also opened up wider discussions and helped sharpen the focus of many members. Regardless of its base in London, the Society actively encouraged all members to write down the living tradition of their own locality, especially songs, stories, tunes, dances, games, general sayings, seasonal and other customs, weather and medical lore, as well as domestic, farming, fishing and hunting practices. Among the Scottish members, rural and urban, there were parish ministers, school-teachers, policemen and doctors whose collections in Scots and Gaelic record the vitality of the living tradition of their day.[1] With such a broad interest range, not surprisingly other societies followed, notably the Folk-Song Society in 1898[2] co-founded by an English music-teacher and composer with a passion for dance, Cecil Sharp. His groundbreaking research, capturing the actual sound of the singer's voice on wax cylinder recordings, was the beginning of a new era that not only revolutionised research methods across Europe and on both sides of the Atlantic, but also opened up new avenues for the tradition-bearers themselves.[3]

Among the earliest to follow Sharp's method was a classically-trained singer from Perth, Marjory Kennedy Fraser (1857–1930), who set out in 1905 to record Gaelic songs in the Hebrides. As a member of a large musical family, which, much like the modern cruise-line entertainer, travelled the world on singing tours, Marjorie chanced to hear Gaelic songs. So captivated was she that she determined to bring them to an international audience. So, along with her daughter Patuffa, who helped transcribe music, she made several trips to the Inner and Outer Hebrides until the outbreak of World War One. The Rev. Kenneth MacLeod from the Isle of Eigg provided translations and collaborated with her to produce English versions and notes for her four-volume publication, *Songs of the Hebrides*. Arranged for voice and pianoforte or clarsach, Marjory Kennedy Fraser's magnum opus is a fine collection of songs from Gaeldom. Though it does not truly represent the living tradition she recorded,[4] it is an important work as far as Gaelic song is concerned: the collection generated widespread interest in Gaelic song and inspired several fine musicians and collectors, including a young American classical pianist, Margaret Fay Shaw (1903–2004). So taken was she by these Gaelic songs that in 1929 she travelled to the Outer Hebrides, settled in South Uist, learnt the language and devoted the rest of her life to Gaelic culture. Shaw, however, recognised not only the importance of conserving the actual words and music, but also the context of the songs. Her *Folklore and Folksongs of South Uist*, containing annotations and photographs as well as careful transcriptions of texts and melodies, sets an exemplary standard for folklorists and song collectors.[5]

In folk song and storytelling, the cross-fertilisation of ideas is evidenced in a remarkable number of worldwide connections, which both surprise and excite singers and scholars alike. Concert platforms, like those on which Kennedy Fraser and her family sang, fireside cèilidhs, farm bothies, local and professional interest clubs and societies have all made, and continue to make, vital connections. In the north-east, for example, a member of the Buchan Field Club and also of the Spalding Club,[6] William Walker, corresponded with Professor Child,[7] initially regarding the ballad texts collected by Peter Buchan, on whose work Walker was an authority.[8] He also advised Child on place-names and dialect words, then, responding to Child's interest in ballads that were still sung,[9] informed him about a ballad-collecting project that had its beginnings in the New Spalding Club. Two of the members, Mr Gavin Greig (1856–1914), a schoolmaster from New Deer and the Rev. Mr. Duncan (1848–1917), minister at Lynturk, were collaborating on the project and giving lectures at clubs and societies which then, as now, stimulated discussion between members and speakers alike. On many visits throughout the north-east, as well as via a weekly newspaper column in the *Buchan*

Observer,[10] Greig and Duncan amassed over 3,000 songs and tunes, producing Scotland's largest collection from the living tradition. Neither of the men lived to see the publication in its entirety, though, with the help of William Walker who compiled an index, Greig published *Folk-Song of the North-East: Articles Contributed to the 'Buchan Observer'*, covering the period 1909–14. In 1925 a selection of songs was published as *Last Leaves of Traditional Ballads and Ballad Airs*[11] and, in 1963, Greig's grandson Arthur Argo co-published further selections.[12] The entire collection, *The Greig–Duncan Folk Song Collection*, was at last published in eight volumes between 1981 and 2002, an unmatched resource for singers and researchers alike.[13]

While this invaluable work preserves the songs and retains the social history of the north-east, of both wealthy farmers and labourers, it does not represent every class of that society. Conspicuous by its absence is the population sector that, arguably, kept alive the richest store of tradition of all: the travelling people, or, as they were once known, 'tinkers'. Apart from John Francis Campbell's inclusion in his *Popular Tales*,[14] it was not until the middle of the twentieth century that the general population, far less folksong and narrative collectors, took account of the treasury of songs and stories kept alive around campfires or inside bow-tents, 'gellies' and caravans.

Scotland's living tradition would have been very much poorer today were it not for Hamish Henderson (1919–2002) and his integration of folklore, literature, philosophy and politics. From earliest childhood in Highland Perthshire, where every aspect of his life was connected to songs and stories, Scots and Gaelic, Henderson was as much at home by a tinker's campfire as alone, engrossed in the pages of Burns, Scott, Campbell and Child, not to mention the works of German, French and Italian writers. Poet, philosopher, scholar, soldier, linguist, teacher, broadcaster and political activist, Henderson may be best known as Scotland's greatest twentieth-century folklorist. A pen-and-notebook collector till after World War Two, he is also regarded as 'father of the Scottish folk revival', a flourishing phenomenon, which Henderson himself attributed to 'a number of different historical events and accidents':

> [O]ne of the latter was the decision in 1947 to found a large-scale International Festival of the Arts in Edinburgh [. . .] and the second 'accident' was that [the festival . . .] coincided with the appearance in Britain of the distinguished American collector Alan Lomax [. . . he] had been a member during the Second World War of a Music Committee formed under the auspices of various US left-wing groupings. This committee had fostered and encouraged the work of Woody Guthrie, Pete Seeger, and the Weavers, but with the advent of the Cold War its activities had become more and more suspect in the eyes of authorities. Finally when full-scale McCarthyishm came into operation, many of its members felt that the US was becoming too hot to hold them.

It was this ugly right-wing reaction to the 'liberalism' of the war years which led Alan Lomax to accept a job which would keep him out of the States for several years – namely, a commission from Columbia Records to edit a series of LPs covering the 'folk and primitive music' of the world [. . .] Scotland was to be volume VI in the series. And so it came about that when [we] organized the first People's Festival (1951) Alan Lomax was there to record it on tape.[15]

For the first time ever tinkers, crofters, housewives and even a mole-catcher were featured during the Edinburgh Festival, albeit outside the 'official festival'. So it was that the People's Festival Ceilidh[16] is remembered as part of the Edinburgh Festival Fringe founded in 1947 by, inter alia, Glasgow Unity Theatre.[17]

Alan Lomax's tour with his reel-to-reel tape-recorder marked the beginning of a new era for folksong collectors, scholars and singers. With the assistance of well-chosen guides – Calum MacLean with his brothers Sorley and Alasdair for Gaeldom along with Hamish Henderson and William Montgomerie[18] for Lowland Scotland and the north-east – Lomax made high quality reel-to-reel tape-recordings of over 400 songs as well as a selection of stories and instrumental music. As the University of Edinburgh founded the School of Scottish Studies that same year, Lomax gifted copies of his recordings to the new department, thus helping to lay the foundation for the nation's most important sound archive of Scotland's living tradition. With Calum MacLean (former fieldworker with the Irish Folklore Commission) and Hamish Henderson as their leading folklorists, the work of recording, documenting and disseminating continued and the department expanded, adding photography, film and manuscripts to its scope as well as additional members of staff and a university degree programme in Scottish Ethnology.

The work of Henderson and MacLean brought world fame to some of the tradition-bearers they recorded, possibly none more memorable than Jeannie Robertson (1908–75). After the production of a commercial LP recording, her striking voice and outstanding repertoire of Scots songs, ballads and stories soon earned her an international reputation and invitations outside of Scotland. In North America, there was considerable interest, especially among ballad enthusiasts and scholars whose work related to Child's *English and Scottish Popular Ballads*. Although Child had left the impression that it was rare to find 'living versions' of a ballad, fieldwork recordings of descendants of British immigrants soon changed opinion that ballad singing belonged to the past. Child had singled out, for example, 'The Two Sisters' (Child 10) as being 'one of the very few ballads which are not extinct as tradition in the British Isles'. His remark that 'drawing-room versions are spoken of as current, generally traced to some old nurse who sang them to the young ladies'[19] may have given the impression that a more vibrant tradition continued among immigrants in North America where dozens of versions of that very ballad had been recorded.[20]

When Jeannie Robertson arrived on the scene, not only did she sing a version of 'The Twa Sisters', but so did many of her kinsfolk. Hamish Henderson later remarked that *'The Twa Sisters* or *Binnorie* as many singers call it, enjoys a robust and even expanding popularity.'[21] In North America, where neither singers nor scholars had doubted the robustness of the ballad tradition, Henderson's collection, as well as Lomax's, had the effect of sparking off new lively discussion. Even an authoritative collection like Cecil Sharp's *English Folksongs of the Southern Appalachians* could be viewed in a new light. Sharp's own 1915 'starting point' had been a manuscript collection of over 200 ballads 'taken down from the lips of singers' by a Mrs Campbell of Asheville, North Carolina. His extensive fieldwork had drawn worldwide attention to the richness of the ballad tradition in the American South and inspired many collectors including his co-fieldworker Maud Karpales, who continued the work after his death.[22] When Henderson introduced Robertson's magnificent voice and repertoire to North America, it was not surprising that she was celebrated in a country that had already enjoyed more than a half-century of folksong scholarship, with 'live' recordings that had built several prestigious folklore archives. While tradition-bearers themselves may never refer to the work of scholars and collectors, nevertheless they are affected by the attention it brings to their tradition, recognising that one of the rewards of being 'collected' is that singers, as well as families and communities, begin to realise the value of their cultural heritage. This had already begun to happen in North America where young ballad singers like Jean Ritchie (b. 1922) became well known among audiences as well as students of folklore and traditional culture. Before long, she visited Robertson in Scotland, as did many others drawn to Scottish traditions or driven by desire to further scholarship in the field of ballad studies. Henderson's work among the Scottish travelling people played no small part in inspiring groundbreaking studies and fieldwork, including that of Bertrand H. Bronson[23] (world authority on the tunes of the Child ballads), as well as Fulbright scholars Kenneth S. Goldstein who extensively recorded Lucy Stewart of Fetterangus (1901–82)[24] and Herchell Gower whose work revealed that more than half the ballads in Sharp's *English Folksongs of the Southern Appalachians* are, in fact, Scottish.[25]

So also with folk tales: Jeannie Robertson's telling of 'Silly Jack and the Factor'[26] is only one example of hundreds of 'Jack Tales' told in Scotland (largely by the travelling people) and also in the Appalachians.[27] In 1988, while guest of an American university, storyteller Duncan Williamson (1928–2007) was invited to share stories with Ray Hicks from Beech

Mountain, North Carolina, whose enormous repertoire and sole reliance on oral tradition seemed to suggest a match for the Scottish traveller. No sooner had they begun to exchange their stories than each showed delighted surprise at the familiarity of characters and plots, the main differences being the social setting of tinker's tent and hill-billy cabin, the 'didnae hae a crust o' bread' equally conveyed in 'ain't had a bite ti eat'. So animated did they become that, to great satisfaction, they turned their session into a game along the lines of 'as soon as you recognise my story, *you* finish it!'[28] And, with a remarkable degree of success, they did.

Songs and stories kept alive in the tradition of Scots at home and abroad also illuminate the work of students and scholars of emigration and migration, as they fill in details of historical, social and cultural significance where no written records exist. A version of 'John of Hazelgreen' (Child 293) in the repertoire of Appalachian singers suggests that the original settlers, of Scottish extraction, arrived in the area before Sir Walter Scott composed 'Jock of Hazeldean' which he based on that ballad. Another old song popular in areas of the South States, 'A-Rovin on a Winter's Night', has a verse that begins 'I love you till the seas run dry, and the rocks all melt with the sun [. . .]' reminiscent of Burns's 'Till a' the seas gang dry my dear / And rocks melt wi' the sun' ('My Love is Like a Red, Red Rose'). Yet this remote area of North America was settled by Scottish and Irish immigrants in the early 1700s – before Burns was born. Yet another verse of the same song begins 'Who's gonna shoe yo' pretty li'l feet? Who's gonna glove yo' han'?' suggesting a connection to a more ancient ballad, 'The Lass of Roch Royal' (Child 76), or 'Lord Gregory' as it is known in Scotland.

Despite time's passing, countless songs and stories are still part of Scotland's living tradition. While there may be variations in texts from performer to performer, many are essentially the same. What has changed most in intervening decades is the context of the performance, especially the singers' and storytellers' way of life. Even in Burns's and Scott's days, the travelling minstrels were but a memory of times past. Gone now are hiring fairs, 'feein' time' at Whitsun and Martinmas, the sax-month 'term', 'arles' and the mysterious 'horseman's word'. Gone are bothies where – never heed the lumpy beds, the meal kists, the iron rations – the night's entertainment wove together tunes on melodeon, fiddle and 'moothie' with ancient ballads, broadsides bought for a penny at a hiring fair, as well as hundreds of ephemeral songs, some composed collectively, scribbled on a scrap of paper that lit a pipe as soon as the song was ready to sing. Gone are the fisher lasses, the *clann-nighean na sgadain*, or herring gutters; the tattie-howkers and berry-pickers have been replaced, and the tramps and hawkers are no longer. Fife song-maker Matt Armour (1935–2009) summed up transitions within his lifetime in his song 'Generations of Change':

> My faither was a baillie on a wee fairm at Caiplie
> He worked on the land a' the days o' his life
> By the time he made second, he said that he reckoned
> He'd ploughed nearly half o' the East Neuk o' Fife [. . .]

Times change and three generations on, the boys have none of the skills of the old ploughman:

> My sons they have grown, and away they have gone
> To search for black oil in the far northern sea
> Like oilmen they walk and like Texans they talk
> There's no much in common 'tween my sons and me.

Yet the songs that belong to an older way still live on, as do the families who experienced a way of life that endured till the 1950s, 1960s and, for some, to the present. Singers, like Gordon Easton from Tyrie (b. 1923) and Jock Duncan from Pitlochry (b. 1925), the late Tom (1929–2003) and Anne (1939–2006) Reid from Cullerlie, Flora MacNeil of Barra (b. 1928), soon found other platforms for their songs, which, by the mid-1990s, included a stage at the Edinburgh International Festival.[29] The richness of language and authenticity of each performance turned a concert into a cultural experience shared with singers who had clearly lived the life. A surprised audience delighted to see Jock Duncan abandon the stage and microphone to plough an imaginary furrow through the audience while 'hup-hup-hupping' his invisible horse. When he returned to the stage to finish his song, the audience understood:

> Noo Mairtinmas term is come at last, oor fee is safely won,
> And we'll awa tae Rhynie Fair, and there we'll hae some fun.
>   An sing airy arity adie O, Sing airy arity ann.
>
> Fan we are ower in Alford, boys, we'll gar the gless ging roun,
> An we'll tell them aa the usage at we hud at Sleepytoon.
>   An sing airy arity adie O, Sing airy arity ann.
>
> I still see Adam Mitchell yet, a-suppin at his brose,
> So I'll gie him a len o ma hankie jist tae dicht his snottery nose.
>   An sing airy arity adie O, Sing airy arity ann.

Within a few years, storytellers also found themselves transported from fireside to village hall, theatre or classroom to recount stories handed down through generations. Possibly none became better known than Duncan Williamson, born in a bow tent in Argyll and who settled in Fife as a young man. Traveller and horseman, Williamson had an enormous repertoire of stories, many of which were recorded, transcribed and published by his wife, folklorist Linda (Headlee) Williamson.[30] The first traveller to write her own story was one of Duncan's kin, Betsy Whyte (1919–88)[31] and soon thereafter so did Stanley Robertson (1940–2009), Jeannie's grand-nephew. Their good friend Willie MacPhee, or 'Big Wullie' (1910–2001), was also one of the finest and best loved storytellers of his time.

In 1992, growing interest in the tradition led to the formation of the Scottish Storytelling Forum, initially to raise awareness of storytelling's significance, and create a directory of recognised storytellers willing to accept invitations to share their stories. Three years later, the Scottish Storytelling Centre in Edinburgh's Netherbow Theatre became the Forum's base. There workshops, 'sessions' and festivals draw packed houses of enthusiasts. From the outset, the Centre's director, Donald Smith, invited storytellers deeply rooted in their tradition, like Duncan Williamson, Stanley Robertson, Betsy Whyte, Willie MacPhee, the Stewarts of Blair and the Gaelic-speaking Essie Stewart (b. 1941), who not only spell-bound their audiences, but also became 'models' of masterful storytelling as a new generation of storyteller began to emerge.

Handing on tradition from generation to generation carries great responsibility – not only to earlier storytellers, but also to a living tradition that has survived for centuries. It seems clear that anyone aspiring to earn a living as a professional storyteller must guard against any reinvention of a tradition they neither saw nor experienced first-hand. Fortunately, from the time of Iain Òg Ìle to the present, dedicated fieldworkers have recorded multiple 'models of authenticity', demonstrating the scope of Scotland's living tradition. Sheila Douglas, for example, spent many years recording traveller storytellers, including Willie, piper and singer as well as storyteller. There may be little sophisticated in the bow tent in Dunbarton where MacPhee was born, yet there he learned his true art, both in oral tradition and tinsmithing. In *Last of the Tinsmiths: The Life of Willie MacPhee*, Douglas gives transcriptions of 'Big Willie's' stories, including an old favourite, 'Friday, Saturday'. Two brothers seek fortune, fame and the princess's hand in marriage: at the point of the wedding night:

[Then] out from below the bed comes this big broon hare.
'I'm gonnae get this broon hare,' he says. He's doon the stair an oot on his horse eftir this broon hare an it's goin roon aboot him in circles an he couldnae blaw saut on this hare's tail. He's eftir this hare on this clear moonlight night an he's ower fences an ower dykes an ower ditches. The hare would go a wee bit before him, then it wad stop an he wad come up on it an it wad go away again, till it led him away miles an miles fae the big hoose intae the moorland' [. . .] [32]

MacPhee's outstanding gift for bringing the story alive was evident in every tale he told. As if watching a film or listening to radio theatre, we follow the hare's every move. Such was the art of the old tinsmith who, even at the age of ninety, could take centre-stage as a great storyteller.

Donald Sinclair from Tiree, referred to in Chapter 1 of this book, who told the story of Diarmaid and Gràinne, also left a legacy of Gaelic stories, which could be learned from the recordings that keep his voice alive. As important as learning Sinclair's repertoire, however, is acquiring insight into the context of his telling as well as his style, masterfully described by Eric Cregeen, the folklorist who sat by his fireside:

> It was more than superb entertainment; it was true art. When he was telling of the great storm, you were there on the shore, watching the boats founder, and felt the terror and the pity of it. Then the melancholy would go from his voice, and his face would light up and his eyes shine as he recounted some wild escapade of one of his ancestors. The width of his sympathies and the rich complexity of his nature were part of his greatness as a *seanchaidh*. Within the space of an evening you saw him as the devout Christian, wondering about life and death and the judgement; as the humorist who loved to tease and outrage and mock at the *unco' guid*; the believer in charms and spells; the man of reason deprecating 'old superstitions'; the singer of songs and teller of tales; the satirical bard, reluctant to sing his own songs; the affectionate and dutiful son, recalling his parents; the boisterous, warm-hearted friend.
> [. . .]
> Donald, and others who are still alive and remarkable as *seanchaidhs*, were in time to save a great part of the lore of their island and of the Highlands for posterity. I wonder if he realised this when he said: 'Isn't it queer? My voice will be heard when I'm a goner.'[33]

Such is the power of Scotland's continuing living tradition.

Endnotes

Introduction – Dunnigan and Gilbert

1. Angela Carter (ed.), *The Virago Book of Fairy Tales* (London: Virago Press, 1990), 'Introduction', p. xxi.
2. James Porter and Herschel Gower, *Jeannie Robertson. Emergent Singer, Transformative Voice* (East Linton: Tuckwell; Knoxville: University of Tennessee Press, 1995), p. 66.
3. Alan Bruford and Donald A. MacDonald (eds), *Scottish Traditional Tales* (Edinburgh: Birlinn, 2003), p. 106; recorded from 'Mrs MacMillan, Bridge Cottage, Strathtay on 3 June 1891' (fn. 11, p. 448).
4. Adam Fox, *Oral and Literate Culture in England 1500–1700* (Oxford: Oxford University Press, 2002), p. 9.
5. John MacInnes, 'The Oral Tradition in Scottish Gaelic Poetry', *Scottish Studies*, 12 (1968), p. 29.
6. Macinnes, 'The Oral Tradition', p. 29.
7. Edward J. Cowan and Mike Paterson (eds), *Folk in Print. Scotland's Chapbook Heritage 1750–1850* (Edinburgh: John Donald, 2007), p. 13.
8. Bruford and MacDonald, p. 55; recorded from Jeannie Robertson (fn 7, p. 445).
9. Porter, p. 46.
10. Bruford and MacDonald, p. 45; recorded from Tom Tulloch (fn 3b, p. 442).

1 – Bennett

1. Robert Burns, Letter to Dr John Moore (Letter 125, 2 Aug. 1787), in *Letters of Robert Burns*, ed. G. Ross Roy, 2 vols (Oxford: Oxford University Press, 1985), vol. 1, p. 135.
2. Walter Scott, 'Memoirs', in David Hewitt (ed.), *Scott on Himself: A Selection of the Autobiographical Writings of Sir Walter Scott* (Edinburgh: Scottish Academic Press, 1981), p. 13.
3. Allan Ramsay, *The Tea-Table Miscellany: A Collection of Choice Songs Scots and English*, 2 vols (Edinburgh: Ruddiman, 1724), vol. 1.

4. The Easy Club was one of Edinburgh's many all-male, common-interest drinking clubs – evenings were spent reciting and discussing poems, and singing songs in a very convivial atmosphere.
5. A *pastorale* is a theatre piece with songs woven through the script. The term 'ballad opera' is defined by *The Concise Oxford Dictionary of Music* as 'an opera with spoken dialogue and using popular tunes of the day provided with new words'. The form's 'invention' is attributed to Allan Ramsay's production of *The Gentle Shepherd*.
6. Further research indicates that several had been printed by broadside-ballad sellers, though Scott recorded them from oral tradition.
7. Apart from *Gleanings of Scotch, English and Irish Scarce Old Ballads*, which was published in 1825, most of Buchan's work remained unpublished till after his death. Part of his collection, *Ancient Scottish Tales*, was published by the Buchan Field Club (1908). Ian Spring edited Buchan's work as *Secret Songs of Silence* (Edinburgh: Hog's Back, 2010).
8. The richly expressive speech of the Northern Isles, Orkney and Shetland, is rooted in Norse.
9. The story is also referred to as 'The Frog Prince'and 'The Enchanted Frog'; it is listed as Tale-Type 440 in the Aarne–Thompson classification of the folk tale.
10. Tale number XXXIII in J. F. Campbell, *Popular Tales of the West Highlands: Orally Collected, with a Translation*, 4 vols (Edinburgh: Edmonston and Douglas, 1860–2), vol. 2, pp. 130–2.
11. Dasent, who was appointed to a diplomatic post in Sweden in 1840, published *A Grammar of the Icelandic or Old Norse Tongue* (London, 1843) translated from Erasmus Rask's original Swedish book. On return to England in 1845 he continued working on translations of Norse folk tales collected by Peter Christen Asbjørnsen and Jørgen Moe (*Norske folkeeventyr*, 1842–4, published as *Popular Tales from the Norse*, Edinburgh, 1859, many later editions).
12. Patronage of the arts was an ancient tradition of Highland chiefs. Though there were drastic changes after the collapse of the clan system (1746), the 8th Duke, himself an author, actively supported the arts.
13. Campbell's advice on methodology, described at length in his Introduction (*Popular Tales*, vol. 1), influenced and encouraged many significant collectors including the treasury of Perthshire stories written down by Lady Evelyn Stewart Murray in *Tales from Highland Perthshire*.
14. See Margaret Bennett, 'John Francis Campbell of Islay: Iain Og Ile', *Journal of the Clan Campbell Society (U. K.)*, 29 (2002), p. xxx.
15. Robert Chambers, *Popular Rhymes of Scotland* (Edinburgh: Chambers, 1841). Chambers includes a version titled 'The Paddo' in his new edition of 1870, noting that it is 'from the memory of the late Charles K. Sharpe, Esq., who would be sitting at the knee of Nurse Jenny, in his father's house of Hoddam in Dumfriesshire, about the year 1784', pp. 87–9.

16. Campbell, *Popular Tales*, vol. 2, pp. 133–4.
17. Jan Harold Brunvand gives a reliable guide in his book *The Study of American Folklore*, and addresses issues of classification and analysis, which apply outwith America.
18. There are many published collections, including J. G. Campbell's *Witchcraft & Second Sight in the Highlands & Islands of Scotland* or Hugh Miller's *Scenes and Legends*, which recount experiences 'told as true'. See also Herbert Halpert's discussion on categories of legend and issues of defining legend in *Folklore: An Emerging Discipline: Selected Essays of Herbert Halpert*, ed. Martin Lovelace, Paul Smith and J. D. A. Widdowson (St John's: Memorial University of Newfoundland, Folklore and Language Publication, 2002), pp. 205–27.
19. See T. O. Clancy, 'Scottish Saints and National Identities in the Early Middle Ages', in Richard Sharpe and Alan Thacker (eds), *Local Saints and Local Churches in the Early Medieval West* (Oxford: Oxford University Press, 2003) pp. 397–421.
20. Luke 5 tells the story, concluding (v. 9) Simon Peter 'was astonished, and all that were with him, at the draught of the fishes which they had taken'. There is no mention of a haddock.
21. Traditional stories, thought to be 'in the Bible', but, on further investigation, are not, are discussed by F. Lee Utley, 'The Bible of the Folk', *California Folklore Quarterly*, 4 (Jan. 1945), pp. 1–17.
22. John Francis Campbell heard an old man in Barra recite a long poem which he wrote down and included in volume 3 of *Popular Tales* and also in his *Leabhar na Feine*, which contains over 54,000 lines of poetry that Campbell gleaned from manuscripts. Norah Montgomerie (1908–98) made a significant collection, posthumously edited by her grandson, Julian Brooks: *The Fantastical Feats of Finn MacCoul* (Edinburgh: Birlinn, 2009).
23. Lomax's field notebook. I am grateful to Lomax's daughter Anna and the Lomax archive in New York for access to the tapes, notebooks and journals.
24. First printed in 1800, *Lyric Gems* appeared in many editions, often without date or publication details. Mackenzie's *Sàr-Obair*, with biographical essays about the bards, has Gaelic texts of songs with MacKenzie's translations, and was first published in Glasgow in 1841. It became popular among Gaels on both sides of the Atlantic, as did *An t-Òranaiche*, the collection by Rev. Alexander Maclean Sinclair (1840–1924), grandson of Tiree bard John Maclean.
25. The edition was printed and published in Halifax, Nova Scotia in 1863.
26. MacArthur's paternal grandparents emigrated from the Isle of Canna. Fieldwork recordings are collected at Memorial University of Newfoundland Folklore Archive, St John's, Newfoundland.
27. See Margaret Bennett, *The Last Stronghold: Scottish Gaelic Traditions of*

Newfoundland (Edinburgh: Canongate, 1989), p. 180. The song, 'Òran na Cailliche', composed by Allan MacDougal – Ailean Dall (blind Allan) – of Glencoe is in *Sàr-Obair*, p. 336, while the biography of the bard begins p. 298.
28. All are archived in Harvard University's collections.
29. Texts in approximately thirty languages are identified; Child collaborated with colleagues and correspondents with expertise in a range of languages.

2 – Lyle, Bold and Russell

1. Letter of William Shenstone to Thomas Hull, dated 24 December 1761, in Margaret Williams (ed.), *The Letters of William Shenstone* (Oxford: Basil Blackwell, 1939), p. 613.
2. Tristram Potter Coffin, *The British Traditional Ballad in North America*, rev. edn (Austin and London: University of Texas Press, 1977), p. 165.
3. Letter to Mrs Dunlop, 25 January 1790, No. 385, in G. Ross Roy (ed.), *The Letters of Robert Burns*, 2 vols (Oxford: Clarendon Press, 1985). This ballad version is Child No. 173–R, F. J. Child, *The English and Scottish Popular Ballads* (London: Houghton Mifflin, 1882–98), vol. 3, p. 397.
4. Child No. 173–D, Child 1882–98: 3.387–8.
5. Child No. 173–E, 173–F, Child 1882–98: 3.388–90.
6. See Matthew Gelbart, *The Invention of 'Folk Music' and 'Art Music': Emerging Categories from Ossian to Wagner* (Cambridge: Cambridge University Press, 2007).
7. See Katherine Campbell, 'Collectors of Scots Song', in John Beech et al. (eds), *Scottish Life and Society: A Compendium of Scottish Ethnology. Oral Literature and Performance Culture* (Edinburgh: John Donald in association with The European Ethnological Research Centre, 2007), pp. 427–39.
8. Emily Lyle, *Fairies and Folk: Approaches to the Scottish Ballad Tradition* (Trier: Wissenschaftlicher Verlag Trier, 2007), pp. 215–38.
9. Emily Lyle (ed.), *Andrew Crawfurd's Collection of Ballads and Songs*, 2 vols (Edinburgh: Scottish Text Society, 1975, 1996); David Buchan and James Moreira (eds), *The Glenbuchat Ballads Compiled by the Rev. Robert Scott* (Jackson: University Press of Mississippi in association with the Elphinstone Institute, University of Aberdeen, 2007).
10. See further Derek Attridge, *The Rhythms of English Poetry* (London: Longman, 1982), pp. 80, 84, 89–90, 93, 95, 161–2, 180, 358.
11. See Brian Paltridge, *Genre, Frames and Writing in Research Settings* (Amsterdam and Philadelphia: John Benjamins, 1997).
12. David C. Fowler, *A Literary History of the Popular Ballad* (Durham, NC: Duke University Press, 1968), pp. 6–13.
13. Child No. 178–A, Child 1882–98: 3.430.

14. James Porter, *Genre, Conflict, Presence: Traditional Ballads in a Modernizing World* (Trier: Wissenschaftlicher Verlag Trier, 2009), pp. 26–9, 138–9, 141, 146–7.
15. Porter, *Genre*, pp. 7–9, 186.
16. Child No. 11–A, from Anna Gordon, Mrs Brown; Child 1882–98: 1.145.
17. Ailie Munro, *The Democratic Muse: Folk Music Revival in Scotland* (Aberdeen: Aberdeen Cultural Press, 1996).
18. Qtd from Valentina Bold and Thomas A. McKean (eds), *Northern Folk: Living Traditions of North East Scotland* (Aberdeen: Elphinstone Institute, 1999): 'Gallery', interactive CD-Rom.
19. M. J. C. Hodgart, *The Ballad*, 2nd edn (London: Hutchison's University Library, 1969), p. 10.
20. Elliot Oring, *Folk Groups and Folklore Genres* (Logan: Utah State University Press, 1986).
21. See, for instance, Brian Hayward, *Galoshins: The Scottish Folk Play* (Edinburgh: Edinburgh University Press, 1992).
22. See, for instance, Helen Creighton, *Bluenose Ghosts* (Toronto: Ryerson, 1959) and Michael Taft and Ronald Caplan (eds), *A Folk Tale Journey through the Maritimes* (Wreck Cove, Cape Breton Island: Breton Books, 1993); also http://john.curtin.edu.au/folklore/ and Graham Seal, *Great Australian Stories: Legends, Yarns and Tall Tales* (Sydney: Allen and Unwin, 2001).
23. http://www.tobarandualchais.co.uk/; http://www.pearl.arts.ed.ac.uk/; http://www.ambaile.org.uk/; http://www.nefa.net/; http://www.scran.ac.uk.
24. The Grampian Association of Storytellers, www.grampianstorytellers.org.uk, for instance, whose website has a section of useful links.
25. http://www.scottishstorytellingcentre.co.uk
26. Stith Thompson, *The Folktale*, 2nd edn (Berkeley: University of California Press, 1977); Richard Dorson, *Folklore and Folk Life* (Chicago: University of Chicago Press, 1972); Archer Taylor, *English Riddles from Oral Tradition* (Berkeley: University of California Press, 1951); Archer Taylor, *The Proverb* (Cambridge, MA: Harvard University Press, 1931); Archer Taylor (ed.), *A Collection of Scotch Proverbs (1663) Pappity Stampoy* (Los Angeles: William Andrews Clark Memorial Library, 1955).
27. See Jan Harold Brunvand, *Encyclopedia of Urban Legends* (New York: W. W. Norton, 2001) and Paul Smith and Gillian Bennett, *Perspectives on Contemporary Legend*, 5 vols (Sheffield: Centre for English Cultural Tradition and Language, 1984–90).
28. Vladimir Propp, *Morphology of the Folktale*, rev. Louis A. Wagner, 2nd edn (Austin: University of Texas Press, 1968); Sigmund Freud, *Jokes and their Relation to the Unconscious*, ed. James Strachey (New York: Norton, 1989); Carl Gustav Jung, *Dreams*, trans. R. F. C. Hull (London: Routledge, 2002); see, for instance, Alan Dundes, *From Game to War and Other Psychoanalytical*

Essays on Folklore (Lexington: University of Kentucky Press, 1997) and Marina Warner, *From the Beast to the Blonde: On Fairy Tales and Their Tellers* (London: Chatto and Windus, 1994).

29. Ernest W. Marwick, *The Folklore of Orkney and Shetland* (Edinburgh: Birlinn, 2011); Alan Temperley, *Tales of Galloway* (Edinburgh: Mainstream, 1986 [1979]).
30. Ian A. Olson, 'The Influence of Nineteenth-Century Migrant Workers on the Greig–Duncan Folk Song Collection', *Review of Scottish Culture*, 9 (1995–6), pp. 113–27; Patrick Shuldham-Shaw, Emily B. Lyle et al., *The Greig–Duncan Folk Song Collection*, 8 vols (Aberdeen: Aberdeen University Press; Edinburgh: Mercat Press for the University of Aberdeen in association with the School of Scottish Studies, University of Edinburgh, 1981–2002).
31. Roger D. Abrahams and George Foss, *Anglo-American Folksong Style* (Englewood Cliffs, NJ: Prentice-Hall, 1968), pp. 19–24.
32. See Elizabeth Stewart, *Binnorrie: Songs, Ballads, and Tunes*, Traveller Traditions of North-East Scotland 1, double CD EICD002, Elphinstone Institute, University of Aberdeen, 2004, CD1 track 1. See also James Porter and Herschel Gower, *Jeannie Robertson: Emergent Singer, Transformative Voice* (East Linton: Tuckwell; Knoxville: University of Tennessee Press, 1995), no. 68, pp. 236–8.
33. A. L. Lloyd, *Folk Song in England* (London: Lawrence and Wishart, 1967), pp. 235–6.
34. See 'Bonnie Udny', in Jane Turriff, *Singin Is Ma Life*, CD SPRCD 1038, Springthyme, Kingskettle, Fife, 1995, track 21; Porter and Gower, *Jeannie Robertson*, no. 69, pp. 239–40.
35. From 'The Irish Boy', as sung by Phyllis Martin of Dumfries. See Sheila Douglas (ed.), *Come Gie's a Sang: 73 Traditional Scottish Songs* (Edinburgh: Hardie Press, 1995), p. 105.
36. See Belle Stewart, *Queen among the Heather: Scots Traditional Songs and Ballads*, LP 12TS307, Topic Records, 1977, re-issued as CD CDTRAX 9055, Greentrax, 1998, track 9.
37. For scans of broadside from the Poet's Box, see *The Word on the Street: How Ordinary Scots in Bygone Days Found out what was Happening*, National Library of Scotland, 2004, http://digital.nls.uk/broadsides/index.html [accessed 10 January 2011].
38. David Atkinson, *The English Traditional Ballad: Theory, Method, and Practice* (Aldershot: Ashgate, 2002), pp. 21–2.
39. David Buchan (ed.), *Scottish Tradition: A Collection of Scottish Folk Literature* (London, Boston, Melbourne and Henley: Routledge and Kegan Paul, 1984), p. 89. Buchan is citing Rev. James Bruce Duncan's 1908 lecture.
40. See Norman Buchan (ed.), *101 Scottish Songs* (Glasgow and London: Collins, 1962), pp. 15, 19.

41. *Lyric Gems of Scotland: A Collection of Scottish Songs, Original and Selected, with Music* (Glasgow: D. Jack, 1856), pp. 26–7; 16–17.
42. Learning and Teaching Scotland provides a recommended list of 'Songs for Secondary Schools'; see http://www.ltscotland.org.uk/scotlandssongs/secondary/index.asp [accessed 11 January 2011].
43. For a film of Sheila's performance, see http://ssa.nls.uk/film.cfm?fid=8217 [accessed 12 January 2011]. See http://www.tobarandualchais.co.uk/examples [accessed 12 January 2011] for Belle's singing.
44. Hamish Henderson, 'Folk-Songs and Music from the Berry Fields of Blair' [1962], in *Alias MacAlias: Writing on Songs, Folk and Literature* (Edinburgh: Polygon, 2004), pp. 101–3.
45. Gavin Greig writes in these terms, referring to the 'folk song hallmark' of anonymity or obscurity of origins, in 'Folk Song in Buchan', *Transactions of the Buchan Field Club*, 9 (1906–7), pp. 2–76, reprinted in Stephen Miller (ed.), *Gavin Greig, 'The Subject of Folksong': Collected Writings on Scottish Folk Song* (Isle of Man: Chiollagh Books, 2000), pp. 35–8.
46. The McPeake Family, 'Will Ye Go Lassie Go', in *Wild Mountain Thyme*, CD TSCD583, Topic Records, [1962] 2009, track 1. The McPeake Family is from Belfast.
47. First published in R. A. Smith, *Scottish Minstrel: A Selection from the Vocal Melodies of Scotland, Ancient & Modern*, 6 vols (Edinburgh: Robert Purdie, 1821–4), I, p. 49.
48. The song is a tribute to Betsy Whyte and her autobiography, *The Yellow on the Broom* (Edinburgh: Chambers, 1979).
49. Adam McNaughtan, *Words, Words, Words*, CD CDTRAX013, Greentrax, 1988.
50. *Singing the Fishing*, Radio Ballad produced by Charles Parker, BBC Home Service, 16 August 1960. See Ewan MacColl, Charles Parker and Peggy Seeger, *Singing the Fishing*, CD TSCD 803, Topic, 1999.
51. Tom McKean, 'The Gatherer of Songs', in *Leopard: The Magazine for North-East Scotland*, November 2002, http://www.leopardmag.co.uk/feats/29/alan-lomax [accessed 11 January 2011].
52. John Mearns, 'Bonnie Lass of Fyvie', *John Mearns Sings Folk-Songs of the North-East*, EP SR4510, Scottish Records, Aberdeen, c. 1964.
53. The traditional stone-built bunk houses for male farm servants are known as bothies. For Alan Lomax's recordings of these singers, see John Strachan, *Songs from Aberdeenshire*, CD 82161–1835–2, Rounder Records, 2002; Jimmie MacBeath, *Tramps & Hawkers*, CD 82161–1834–2, Rounder Records, 2002; Davie Stewart, *Go on, Sing Another Song*, CD82161–1833–2, Rounder Records, 2002.
54. Henderson, *Alias MacAlias*, p. 194.
55. Davie Stewart CD, track 1, liner notes, pp. 12–13, 'Hame Drunk Cam I,' as sung by Cameron Turriff, in Douglas, *Come Gie's a Sang*, pp. 18–19.

56. John Strachan CD, track 11.
57. See *A Soldiers Life for Me*, The Folk Songs of Britain, Vol. 8, LP 12T196, Topic Records, 1971, track B11; (re-issue of LP TC 1164, Caedmon, 1961), as sung by Jimmy McBeath [sic].
58. Jane Turriff CD, track 21.
59. Jimmy MacBeath CD, track 1.
60. Verses written by Mary Brooksbank (1897–1978) about the conditions in the Dundee jute mills in the early twentieth century. From her collection of poems, *Sidlaw Breezes* (Dundee: the author, n. d.), p. 41. See also Norman Buchan and Peter Hall (eds), *The Scottish Folksinger* (London and Glasgow: Collins, 1973), pp. 33–4. For a recording of her singing the song, see *Festival at Blairgowrie*, LP 12T181, Topic Records [1967], 1977, track A6.
61. Verses written by Ewan McVicar about the Paisley thread mills. See Ewan McVicar (ed.), *One Singer One Song; Songs of Glasgow Folk* (Glasgow: Glasgow City Libraries, 1990), pp. 142–3.
62. Jimmy MacBeath CD, track 20.
63. Davie Stewart CD, track 22.
64. The disaster happened on 22 October 1877 in High Blantyre near Glasgow; 207 men were killed. See A. L. Lloyd, *Come All Ye Bold Miners: Ballads and Songs of the Coalfields* (London: Lawrence and Wishart [1952], 1978), pp. 179–81, 351–2.
65. This Fife mining disaster occurred on 26 August 1901; eight miners and three rescuers lost their lives. As sung by J. Ferguson of Markinch, see Lloyd, *Come All Ye Bold Miners*, pp. 186–7, 352–3; Buchan and Hall, *Scottish Folksinger*, p. 21.
66. Shuldham-Shaw, Lyle et al., *The Greig–Duncan Folk Song Collection*; Katherine Campbell (ed.), *Songs from North-East Scotland: A Selection for Performers from the Greig–Duncan Folk Song Collection* (Edinburgh: John Donald, 2009).
67. See http://www.hrionline.ac.uk/carpenter/ and http://www.abdn.ac.uk/elphinstone/carpenter/ [accessed 12 January 2011].
68. See Buchan and Hall, *The Scottish Folksinger* and Buchan, *101 Scottish Songs*.
69. See Douglas, *Come Gie's a Sang* and Sheila Douglas (ed.), *The Sang's the Thing: Voices from Lowland Scotland* (Edinburgh: Polygon, 1992).
70. See http://www.tobarandualchais.co.uk/ [accessed 12 January 2011].
71. See http://www.ltscotland.org.uk/scotlandssongs/ [accessed 11 January 2011].

3 – Henderson

1. Lizanne Henderson, 'Studying the Supernatural History of Scotland', in Lizanne Henderson (ed.), *Fantastical Imaginations: The Supernatural in Scottish History and Culture* (Edinburgh: John Donald, 2009), p. xvi.
2. On the unitary, binary, trinary and general characteristics of folk tale see

Axel Olrik, 'Epic Laws of Folk Narrative' [1909], reprinted in Alan Dundes (ed.), *The Study of Folklore* (Englewood Cliffs: Prentice-Hall, 1965), pp. 131–41; Vladimir Propp, *Morphology of the Folktale* [1928] (Austin: n. p., 1968).
3. Reidar Thoralf Christiansen, *The Migratory Legends* (Helsinki: Folklore Fellows Communications, 1958); Stith Thompson, *Motif-Index of Folk Literature*, 6 vols (Bloomington: Indiana University Press, 1955–8) and Antti Aarne and Stith Thompson, *The Types of the Folktale* (Helsinki: Academia Scientiarum Fennica, 1961).
4. William Motherwell, 'Preface', in Andrew Henderson, *Scottish Proverbs* (Edinburgh: Oliver and Boyd, 1832), p. xxix.
5. Robert Chambers, *The Popular Rhymes of Scotland* [1826] (London and Edinburgh: W. & R. Chambers, 1870), pp. vi, 48.
6. David Buchan, *Scottish Tradition* (London: Routledge and Kegan Paul, 1984), p. 11.
7. Lizanne Henderson, '"Detestable Slaves of the Devil": Changing Attitudes to Witchcraft in Sixteenth-Century Scotland', in Edward J. Cowan and Lizanne Henderson (eds), *A History of Everyday Life in Medieval Scotland* (Edinburgh: Edinburgh University Press, 2011), pp. 226–53; Lizanne Henderson, 'Witch, Fairy and Folktale Narratives in the Trial of Bessie Dunlop', in *Fantastical Imaginations*, pp. 141–66.
8. 'The Legend of the Bischop of St Androis Lyfe, callit Mr Patrik Adamsone' [1583], in James Cranstoun (ed.), *Satirical Poems of the Time of the Reformation*, 2 vols, Scottish Text Society (Edinburgh: William Blackwood and Sons, 1891) vol. 1, p. 362 and notes; Lizanne Henderson and Edward J. Cowan, *Scottish Fairy Belief: A History* [2001] (Edinburgh: John Donald, 2007), pp. 165–8.
9. Stewart Sanderson (ed.), *The Secret Common-Wealth of Elves, Fauns and Fairies* (Cambridge: Mistletoe Press, 1976), p. 1.
10. Sanderson, *The Secret Common-Wealth*, pp. 54, 60, 61, 95.
11. On pre-1603 folk narrative see David Buchan, 'Folk Tradition and Literature Till 1603', in J. D. McClure and M. R. G. Spiller (eds), *Bryght Lanternis: Essays on the Language and Literature of Medieval and Renaissance Scotland* (Aberdeen: Aberdeen University Press, 1989), pp. 1–13.
12. Robert H. Cromek, *Remains of Nithsdale and Galloway Song: With Historical and Traditional Notices Relative to the Manners and Customs of the Peasantry* [1810] (Paisley: Alexander Gardner, 1880), pp. xxx–xxi.
13. Cromek, *Remains*, pp. 272–93; Allan Cunningham, *Traditional Tales of the English and Scottish Peasantry*, 2 vols (London, 1822).
14. Cromek, *Remains*, pp. 276–7.
15. Cromek, *Remains*, pp. 277–80.
16. James Grant, *Walks and Wanderings in the World of Literature*, 2 vols (London: Saunders and Otley, 1839) vol. 2, pp. 189–201; William Henderson, *Notes*

on the Folklore of the Northern Counties of England and the Borders [1866] (London: The Folklore Society, 1879).
17. Tale-types 'the youth transformed into a horse' and 'the magic bridle', Aarne and Thompson, *The Types of the Folktale*, AT 314 and AT 594.
18. Cromek, *Remains*, p. 291.
19. Lizanne Henderson, 'The Survival of Witch Prosecutions and Witch Belief in South-West Scotland', *Scottish Historical Review*, LXXXV, 1: 219 (2006), pp. 52–74.
20. Cromek, *Remains*, pp. 330–8.
21. William Henderson noted this tradition in Berwickshire, *Notes on the Folk Lore of the Northern Counties of England and the Borders* (London: Longmans, Green and Co., 1866), p. 209.
22. Cromek, *Remains*, pp. 332–3.
23. William Nicholson, 'The Brownie of Blednoch', *The Poetical Works of William Nicholson*, 3rd edn (Castle Douglas: Samuel Gordon, 1878), pp. 77–82.
24. Edward J. Cowan, 'Miller's Tale: Narrating History and Tradition', in Lester Borley (ed.), *Celebrating the Life and Times of Hugh Miller* (Cromarty Arts Trust and the Elphinstone Institute of the University of Aberdeen, 2003), pp. 76–88.
25. Lizanne Henderson, 'The Natural and Supernatural Worlds of Hugh Miller', in Borley, *Celebrating*, pp. 89–98.
26. James Robertson (ed. and intro.), *Scenes and Legends of the North of Scotland* [1835] (Edinburgh: B. and W. Publishing Ltd., 1994), pp. 269–76.
27. 'Introduction', in Mary Ellen Brown and Bruce A. Rosenberg (eds), *Encyclopedia of Folklore and Literature* (Santa Barbara: ABC-CLIO, 1998).

4 – Porter

1. See such classic essays as Phillips Barry's 'The Transmission of Folk Song', *Journal of American Folklore*, 27 (1914), pp. 67–76.
2. The main contributions to this development are to be found in the *JAF* volume, 'Toward New Perspectives in Folklore', 84 (1971), although some work precedes this date by a few years such as Alan Dundes, 'Text, Texture, Context', *Southern Folklore Quarterly*, 28 (1964), pp. 251–65; Roger Abrahams, 'Introductory Remarks to a Rhetorical Theory of Folklore', *JAF*, 81 (1968), pp. 143–58; Robert A. Georges, 'Toward an Understanding of Storytelling Events', *JAF*, 82 (1969), pp. 313–28.
3. D. K. Wilgus subjected the movement to a critique in '"The Text is the Thing"', *JAF*, 86 (1973), pp. 241–52. Wilgus protested against the attempted dominance of the field by the movement through many of its assertions. The 'sender and receiver' image comes from the well-known work by C. E. Shannon and Warren Weaver, *The Mathematical Theory of Communication*

(Urbana: University of Illinois Press, 1949). A later, more broadly developed concept of communication is the interactive model of David S. Kaufer and Kathleen M. Carley, *Communication at a Distance: The Influence of Print on Sociocultural Organization and Change* (Hillsdale, NJ: Lawrence Erlbaum, 1993). Linda Dégh in *American Folklore and the Mass Media* (Bloomington: Indiana University Press, 1994) deals to some extent with the same topic.

4. See Dan Ben-Amos, 'The Seven Strands of Tradition: Varieties in its Meaning in American Folklore Studies', *Journal of Folklore Research*, 21 (1984), pp. 97–151. The verb 'transmit' is from the Latin roots 'trans-' meaning across or over, and 'mittere', to send or pass. 'Tradition' is derived from the verb, 'tradere', to hand on.

5. See the Special Issue of *JAF*, 108 (1995), *Common Ground: Keywords for the Study of Expressive Culture*. The keywords selected for discussion are 'tradition', 'art', 'text', 'group', 'performance', 'genre' and 'context'. Henry Glassie, discussing 'tradition' (pp. 395–412) mentions 'transmission' only briefly (p. 402). From the mid-1970s, anthropologists like Clifford Geertz, in *The Interpretation of Cultures* [1973] (New York: Basic, 2000) and the sociologist Erving Goffman, in such works as *Frame Analysis: An Essay on the Organisation of Experience* (New York: Harper and Row, 1974), have been influential.

6. In his dictionary of terms, *General Ethnological Concepts* (Copenhagen: Rosenkilde and Bagger, 1960), the Swedish anthropologist Åke Hultkrantz devotes just a few lines to 'transmission of cultural materials', describing it as 'the passing on of cultural materials from older times to later times, or from one place to another, or from one social group (or class) to another'. Ethnology has been associated with an older, cross-cultural and comparative style of scholarship stemming from before World War Two. Its main organs are: *Ethnologia Europaea: A World Review of European Ethnology* (1967–) and *Folk-Liv: Journal for European Ethnology and Folklore* (1937–). For Scotland, see *Bibliography for Scottish Ethnology*, ed. Heather Holmes and Fiona MacDonald (East Linton: Tuckwell, 2003).

7. The term 'oral literature' has drawn extensive comment in a Scottish context: see John D. Niles, *Homo Narrans: The Poetics and Anthropology of Oral Literature* (Philadelphia: University of Pennsylvania Press, 1991); also *Oral Literature and Performance Culture: A Compendium of Scottish Ethnology*, ed. John Beech et al., vol. 10 (Edinburgh: John Donald, 2007).

8. See Helen Child Sargent and George Lyman Kittredge (eds), *English and Scottish Popular Ballads* (Boston: Houghton, Mifflin and Co., 1904), pp. xi–xxxi. More recently, one ballad scholar has insisted on limiting the term 'oral' (as in 'oral literature', 'oral tradition') to mean the literature, tradition and method of composition in conditions of non-literacy; see David Buchan, 'Oral Tradition and Literary Tradition: The Scottish Ballads', in Hans Bekker-Nielsen et al. (eds), *Oral Tradition: Literary Tradition, A Symposium* (Odense: Bekker Nielsen, 1977), pp. 56–68. See further Joseph Harris (ed.),

The Ballad and Oral Literature (Cambridge, MA: Harvard University Press, 1991).

9. For a discussion of 'orality' and 'textuality' see Joseph M. P. Donatelli, '"To Hear With Eyes": Orality, Print Culture, and the Textuality of Ballads', in James Porter (ed.), *Ballads and Boundaries: Narrative Singing in an Intercultural Context* (Los Angeles: UCLA Press, 1995), pp. 347–57.

10. The literature of this particular movement is extensive: see John Miles Foley, *The Theory of Oral Composition: History and Methodology* (New York: Garland, 1988); *Oral-Formulaic Theory: A Folklore Casebook* (New York: Garland, 1990). Lord found that there were many degrees of influence between written and oral versions of epic songs; and even in modern times, epic singers might consult recorded versions in archives and libraries. See Lord, 'The Merging of Two Worlds: Oral and Written Poetry as Carriers of Ancient Values', in *Oral Tradition in Literature: Interpretation in Context* (Columbia: Unversity of Missouri Press, 1986), pp. 19–64.

11. Notably, David Buchan, *The Ballad and the Folk* (London: Routledge and Kegan Paul, 1972); William McCarthy, *The Ballad Matrix: Personality, Milieu, and the Oral Tradition* (Bloomington: Indiana University Press, 1990). For a broader assessment of 'oral literature' and its relationship to folklore, see Elaine J. Lawless, '"Oral Character" and "Literary" Art: A Call for a New Reciprocity between Oral Literature and Folklore', *Western Folklore*, 44, pp. 77–98.

12. Buchan, *The Ballad and the Folk*, p. 52.

13. See James H. Jones, 'Commonplace and Memorisation in the Oral Tradition of the English and Scottish Popular Ballads', *JAF*, 74 (1961), pp. 97–112; Jones's adherence to the oral-formulaic theory for ballads was rebutted by Albert B. Friedman, 'The Formulaic Improvisation Theory of Ballad Tradition – A Counter-statement', *JAF*, 74 (1961), pp. 113–15; Friedman, 'The Oral-Formulaic Theory of Balladry – A Re-Rebuttal', in James Porter (ed.), *The Ballad Image* (Los Angeles: UCLA Press, 1983), pp. 215–40.

14. See Holger Olof Nygard, 'Mrs Brown's Recollected Ballads', in Patricia Conroy (ed.), *Ballads and Ballad Scholarship* (Seattle: University of Washington Press, 1978), pp. 68–87; Flemming G. Andersen and Thomas Pettitt, 'Mrs Brown of Falkland: A Singer of Tales?', *JAF*, 92 (1979), pp. 1–24.

15. For some examples of such spontaneous recreation that also displays *chantefable* elements, see the CD reissued in 1992, *The Muckle Sangs: Classic Scots Ballads*. Scottish Tradition 5 (Greentrax 9005).

16. Even Robert Burns could be conceived of as falling into the notion of 'member of a traditional society', and the fact that he was a great poet and songwriter does not detract from his sensitivity to and uses of a folk tradition with which he identified. His great feat, in contributing songs to James Johnson's *The Scots Musical Museum* from 1787, was to merge his own poetic

sensibilities with those of the traditional songmakers, so that it is often difficult or impossible to know what alterations he made.

17. See Robert Ford, *Vagabond Songs and Ballads of Scotland* (Paisley: A. Gardner, 1899). On the theory of ballad dissemination in Europe, see *The European Medieval Ballad: A Symposium* (Odense: Odense University Press, 1978); also, Sigrid Rieuwerts and Helga Stein (eds), *Bridging the Cultural Divide: Our Common Ballad Heritage* (Hildesheim: Verlag, 2000).

18. School of Scottish Studies Archive, University of Edinburgh, SA 1973/80/6. The song, recorded by Hamish Henderson and James Porter, was entitled 'The Laird o Esslemont'. It concerns an allegedly real episode in which a local landowner, Charlie Napier Gordon, driving home at night after some carousing, attempts to seduce a young woman, but is thwarted when the gig he is driving overturns. Only one other text of this song is extant, namely in the James Madison Carpenter Collection, Archive of Folk Culture, American Folklife Center, Library of Congress AFC 1972/001, MS pp. 01587–01589. See further James Porter, 'The Turriff Family of Fetterangus: Society, Learning, Creation and Re-creation of Traditional Song', *Folk Life*, 16 (1978), pp. 5–26.

19. See David Kerr Cameron, *The Ballad and the Plough: A Portrait of Life in the Old Scottish Farmtouns* (London: Gollancz, 1978); William Alexander, *Rural Life in Victorian Aberdeenshire*, ed. Ian Carter (Edinburgh: Mercat Press, 1992).

20. The classic collection is John Ord, *The Bothy Songs & Ballads of Aberdeen, Banff and Moray/Angus and the Mearns* (Paisley: A. Gardner, 1930). See also Patrick Shuldham-Shaw, E. B. Lyle and Peter A. Hall (eds), *The Greig–Duncan Folk Song Collection*, vol. 3 (Aberdeen: Aberdeen University Press, 1987).

21. See, for example, Charles Joyner, 'A Model for the Analysis of Folklore Performance in Historical Context', *JAF*, 88 (1975), pp. 254–65; also Bruce Jackson, 'Folkloristics', *JAF*, 98 (1985), pp. 95–101; 'Things That from a Long Way Off Look like Flies', *JAF*, 98 (1985), pp. 131–47.

22. Linda Dégh and Andrew Vaszonyi, 'The Memorate and Proto-Memorate', *JAF*, 87 (1974), pp. 225–39. For 'community', one should also note the influence of Benedict Anderson's *The Imagined Community: Reflections on the Origin and Spread of Nationalism* (London: Verso, 1983); also Roger D. Abrahams, 'Phantoms of Romantic Nationalism in Folkloristics', *JAF*, 106 (1993), pp. 3–37.

23. See John A. Robinson, 'Personal Narratives Reconsidered', *JAF*, 94 (1981), pp. 58–85.

24. See Dan Ben-Amos, '"Context" in Context', *Western Folklore*, 52 (1993), pp. 209–26. Ben-Amos here is following the anthropologist Bronislaw Malinowski's distinction between the context of culture in general and that of immediate situation (p. 215).

25. See Trudier Harris, 'Genre', JAF, 108 (1995), pp. 509–27. The term 'dialogic' comes from Bakhtin's influential work, The Dialogic Imagination, trans. Caryl Emerson and Michael Holquist (Austin: University of Texas Press, 1981). See Charles L. Briggs and Richard Bauman, 'Genre, Intertextuality, and Social Power', Journal of Linguistic Anthropology, 2 (1992), pp. 131–72. Further, James Moreira, 'Genre and Balladry', in Tom Cheesman and Sigrid Rieuwerts (eds), Ballads into Books: The Legacies of Francis James Child (Bern: Peter Lang, 1997), pp. 95–109; James Porter, 'The Traditional Ballad: Requickened Text or Performative Genre?', Scottish Studies Review, 4/1 (2003), pp. 24–40; see also the collection of essays, Ballads and Other Genres (Zagreb: International Society for Ethnology and Folklore, 1988).
26. The main proponents of this movement have been Dell Hymes, Richard Bauman and Charles Briggs. See Dell Hymes, 'The Contribution of Folklore to Sociolinguistic Research', JAF, 84 (1971), pp. 42–50; 'Folklore's Nature and the Sun's Myth', JAF, 88 (1975), pp. 345–69; 'Breakthrough into Performance', in Dan Ben-Amos and Kenneth Goldstein (eds), Folklore: Performance and Communication (The Hague: Mouton and Co., 1975), pp. 11–74; Richard Bauman, Verbal Art as Performance (Prospect Heights, IL: Waveland Press, 1977; 2nd edn, 1984); a special issue of JAF (115, 2002) was recently devoted to 'new perspectives' on this last work. Further, Charles Briggs, Competence in Performance: The Creativity of Tradition in Mexicano Verbal Art (Philadelphia: University of Pennsylvania Press, 1988).
27. Donald J. Ward, 'Idionarrating and Social Change', in Lutz Röhrich and Sabine Wienker-Piepho (eds), Storytelling in Contemporary Societies: Report of the Theory Commission, International Society for Narrative Research, Budapest 1989 (Tübingen: Gunter Narr Verlag, 1990), pp. 33–41.
28. See Gary Alan Fine, 'The Third Force in American Folklore: Folk Narrative and Social Structure', Fabula, 29 (1988), pp. 342–53.
29. Victor Turner, The Ritual Process (Chicago: Aldine, 1969) and The Anthropology of Performance (New York: PAJ, 1988) drew on Arnold van Gennep's study of rites of passage (1960); see also Richard Schechner, Essays on Performance Theory (New York: Drama Book Specialists, 1977); Roger D. Abrahams, 'Toward an Enactment-Centered Theory of Folklore', in William Bascom (ed.), Frontiers of Folklore (Boulder, CO: West View Press, 1977), pp. 79–120.
30. See Clifford Geertz, Local Knowledge (New York: Basic Books, 1983).
31. Waulking (fulling) songs in the Highlands, for example, involved a group of young women shrinking cloth by pounding it on a board or wattle frame. Led by at least one older woman, who sang the song lines of various verse types and poetic content, the women would take up the refrains. Men were usually banned from the waulking. See J. L. Campbell and Francis Collinson, Hebridean Folksongs, 3 vols (Oxford: Clarendon Press, 1969, 1977, 1981).

32. Gender and feminist studies have often appeared parallel in such discussions as Rosan A. Jordan and Susan J. Kalcik (eds), *Women's Folklore, Women's Culture* (Philadelphia: University of Pennsylvania Press, 1985); Margaret Mills, 'Feminist Theory and the Study of Folklore: A Twenty-Year Trajectory', *Western Folklore*, 52 (1993), pp. 173–92; Patricia E. Sawin, 'Gender, Context, and the Narrative Construction of Identity: Rethinking Models of "Women's Narrative"', in Mary Bucholtz, Anita C. Liang, and Laurel A. Sutton (eds), *Reinventing Identities: The Gendered Self in Discourse* (New York: Oxford University Press, 1999), pp. 241–58; Venetia Newall, 'Folklore and Male Homosexuality', *Folklore*, 97 (1986), pp. 123–47. For a selection of essays on the topic of gender as it relates to traditional balladry see Maria Herrera-Sobek (ed.), *Gender and Print Culture: New Perspectives on International Ballad Studies* (Irvine, CA: New Impressions, 1991).
33. The classic collections of English-language children's lore in modern times are Iona and Peter Opie, *The Lore and Language of Schoolchildren* (Oxford: Oxford University Press, 1959) and *The Singing Game* (Oxford: Oxford University Press, 1985). For an exploration of legends, songs, child lore and play culture in Scotland, see Beech et al., *Oral Literature and Performance Culture*, pp. 117–18, 162–3, 293–4, 487–504.
34. 'Ethnography' refers to the writing about or interpretation of culture based on directed field research. See James L. Clifford and George E. Marcus (eds), *Writing Culture: The Poetics and Politics of Ethnography* (Berkeley: University of California Press, 1986). Further, by the same author, *The Predicament of Culture* (London: Harvard University Press, 1988).
35. In England, after the turn of the twentieth century, the influential collector Cecil Sharp was motivated by a nationalist ideology that caused him to distort the nature of English song traditions. See Georgina Boyes, *The Imagined Village: Culture, Ideology and the English Folk Revival* (Manchester: Manchester University Press, 1993).
36. Clifford Geertz, '"From the Native's Point of View": On the Nature of Anthropological Understanding', in J. Dolgin et al. (eds), *Symbolic Anthropology* (New York: Columbia University Press, 1977), pp. 480–92. See further James Porter, 'Ballad Singing, Fieldwork, Meaning', in Sigrid Rieuwerts and Helga Stein (eds), *Bridging the Cultural Divide: Our Common Ballad Heritage* (New York: Olms, 2000), pp. 356–74.
37. The 'truth' about its past and traditions may well not accord with the 'objectivity' that many analysts demand. But just as communities construct their past and their identity in imaginative terms, ethnology constructs these 'others' as its object: see Johannes Fabian, *Time and the Other: How Anthropology Makes Its Object* (New York: Columbia University Press, 1983).
38. See George E. Marcus and Michael M. J. Fischer, *Anthropology as Cultural Critique: An Experimental Moment in the Human Sciences* (Chicago: University

of Chicago Press, 1999). Much of this tendency in the human sciences comes from the influence of hermeneutic theory, in particular the work of Gadamer, Habermas, Ricoeur, Merleau-Ponty and others. See, for example, *Paul Ricoeur: Hermeneutics and the Social Sciences: Essays on Language, Action and Interpretation*, ed. John B. Thompson (Cambridge: Cambridge University Press, 1981).

5 – McNamara

1. A famous case is the following description of cultural opposition in John of Fordun's *Chronica Gentis Scotorum* (1380s), which became commonplace in subsequent chroniclers:

   > The manners and customs of the Scots vary with the diversity of their speech [. . .] The people of the coast [and the plains] are of domestic and civilised habits, trusty, patient, and urbane, decent in their attire, affable and peaceful, devout in Divine worship [. . .] The Highlanders and the people of the Islands, on the other hand, are a savage and untamed nation [or race], rude and independent, given to rapine, ease-loving, of a docile and warm disposition, comely in person, but unsightly in dress, hostile to the English people and language, and owing to the diversity of speech [between Scots and Gaelic], even to their own nation, and exceedingly cruel.

   The point to be made here is not simply that this is a distorted, and distorting, cultural stereotype, but that it is a foray into identity politics on behalf of the Lowlanders, who define themselves in opposition to the radical 'otherness' of the peoples of the Highlands and the Islands.
2. Carl Lindahl, 'Folklore', in Carl Lindahl, John McNamara and John Lindow (eds), *Medieval Folklore: An Encyclopedia*, vol. 1 (Santa Barbara: ABC-CLIO, 2000), p. 333.
3. Hamish Henderson, 'The Ballad and Popular Tradition to 1660', in R. D. S. Jack (ed.), *The History of Scottish Literature*, vol. 1 (Aberdeen: Aberdeen University Press, 1988), p. 281.
4. Michael Chesnutt, 'Otterburn Revisited: A Late Medieval Border Ballad and its Transmission', in Sally Mapstone (ed.), *Older Scots Literature* (Edinburgh: John Donald, 2005), pp. 397–409.
5. A. A. M. Duncan (*John Barbour. The Bruce* [Edinburgh: Canongate, 1997], p. 15) also cites numerous references to oral tradition such as 'Bot ik haiff herd syndry men say' (Book 5, line 506).
6. Detailed references may be found in Matthew P. McDiarmid (ed.), *Hary's Wallace*, Scottish Text Society, vol. 1 (Edinburgh: William Blackwood and Sons, 1968), pp. lxviii–lxix.
7. William Hamilton of Gilbertfield, *Blind Harry's Wallace*, intro. Elspeth King (Edinburgh: Luath Press, 1998).

8. This is an instance of the common folk motif of the Headless Revenant, E422.1.1 in Stith Thompson's *Motif-Index of Folk-Literature*, 6 vols (Bloomington: Indiana University Press, 1955–58).
9. Priscilla Bawcutt, 'William Dunbar', in Ian Brown et al. (eds), *The Edinburgh History of Scottish Literature*, vol. 1 (Edinburgh: Edinburgh University Press, 2007), p. 296.
10. John MacQueen (ed.), *St Nynia, with a Translation of the Miracula Nynia Episcopi and the Vita Niniani by Winifried MacQueen* [1990] (Edinburgh: Birlinn, 2005), p. 102.
11. Cynthia Whidden Green (ed. and trans.) (University of Houston thesis, 1998), http://www.fordham.edu/halsall/basis/Jocelyn-LifeofKentigern.asp.
12. Richard Sharpe (ed. and trans.), *The Life of St Columba* (London: Penguin, 1995), p. 330, n. 272.

6 – Dunbar

1. William Gillies, 'Gaelic Literature in the Later Middle Ages: *The Book of the Dean* and Beyond', in Thomas Owen Clancy and Murray Pittock (eds), *The Edinburgh History of Scottish Literature*, vol. 1 (Edinburgh: Edinburgh University Press, 2007), p. 219.
2. See, for example, the Tobar an Dualchais/Kist of Riches project (http://www.tobarandualchais.co.uk/), where the audio collections of the School of Scottish Studies, John Lorne Campbell archive and BBC Scotland are being digitised and made available on-line.
3. The most important initiative was the Nova Scotia Gaelic Folklore Project, between 1978 and 1983, based at St Francis Xavier University, Antigonish, Nova Scotia, where Dr John Shaw was principal fieldworker. About 2,000 separate folklore items were recorded from about 150 informants, including about 1,100 songs and almost 400 traditional folk tales. The collection has largely been digitised and is available on the Sruth nan Gàidheal/Gael Stream website.
4. See Colm Ó Baoill (ed.), *Mairghread nighean Lachlainn: Song-Maker of Mull* (Edinburgh: Scottish Gaelic Texts Society, 2009), p. 19.
5. See, for example, John Shaw (ed.), Lauchie MacLellan and Lisa Ornstein, *Brìgh an Òrain/A Story in Every Song: The Songs and Tales of Lauchie MacLellan* (Montreal: McGill-Queen's University Press, 2000).
6. For more recent developments, see Michael Newton, in this volume.
7. Ronald Black (ed.), *An Lasair: Anthology of 18th Century Scottish Gaelic Verse* (Edinburgh: Birlinn, 2001), p. xii.
8. Alexander Carmichael, *Carmina Gadelica*, vol. 1 (Edinburgh: Oliver and Boyd, 1928), p. xxii. See, also, Black, *An Lasair*, p. xl, n. 11.
9. Carmichael, *Carmina Gadelica*, pp. xxii–xxiv. For a contemporary account, see Maighread A. Challan, *Air Bilean an t-Sluaigh: Sealladh air Leantalachd*

Beul-Aithris Ghàidhlig Uibhist a Tuath (Belfast: Cló Ollscoil na Banríona, 2012), pp. 20–35.
10. Shaw, *Brìgh an Òrain*, p. 13, n. 8.
11. Challan, *Air Bilean an t-Sluaigh*, pp. 35–47, n. 14.
12. Ibid, pp. 47–54.
13. See Anja Gunderloch, *The Gaelic Manuscripts of Glasgow University Library: A Catalogue* (Glasgow: Department of Celtic, University of Glasgow, 2007), p. 16. See also Calum Mac Phàrlain, *Dorlach Laoidhean do sgrìobhadh le Donnchadh Mac Rath, 1688/A Handful of Lays written by Duncan Mac Rae, 1688* (Dun-de: Calum S. Mac Leoid, 1923).
14. John MacInnes, 'The Cultural Background to the Eighteenth-Century Collections of Gaelic Poetry', in *Papers Presented to Kenneth Jackson by some of his Pupils and Colleagues in June 1976* (1976), p. 243.
15. The most recent edition is Robert Kirk, *The Secret Commonwealth of Elves, Fauns and Fairies* (Mineola, NY: Dover Publications, 2008); see also Stewart Sanderson (ed.), Rev. Robert Kirk, *The Secret Common-Wealth* (Cambridge: The Folklore Society, 1974).
16. Donald E. Meek, 'The Pulpit and the Pen: Clergy, Orality and Print in the Scottish Gaelic World', in Adam Fox and Daniel Woolf (eds), *The Spoken Word: Oral Culture in Britain 1500–1850* (Manchester: Manchester University Press, 2002), p. 111.
17. J. L. Campbell and Derick Thomson (eds), *Edward Lhuyd in the Scottish Highlands 1699–1700* (Oxford: Clarendon Press, 1963).
18. Derick S. Thomson, 'The Gaelic Oral Tradition', *The Proceedings of the Scottish Anthropological and Folklore Society*, 5:1 (1954), p. 5.
19. See Rev. George Henderson, 'Lamh-Sgrìobhainnean Mhic-Neacail', *Transactions of the Gaelic Society of Inverness*, 27 (1908–11), pp. 340–409.
20. See Derick S. Thomson (ed.), *The MacDiarmid MS Anthology: Poems and Songs Mainly Anonymous from the Collection Dated 1770* (Edinburgh: Scottish Gaelic Texts Society, 1992).
21. See Derick S. Thomson, 'The McLagan MSS in Glasgow University Library: A Survey', *Transactions of the Gaelic Society of Inverness*, 58 (1993–4), pp. 406–24.
22. Ibid, pp. 409–12.
23. Gunderloch, *Gaelic Manuscripts*, pp. 18–19, n. xviii.
24. Derick Thomson suggests that Dr Maclean began collecting in 1738 and completed the manuscript in 1768: *An Introduction to Gaelic Poetry* (Edinburgh: Edinburgh University Press, 1990), p. 145.
25. Rev. Donald Maclean Sinclair, 'John Maclean: A Centenary', *The Dalhousie Review*, 28: 3 (1948), p. 264.
26. See Colm Ó Baoill, *Maclean Manuscripts in Nova Scotia: A Catalogue of the Gaelic Verse Collections MG15G/2/1 and MG15G/2/2 in the Public Archives of Nova Scotia* (Aberdeen: Aberdeen University Department of Celtic, 2001).

27. For a modern edition, see Rev. Patrick MacDonald, *The Patrick MacDonald Collection: Highland Vocal Airs, Country Dances or Reels of the North Highands and Western Isles (first published 1784)* (Breacais Ard, the Isle of Skye: Taigh na Teud).
28. Morag Macleod, 'Collectors of Gaelic Song', in John Beech, Owen Hand, Fiona MacDonald, Mark A Mulhern and Jeremy Weston (eds), *Scottish Life and Society, a Compendium of Scottish Ethnology: Oral Literature and Performance Culture* (Edinburgh: John Donald, 2007), p. 440.
29. See Peter Cooke, Morag Macleod and Colm Ó Baoill (eds), *The Elizabeth Ross Manuscript: Original Highland Airs Collected at Raasay in 1812 by Elizabeth Jane Ross* (Edinburgh: University of Edinburgh, School of Celtic and Scottish Studies, 2011).
30. Macleod, 'Collectors of Gaelic Song', p. 440; Rev. William Matheson, 'Some Early Collectors of Gaelic Folk-Song', *The Proceedings of the Scottish Anthropological and Folklore Society*, 5: 2 (1955), pp. 69–71.
31. Macleod, 'Collectors of Gaelic Song', p. 440; Matheson, 'Some Early Collectors', pp. 73–4.
32. Matheson, 'Some Early Collectors', p. 68.
33. Macleod, 'Collectors of Gaelic Song', p. 441, note xxxvii.
34. *Orain Ghaidhealach*, le Donnchadh Mac-an-t-saoir. Clódh-bhuailt' ann Dun-eidinn. Le A. MacDhónuil, air son an Ughdair (1768).
35. *Orain Ghaidhealach, agus Bheurla, air an eadar-theangacha* (Inverness, 1792).
36. *Orain Ghaidhealacha, le Ailein Dughallach, fear ciuil ann an Ionbhar Lochaidh. Maille ri Co'-chruinneachadh Oran is Dhan, le Ughdairibh eile* (Edinburgh, 1798). A significantly expanded collection of his poetry was published just after his death: Ailein Dùghalach, *Orain, Marbhrannan agus Duanagan Gaidhealach* (Inbhirnis, 1829).
37. Rev. Alexander Maclean Sinclair, 'The Gaelic Bards and the Collectors of their Works', *Transactions of the Gaelic Society of Inverness*, 24 (1899–1901), p. 272. For a catalogue of the collection, see Ó Baoill, n. xxxiv.
38. A collection first appeared in 1815, and was reprinted several times; see also Hector MacDougall (ed.), *Spiritual Songs by Rev. Peter Grant, Strathspey* (Glasgow: Alexander MacLaren and Sons, 1926).
39. The poet brought out a collection of his own hymns in 1835, although it is extremely rare: Iain Mac Gillean, *Laoidhean Spioradail le Iain Mac Gilleain; a rugadh ann an eilean Thireadh 'S tha 'n drast ann an America mu Thuath* (Glascho: Clodh-bhuailte le Bell agus Bain, agus r'an reic le M. Ogle agus a Mhac, 1835). His grandson, Alexander Maclean Sinclair, produced an edition in 1880, although it was heavily, indeed intrusively, edited: Alexander Maclean Sinclair (ed.), *Dain Spioradail, le Iain Mac-Gillean, maille ri beagan de Laoidhean Mhic Griogair, nach robh gus a so air an clo-bhualadh* (Edinburgh: MacLachlan and Stewart, 1880).

40. George Henderson (ed.), *Dàin Iain Ghobha/The Poems of John Morison* (Edinburgh: Knox Press, 1893–6).
41. Black, *An Lasair*, p. 602, n. xlvii.
42. Black, *An Lasair*, p. 604, n. xlvii.
43. Black, *An Lasair*, p. 606, n. xlvii.
44. Donald E. Meek (ed.), *Caran an t-Saoghail/The Wiles of the World: Anthology of 19th Century Scottish Gaelic Verse* (Edinburgh: Birlinn, 2003), pp. xviii–xix.
45. See Charles W. Dunn, *Highland Settler: A Portrait of the Scottish Gael in Nova Scotia* (Toronto: University of Toronto Press, 1980), pp. 81–2.
46. Frances Tolmie, 'One Hundred and Five Songs of Occupation from the Western Isles of Scotland', *Journal of the Folk-Song Society*, 4: 3 (1911), pp. 143–271, reprinted in 1997 by Llanerch Publishers.
47. Macleod, 'Collectors of Gaelic Song', pp. 441–2, note xxxvii.
48. William Lamb (ed.), *Keith Norman MacDonald's* Puirt-à-Beul, *the Vocal Dance Music of the Scottish Gaels* (Upper Breakish: Taigh na Teud, 2012), p. 31.
49. Lamb (ed.), *Keith Norman MacDonald's* Puirt-à-Beul, p. 31.
50. Lamb (ed.), *Keith Norman MacDonald's* Puirt-à-Beul, p. 33.
51. John Lorne Campbell (ed.) and Francis Collinson, *Hebridean Folksongs: A Collection of Waulking Songs, Made by Donald MacCormick in Kilphedir in South Uist in the year 1893* (Oxford: Clarendon, 1969), p. 26.
52. John MacInnes, 'Gaelic Panegyric Verse', in Beech et al., *Scottish Life and Society*, p. 82, n. xxxvii; the classic work on this is John MacInnes, 'The Panegyric Code in Gaelic Poetry and its Historical Background', *Transactions of the Gaelic Society of Inverness*, 50 (1978), pp. 435–98.
53. See Black, *An Lasair*, p. 100, n. 11.
54. See, generally, Fionnuala Carson Williams (2007), 'Proverbs in Scotland', in Beech et al, *Scottish Life and Society*, pp. 171–89, n. xxxvii.
55. Gaelic MSS LXII and LXV: Derick S. Thomson, 'Proverbs [. . .]', in Derick S. Thomson (ed.), *The Companion to Gaelic Scotland* (Oxford: Blackwell, 1983), p. 243.
56. Alexander MacBain and John Kennedy (eds), *Reliquiae Celticae II: Texts, Papers and Studies in Celtic Philology left by the Late Rev. Alexander Cameron, LL. D.* (Inverness: 'Northern Chronicle' Office, 1892–94).
57. Donald E. Meek, *The Campbell Collection of Gaelic Proverbs and Proverbial Sayings* (Inverness, 1978).
58. Black, *An Lasair*, p. 599, n. xlvii.
59. For accounts of his life and work, see, for example, Frank G. Thompson, 'John Francis Campbell', *Transactions of the Gaelic Society of Inverness* (1984–6), pp. 1–57; *Lamplighter and Story-Teller: John Francis Campbell of Islay 1821–1885* (Edinburgh: National Library of Scotland, 1985); John Shaw, 'The Collectors: John Francis Campbell and Alexander Carmichael',

in Susan Manning (ed.), *Edinburgh History of Scottish Literature*, vol. 2 (Edinburgh: Edinburgh University Press, 2007), pp. 347–52; and Richard Dorson, *The British Folklorists: A History* (London: Routledge and Kegan Paul, 1968), pp. 393–402.
60. Lord Archibald Campbell (ed.), *Waifs and Strays of Celtic Tradition, Argyllshire Series, Vol. I, Craignish Tales* (London: Alfred Nutt, 1889).
61. James MacDougall (ed.) (1891), *Waifs and Strays of Celtic Tradition, Argyllshire Series, Vol. III: Folk and Hero Tales* (London: Alfred Nutt, 1891).
62. For a selection from this collection, see Rev. George Calder (ed.), with Alan Bruford, *Highland Fairy Legends, Collected from Oral Tradition by Rev. James MacDougall* (Cambridge: D. S. Brewer, 1978).
63. See Roger Hutchinson, *Father Allan: The Life and Legacy of a Hebridean Priest* (Edinburgh: Birlinn, 2010).
64. One notebook, a collection of words, has been published: John Lorne Campbell (ed.), *Gaelic Words and Expressions from South Uist and Eriskay, collected by Fr Allan McDonald of Eriskay* (Oxford: Oxford University Press, 1958). Two notebooks are in the Carmichael-Watson Collection and Edinburgh University Library; two in Glasgow University Library. Ronald Black is understood to be editing these.
65. See Sylvia Robertson and Tony Dilworth (eds), *Tales from Highland Perthshire collected by Lady Evelyn Stewart Murray* (Llandysul: Scottish Gaelic Texts Society, 2009).
66. Donald E. Meek, 'Gaelic Printing and Publishing', in Bill Bell (ed.), *The Edinburgh History of the Book in Scotland, Vol. 3: Ambition and Industry, 1800–80* (Edinburgh: Edinburgh University Press, 2007), pp. 107–22.
67. His prose writings were anthologised in 1867: Norman MacLeod and A. Clerk (eds), *Caraid nan Gaidheal: A Choice Selection of the Gaelic Writings of the Late Norman MacLeod D. D. of St. Columba Parish Glasgow* (Edinburgh: John Donald, 1867).
68. See, for example, Sheila Kidd, 'Early Gaelic Periodicals: Knowledge Transfer and Impact', in Colm Ó Baoill and Nancy McGuire (eds), *Rannsachadh na Gàidhlig 6*, Proceedings of the Sixth Conference of Scottish Gaelic Studies (Aberdeen: University of Aberdeen Press), forthcoming.
69. Moray Watson, *An Introduction to Gaelic Fiction* (Edinburgh: Edinburgh University Press, 2011), pp. 14–20.
70. Watson, *An Introduction*, pp. 12–14.

7 – Dunnigan

1. A. M. Stewart (ed.), *The Complaynt of Scotland (c. 1550) by Mr Robert Wedderburn* (Edinburgh: Scottish Text Society, 1979), p. xxxiii.
2. Stewart (ed.), *The Complaynt of Scotland*, p. 50.
3. See, for example, Nicola Royan and Theo van Heijnsbergen (eds), *Literature,*

Letters and the Canonical in Early Modern Scotland (East Linton: Tuckwell Press, 2002).

4. There is not space here for a comprehensive listing of their scholarship but see, for example, Hamish Henderson's 'The Ballad and Popular Tradition to 1660', in Cairns Craig (ed.), *The History of Scottish Literature*, 4 vols (Aberdeen: Aberdeen University Press, 1988), vol. 1, ed. R. D. S. Jack, pp. 263–83; Edward J. Cowan, 'Calvinism and the Survival of Folk', in Cowan (ed.), *The People's Past* (Edinburgh: Polygon, 1980), pp. 30–53; Emily Lyle, *Fairies and Folk: Approaches to the Scottish Ballad Tradition* (Trier: VWT, 2008). See also Mary Ellen Brown, 'Balladry: A Vernacular Poetic Resource', in Ian Brown et al. (eds), *The Edinburgh History of Scottish Literature*, 3 vols (Edinburgh: Edinburgh University Press, 2007), vol. 1, pp. 263–72.

5. Cf. Adam Fox, *Oral and Literate Culture in England, 1500–1700* (Oxford: Clarendon Press, 2002) and Adam Fox and D. R. Woolf (eds), *Spoken Word: Oral Culture in Britain 1500–1850* (Manchester: Manchester University Press, 2004); Alison Shell, *Oral Culture and Catholicism in Early Modern England* (Cambridge: Cambridge University Press, 2007); Mary Ellen Lamb and Karen Bamford (eds), *Oral Traditions and Gender in Early Modern Literary Texts* (Aldershot: Ashgate, 2008).

6. But see Sarah Carpenter, 'Scottish Drama until 1650' and Michael Newton, 'Folk Drama in Gaelic Scotland', in Ian Brown (ed.), *The Edinburgh Companion to Scottish Drama* (Edinburgh: Edinburgh University Press, 2011), pp. 6–21 and 41–6; John J. McGavin, *Theatricality and Narrative in Medieval and Early Modern Scotland* (Aldershot: Ashgate, 2007).

7. Peter Burke, *Popular Culture in Early Modern Europe* (Aldershot: Scolar Press, 1994), pp. 72–3.

8. There are a few exceptions that date from earlier (i.e. sixteenth-century) manuscripts e.g. 'Sir Cawline' (Child 61); see Brown, 'Balladry', p. 269.

9. On the Bannatyne manuscript's social contexts and circulation, see Theo van Heijnsbergen, 'The Interaction between Literature and History in Queen Mary's Edinburgh: the Bannatyne Manuscript and its Prosopographical Context' in A. A. MacDonald, Michael Lynch and Ian B. Cowan (eds), *The Renaissance in Scotland: Studies in Literature, Religion, History, and Culture Offered to John Durkan* (Leiden: Brill, 1994), pp. 183–225; on the antiquarian recovery of the Bannatyne and other early modern manuscripts, see Brown, 'Balladry', p. 265.

10. Brown, 'Balladry', p. 265.

11. See W. Tod Ritchie (ed.), *The Bannatyne Manuscript Writtin in Tyme of Pest 1568*, 4 vols (Edinburgh: Blackwood, 1928), vols 2 and 3; Joan Hughes and W. S. Ramson (eds), *Poetry of the Stewart Court* (Canberra: Australian University Press), pp. 277–411.

12. See Allan H. MacLaine (ed.), *The Christis Kirk Tradition. Scots Poems of Folk*

Festivity (Glasgow: ASLS, 1996), pp. 155–7, for an account of the poem's problematic dating, provenance, printing history and authorship.
13. MacLaine, *Christis Kirk*, p. xiii.
14. Text taken from MacLaine, *Christis Kirk*, p. 10.
15. Joyce Crick (ed.), *Selected Tales* (Oxford: Oxford World's Classics, 2009), p. 317ff.
16. Priscilla Bawcutt (ed.), *The Shorter Poems of Gavin Douglas* [1967] (Edinburgh: The Scottish Text Society, 2003), p. 109, ll. 1711–19. It is interesting that this stanza is omitted from the London print (c. 1553).
17. In the notes to his TEAMS edition (http://www.lib.rochester.edu/camelot/teams/parkinso.htm), David Parkinson comments: 'Goll Mac Morna, leader of the Fianna Fiall, the bodyguard of the High King of Ireland; and Finn Mac Cumhal, who took the place of Goll (his father's slayer) at the head of the Fianna and became one of the great heroes of Ireland. The Gaelic-speaking districts of West and North Scotland retained familiarity with Irish traditions well into the nineteenth century'; see also Bawcutt (ed.), *The Shorter Poems*, pp. 205–6, for explication of some of these allusions.
18. Parkinson notes that 'Douglas may be referring to a localized version of one of the widespread folktales in which a wren plays a prominent part: nineteenth-century Scottish versions of "The Battle of the Birds and the Beasts" and "The King of the Birds"' have been recorded; the wren has an interesting folkloric heritage in both Scottish and Irish tradition.
19. Janet Hadley Williams (ed.), *Sir David Lyndsay. Selected Poems* (Glasgow: ASLS, 2000), p. 2, ll. 43–6. The prophecies of Thomas the Rhymer, popularly printed throughout the seventeenth and eighteenth centuries, were evidently long established in oral circulation; the tale of the 'Red Etin' is alluded to in the *Complaynt*, though the earliest textual versions appear in the nineteenth century; the 'Gyir Carling' refers to the Bannatyne poem about the mother-witch, again showing the tale's popular oral currency.
20. See Lizanne Henderson and Edward J. Cowan (eds), *Scottish Fairy Belief* (East Linton: Tuckwell Press, 2001), p. 152.
21. Keely Fisher, 'Eldritch Comic Verse in Older Scots', in Sally Mapstone (ed.), *Older Scots Literature* (Edinburgh: John Donald, 2005), pp. 292–313.
22. Significantly, these women are defined by age and status: older (as in 'carlingis') and married ('wyffiss'), characterising these topsy-turvy 'fairy stories' as licensed by, or associated with, the older, experienced female figures of a popular storytelling tradition.
23. John Purser, *Scotland's Music* (Edinburgh: Mainstream, 1992), p. 105; see also Helena Shire, *Song, Dance and Poetry of the Court of Scotland under King James VI* (Cambridge: Cambridge University Press, 1969).
24. See R. D. S. Jack, *Alexander Montgomerie* (Edinburgh: Scottish Academic Press, 1985), p. 47.
25. Mark C. Amodio, *Writing the Oral Tradition: Oral Poetics and Literate Culture*

in Medieval England (Notre Dame: University of Notre Dame Press, 2005), p. 7.
26. Cf. Jack, *Montgomerie*, p. 27. On the genre of Scots flyting see, for example, Sally Mapstone, 'Invective as Poetic: The Cultural Contexts of Polwarth and Montgomerie's Flyting', *Scottish Literary Journal*, 26: 2 (1999), pp. 18–40; Paul Robichaud, '"To Heir Quhat I Sould Wryt": The Flyting of Dunbar and Kennedy and Scots Oral Culture', *Scottish Literary Journal*, 25:2 (1998), pp. 9–16.
27. Amodio, *Writing the Oral Tradition*, p. 3.
28. David Parkinson (ed.), *Alexander Montgomerie. Poems*, 2 vols (Edinburgh Scottish Text Society, 2000), vol 1, pp. 143–4.
29. See Henderson and Cowan, *Scottish Fairy Belief*, Chap. 4.
30. Amodio, *Writing the Oral Tradition*, p. 14.
31. Henderson, 'The Ballad and Popular Tradition to 1660', p. 275; cf. James Reed, *The Border Ballads* (London: Athlone Press, 1973).
32. Child No. 169–A, F. J. Child, *The English and Scottish Popular Ballads* (London: Houghton Mifflin, 1882–98), vol. 3, p. 368; Child No. 169–C, 3.371. The Scots ballad was printed in Allan Ramsay's *Ever Green*, 'copied from a gentleman's mouth of the name of Armstrang, who is the 6th generation from this John' (p. 370).
33. Child No. 174, 3.400; 401.
34. See Edward D. Ives, *The Bonny Earl of Murray: The Man, the Murder, the Ballad* (East Linton: Tuckwell Press, 1997).
35. Child No. 181–A, 3.448; 181–B, 3.448. The printed versions are in Allan Ramsay's *Tea-Table Miscellany* (1763) and John Finlay's *Scottish Historical and Romantic Ballads* (1808).
36. Henderson, 'The Ballad and Popular Tradition to 1660', p. 277.
37. Extracted from David Moysie's *Memoirs* in Child, *Popular Ballads*, vol. 3, p. 449 (cf. Emily Lyle, *Scottish Ballads* (Edinburgh: Canongate, 1998), pp. 278–9).
38. Child, vol. 3 (discursive notes), p. 450, from the *History of the Church of Scotland* (1666).
39. Child No. 182–A, 3.452.
40. Child No. 181–D, 3.453.
41. Child No. 173–A, 3.384.
42. Child No. 173–B, 3.385; 173–A, 3.384; 173–E, 3.389.
43. Child No. 173–F, 3.390.
44. Child No. 173–C, 3.387.
45. Child, vol. 3 (discursive notes), p. 382.
46. Lyle, *Scottish Ballads*, p. 283.
47. Jonathan Barry in Tim Harris (ed.), *Popular Culture in England* (Basingstoke: Macmillan, 1995), p. 82.
48. Child, vol. 3 (discursive notes), p. 382.

49. Harris (ed.), *Popular Culture in England*, p. 5.
50. There is a vast critical literature on the Scottish Reformation but see, for example, Jane Dawson, *Scotland Re-formed 1488–1587* (Edinburgh: Edinburgh University Press, 2007), Chapter 10.
51. Cf. Lamb and Bamford (eds), *Oral Traditions and Gender*, p. 211.
52. For general context, see Patricia Fumerton, Anita Guerrini and Kris McCabe (eds), *Ballads and Broadsides in Britain 1500–1800* (Aldershot: Ashgate, 2010).
53. R. D. S. Jack and P. A. T. Rozendaal (eds), *The Mercat Anthology of Scottish Literature* (Edinburgh: Mercat Press, 1997), p. 201. See also *The Sempill Ballates* (Edinburgh: Thomas George Stevenson, 1872); James Cranston (ed.), *Satirical Poems of the Time of the Reformation*, 2 vols (Edinburgh: Blackwood, 1891–3).
54. Shire, *Song, Dance and Poetry*, p. 28.
55. Burke, *Popular Culture*, p. 227.
56. See Crawford Gribben and David George Mullan (eds), *Literature and the Scottish Reformation* (Farnham: Ashgate, 2009); cf. Margo Todd, *The Culture of Protestantism in Early Modern Scotland* (New Haven, CT: Yale University Press, 2002).
57. Burke, *Popular Culture*, p. 215.
58. Prologue quoted in Shire, *Song, Dance and Poetry*, p. 26.
59. Barry, in Harris (ed.), *Popular Culture in England*, pp. 69–94 (p. 70).
60. Burke, *Popular Culture*, p. 87.
61. Stewart (ed.), *The Complaynt of Scotland*, p. 53.

8 – Gunderloch

1. Neil Ross (ed. and trans.), *Heroic Poetry from the Book of the Dean of Lismore*, Scottish Gaelic Texts Society, vol. 2 (Edinburgh: Oliver and Boyd, 1939). John MacInnes, 'Twentieth-Century Recordings of Scottish Gaelic Heroic Ballads', in Bo Almqvist, Seán Ó Catháin and Pádraig Ó Héalaí (eds), *The Heroic Process – Form, Function and Fantasy in Folk Epic* (Dun Laoghaire: The Glendale Press, 1987), pp. 101–30.
2. John Francis Campbell (ed. and trans.), *Popular Tales of the West Highlands*, vol. 3, 2nd edn (Paisley/London: Alexander Gardener, 1892), pp. 46–102, 120–6, 136–60, 309–440; John Gregorson Campbell (ed. and trans.), *The Fians; Or Stories, Poems, and Traditions of Fionn and his Warrior Band* (London: David Nutt, 1891).
3. Irish texts that can be compared with the Scottish Gaelic evidence are plentiful in an extensive corpus of manuscripts that includes the important collection of the Royal Irish Academy in Dublin; see Elizabeth FitzPatrick and Siobhán Fitzpatrick [1988], *The Catalogue of Irish Manuscripts in the Royal Irish Academy: A Brief Introduction* (Dublin: Royal Irish Academy, rev. 2003).

4. Donald E. Meek, 'The Gaelic Ballads of Medieval Scotland', *Transactions of the Gaelic Society of Inverness*, 55 (1986–8), p. 49.
5. Eleanor Knott, *Irish Syllabic Poetry 1200–1600*, 2nd edn (Cork: Cork University Press, 1935), pp. 1–20.
6. Knott, *Irish Syllabic Poetry*, pp. 13–20.
7. Much of the manuscript material from the eighteenth century onwards has been taken down from such contemporary reciters and is now held by repositories such as the National Library of Scotland, Edinburgh University Library and Glasgow University Library.
8. For early texts, see Kuno Meyer, *Fianaigecht*, Royal Irish Academy, Todd Lecture Series vol. XVI (Dublin: Hodges, Figgis and Co., 1910). See also S. Arbuthnot and G. Parsons (eds), *The Gaelic Finn Tradition* (Dublin: Four Courts Press, 2012).
9. Oisín and Caílte in Middle Irish spelling. J. E. Caerwyn Williams and Patrick K. Ford, *The Irish Literary Tradition* (Cardiff: University of Wales Press, 1992), pp. 126–8.
10. Ann Dooley and Harry Roe (trans.), *Tales of the Elders of Ireland: Acallam na Senórach* (Oxford: Oxford University Press, 1999), pp. xxii–xxviii.
11. Alexander Cameron, *Reliquiae Celticae*, vol. 1 (Inverness: Northern Chronicle Office, 1892), p. 266. My translation.
12. John MacInnes, 'The Panegyric Code in Gaelic Poetry and its Historical Background', *Transactions of the Gaelic Society of Inverness*, 50 (1976–8), pp. 435–98.
13. Derick S. Thomson, *The Gaelic Sources of Macpherson's 'Ossian'* (Edinburgh/London: Oliver and Boyd, 1952), pp. 9–12.
14. J. E. Caerwyn Williams and Patrick K. Ford, *The Irish Literary Tradition* (Cardiff: University of Wales Press, 1992), pp. 94–6.
15. Donald E. Meek, 'The Gaelic Ballads of Scotland: Creativity and Adaptation', in Hugh Gaskill (ed.), *Ossian Revisited* (Edinburgh: Edinburgh University Press, 1991), pp. 19–48 (pp. 34–5).
16. Derick S. Thomson (ed. and trans.), *The MacDiarmid MS Anthology: Poems and Songs Mainly Anonymous from the Collection Dated 1770* (Edinburgh: Scottish Academic Press, 1992), pp. 169, 171.
17. John Gillies (ed.), *Sean dain agus orain Ghaidhealach* (Perth, 1786), p. 165.
18. Thomson, *Gaelic Sources*, pp. 42–3, 58.
19. Fiona Stafford, *The Sublime Savage: James Macpherson and the Poems of Ossian* (Edinburgh: Edinburgh University Press, 1988), pp. 113–25.
20. Ross, *Heroic Poetry*. William J. Watson (ed. and trans.), *Scottish Verse from the Book of the Dean of Lismore*, Scottish Gaelic Texts Society, vol. 1 (Edinburgh: Oliver and Boyd, 1937).
21. The Book of the Dean of Lismore (NLS Adv. MS 72. 1. 37) has been digitised and is available on http:www.isos.dias.ie/english/index.html [consulted 5 Feb. 2013].

22. Donald E. Meek, 'The Scots-Gaelic Scribes of Late Medieval Perthshire: An Overview of the Orthography and Contents of the Book of the Dean of Lismore', in J. Derrick McClure and Michael R. G. Spiller (eds), *Bryght Lanternis* (Aberdeen: Aberdeen University Press, 1989), pp. 387–404.
23. Meek, 'Scots-Gaelic Scribes', pp. 397–9.
24. John Francis Campbell, *Leabhar na Féinne* (London: Spottiswoode and Co., 1972), pp. xv, 218–24.
25. Derick S. Thomson, 'The McLagan MSS in Glasgow University Library: A Survey', *Transactions of the Gaelic Society of Inverness*, 58 (1992–4), pp. 406–24 (p. 407).
26. Stana Nenadic, *Lairds and Luxury: The Highland Gentry in Eighteenth-Century Scotland* (Edinburgh: John Donald, 2007), pp. 45–64, 186–8.
27. Thomson, 'McLagan MSS', pp. 407–8.
28. Glasgow University Library MS Gen 1042.
29. Thomson, 'McLagan MSS', p. 423.
30. Cameron, *Reliquiae Celticae*, vol. 1, pp. 295–370. Thomson, *Gaelic Sources*, pp. 91–100.
31. Thomson, 'McLagan MSS', p. 409. John Gillies (ed.), *Sean dain agus orain Ghaidhealach* (Perth, 1786).
32. Campbell, *Leabhar na Féinne*, p. xxxii.
33. Francis Thompson, 'John Francis Campbell', *Transactions of the Gaelic Society of Inverness*, 54 (1984–6), pp. 1–57 (33–9, 55–7).
34. NLS Adv. MS. 50. 1. 12, ff. 118–20.
35. Carmichael-Watson Collection, Edinburgh University Library, C.-W. 340.
36. Thompson, 'John Francis Campbell', pp. 53–4.
37. http://www.carmichaelwatson.lib.ed.ac.uk/cwatson/ [consulted 27 July 2011].
38. MacInnes, 'Twentieth-Century Recordings'.
39. The motifs present in the story are A515. 5. *'Culture hero fights with son without recognising him' and N731. 2. 'Father-son combat'. Tom Peete Cross, *Motif-index of Early Irish Literature* (Bloomington: Indiana University Publications 1952), pp. 16, 411.
40. 'Aided Óenfhir Aífe', 'The Death of Aífe's Only Son' in Jeffrey Gantz, *Early Irish Myths and Sagas* (London: Penguin Books Ltd, 1981), pp. 147–52.
41. Ross, *Heroic Poetry*, pp. 168–75. Wilson McLeod and Meg Bateman (eds and trans.), *Duanaire na Sracaire – Songbook of the Pillagers: Anthology of Scotland's Gaelic Verse to 1600* (Edinburgh: Birlinn, 2007), pp. 180–1.
42. William J. Watson (ed. and trans.), *Scottish Verse from the Book of the Dean of Lismore* (Edinburgh: Scottish Gaelic Texts Society, 1937), pp. 82–9.
43. Watson, *Scottish Verse*, pp. 277–8.
44. Linda Gowans, *Am Bròn Binn – An Arthurian Ballad in Scottish Gaelic* (Eastbourne, 1992), pp. 1–2.

45. Gowans, *Am Bròn Binn*, pp. 19–29.
46. Ross, *Heroic Poetry*, pp. 32–3.
47. Tom Peete Cross, 'The Gaelic "Ballad of the Mantle"', *Modern Philology*, XVI (1918–19), pp. 653–7.
48. Gillies, *Sean dain*, pp. 162–3. My translation.
49. Gillies, *Sean dain*, p. 285. My translation.
50. Gillies, *Sean dain*, p. 109. My translation.
51. Donald Archie MacDonald: 'A Visual Memory', in *Scottish Studies*, 22 (1978), pp. 1–26. For visualisation of poetry, see Dòmhnall Iain MacDhòmhnaill, *Chì Mi*, ed. Bill Innes (Edinburgh: Birlinn, 1998), p. xvii.
52. From McLagan manuscript 113, printed in Cameron, *Reliquiae Celticae*, pp. 345–6. My translation.
53. Correcting the printer's error 'cheann'.
54. Cameron, *Reliquiae Celticae*, p. 352.
55. Cameron, *Reliquiae Celticae*, p. 346. My translation.
56. Cameron, *Reliquiae Celticae*, p. 351. My translation.
57. Gillies, *Sean dain*, p. 111. My translation.
58. Donald E. Meek, '*Táin Bó Fraích* and Other "Fráech" Texts: A Study in Thematic Relationships', *Cambridge Medieval Celtic Studies*, 7 (1984), pp. 6, 13–15.
59. Thomas Pennant, *A Tour in Scotland 1769* (Edinburgh: Birlinn, 2000), pp. 144–5.
60. Gillies, *Sean dain*, p. 107.
61. Campbell, *Leabhar na Féinne*, pp. 32–3.
62. Campbell, *Leabhar na Féinne*, p. 33.
63. William Matheson, 'Laoidh Fhraoich', *Tocher*, 35 (1981), pp. 292–7.

9 – Bold

1. See Charles G. Zug III, 'The Ballad Editor as Antiquary: Scott and the *Minstrelsy*', *Journal of the Folklore Institute*, 13: 1 (1976), pp. 57–73 and, for Scott's impact on the conceptual development of another antiquarian pursuit, archaeology, see Shawn Malley, 'Walter Scott's Romantic Archaeology: New/Old Abbotsford and "The Antiquary"', *Studies in Romanticism*, 40: 3 (Summer 2001), pp. 233–51.
2. See, for instance, George Chalmers, *Caledonia*, 3 vols (Edinburgh: Caddell and Davies, 1807–24) and John Jamieson *The Etymological Dictionary of the Scottish Language*, 2 vols (Edinburgh: Creech, Constable and Blackwood, 1808).
3. See Richard Dorson, *The British Folklorists: A History* (Chicago: University of Chicago Press, 1968), Chap. 1 'The Antiquaries'.
4. Qtd Ronald C. Gant, 'David Steuart Erskine, 11th Earl of Buchan: Founder of the Society of Antiquaries of Scotland', in A. S. Bell (ed.), *The Scottish*

Antiquarian Tradition. Essays to Mark the Bicentenary of the Society of Antiquaries of Scotland and its Museum, 1780–1980 (Edinburgh: John Donald, 1981), p. 9.
5. See R. A. Gardiner, 'William Roy, Surveyor and Antiquary', *The Geographical Journal*, 143: 3 (November 1977), pp. 439–50.
6. Rosemary Sweet, *Antiquaries. The Discovery of the Past in Eighteenth-Century Britain* (London: Cambridge University Press, 2004), p. 69.
7. See Sigrid Rieuwerts (ed.), 'The Ballad Repertoire of Anna Gordon, Mrs Brown of Falkland'. *The Scottish Text Society Fifth Series*, 8 (Woodbridge: Boydell and Brewer, 2011).
8. *Society of Antiquaries of London*: http://www.sal.org.uk
9. See, for instance, Robert Crawford, *Devolving English Literature* (Oxford: Clarendon Press, 1992).
10. See Leah Dennis, 'Thomas Percy: Antiquarian vs. Man of Taste', *PMLA*, 57: 1 (March 1942), pp. 140–54.
11. See for instance, Bell, *The Scottish Antiquarian Tradition*. See also H. S. V. Jones, 'Joseph Ritson: A Romantic Antiquarian', *The Sewanee Review*, 22: 3 (July 1914), pp. 341–50.
12. See Thomas Pennant, *The Literary Life of Thomas Pennant Esq. by Himself* (London, 1793) and Ralph E. Jenkins, '"And I Travelled After Him": Johnson and Pennant in Scotland', *Texas Studies in Literature and Language*, 14: 3 (Fall 1972), pp. 445–62; *Boswell's Journal of a Tour to the Hebrides with Samuel Johnson LLD*, ed. F. A. Pottle and C. H. Bennett (London: Heinemann, 1936).
13. Earle qtd Sweet, *Antiquaries*, p. xiii; see too Rosemary Sweet, 'Antiquaries and Antiquities in Eighteenth-Century England', *American Society for Eighteenth Century Studies*, 34: 2 (Winter 2001), pp. 181–206.
14. See Yoo Sun Lee, 'A Divided Inheritance: Scott's Antiquarian Novel and the British Nation', *ELH*, 64: 2 (Summer 1997), pp. 537–67.
15. Sweet, *Antiquaries*, p. xiv.
16. Lee, 'A Divided Inheritance', p. 539.
17. *Dictionary of National Biography* (London: Smith, Elder, 1885–1900).
18. See Domhnall Uilleam Stiùbhart, 'Martin Martin', *Oxford Dictionary of National Biography*, www.oxforddnb.com
19. Glasgow University Library Special Collection.
20. See Thomas A. McKean, 'The Fieldwork Legacy of James Macpherson', *Journal of American Folklore*, 114: 454 (Autumn 2001), pp. 447–63 and, on the Gaelic sources, Derick Thomson, *The Gaelic Sources of Macpherson's "Ossian"* (Edinburgh: Oliver and Boyd, 1952).
21. Amy Gazin-Schwartz, 'Imaging the Scottish Highlands', *Historical Archaeology*, 41: 1 (2007), p. 76.
22. David Herd, 'Preface', in *Ancient and Modern Songs, Heroic Ballads, etc.*, reprinted in 2 vols (Glasgow: Kerr and Richardson, 1869), pp. v–vii.

23. See James Johnson, *The Scots Musical Museum, 1787–1803*, ed. Donald A. Low (Aldershot: Scolar, 1991).
24. See Robert Burns, *The Merry Muses of Caledonia*, ed. Valentina Bold et al. (Edinburgh: Canongate, 2009).
25. See Valentina Bold, '"The Apple at the Glass": Halloween and Scottish Poetry', in H. O'Donnell and M. Foley (eds), *Treat or Trick: Halloween in a Globalising World* (Newcastle-upon-Tyne: Cambridge Scholars, 2009), pp. 56–66; and Burns, *The Poems of Robert Burns*, ed. James Kinsley (Oxford: Clarendon, 1968), poems 73, 562 and 512.
26. See Charles J. Withers, 'The Social Nature of Map Making in the Scottish Enlightenment c. 1682–c. 1832', *Imago Mundi*, 54 (2002), pp. 46–66; Dorson, *The British Folklorists*, p. 26.
27. Burns, *Poems*, poems 275, 321.
28. See Bell, *The Scottish Antiquarian Tradition*.
29. Gant in Bell, *The Scottish Antiquarian Tradition*, pp. 1–30; Walter Scott *The Journal of Walter Scott*, ed. W. K. Anderson (Oxford: Clarendon, 1972), p. 550.
30. Appendix 1, 'The Society's charter, read to a meeting of the Society of Antiquaries of Scotland, 6 May 1783, translated from the Latin', qtd Bell, *The Scottish Antiquarian Tradition*, pp. 273–6.
31. See Ian Stewart, 'Two Centuries of Scottish Numismatics', in Bell, *The Scottish Antiquarian Tradition*, pp. 227–65.
32. See R. B. K. Stevenson, 'The Museum, its Beginnings and its Development. Part I: to 1858: the Society's Own Museum', in Bell, *The Scottish Antiquarian Tradition*, p. 39.
33. See Stevenson, 'The Museum', pp. 31–85; http://www.gla.ac.uk/hunterian/; http://www.abdn.ac.uk/about/marischal-museum.php; http://www.museum.rcsed.ac.uk/content/content.aspx

10 – Campbell and McCue

1. See Katherine Campbell, 'Scots Song Collectors', in John Beech et al. (eds), *Scottish Life and Society: Oral Literature and Performance Culture* (A Compendium of Scottish Ethnology, vol. 10) (Edinburgh: John Donald, in association with the European Ethnological Research Centre, 2007), pp. 427–39. Also Karen McAulay, 'Our Ancient National Airs: Scottish Song Collecting c. 1760–1888', PhD thesis, University of Glasgow (2009). Also Clare Nelson, 'Tea-table Miscellanies: Song Culture in Late Eighteenth-Century Scotland', *Early Music*, 28: 4 (2000), pp. 596–618. For the connections with Scotland and Germany, see Kirsteen McCue, 'Scottish Song, Lyric Poetry and the Romantic Composer', in Murray Pittock (ed.), *The Edinburgh Companion to Scottish Romanticism* (Edinburgh: Edinburgh University Press, 2011), pp. 39–48.

2. See E. J. Cowan and M. Paterson, *Folk in Print: Scotland's Chapbook Heritage, 1750–1850* (Edinburgh: John Donald, 2007). Also C. M. Simpson, *The British Broadside Ballad and its Music* (New Brunswick, NJ: Rutgers University Press, 1966).
3. See T. Crawford, *Society and the Lyric: A Study of the Song Culture of Eighteenth-Century Scotland* (Edinburgh: Scottish Academic Press, 1979), p. 8 and pp. 216–19. See also Thomas Crawford (ed.), *Love, Labour and Liberty: The Eighteenth-Century Scottish Lyric* (Cheadle: Carcanet Press, 1976).
4. Crawford, *Society and the Lyric*, p. 7.
5. James Hogg, *The Forest Minstrel*, ed. Peter D. Garside and Richard D. Jackson (Edinburgh: Edinburgh University Press, 2006), p. xxvii.
6. The complexities of the bibliographies of both Ramsay texts are accounted for in Burns Martin's *Bibliography of Allan Ramsay* (Glasgow: Jackson, Wylie and Co., 1931). The *Miscellany* thereafter typically appeared in either two or four volumes.
7. Clear comparisons can be made here with John Gay's *The Beggar's Opera*, which first appeared in print in 1728 and also included a number of popular tunes with new sets of lyrics, some of them Scottish.
8. See Steve Newman, 'The Scots Songs of Allan Ramsay: "Lyrick" Transformation, Popular Culture and the Boundaries of the Scottish Enlightenment', *Modern Language Quarterly*, 63: 3 (September 2002), pp. 277–314.
9. See J. C. Dick (ed.), *The Songs of Robert Burns* (Philadelphia: Henry Frowde, 1903/1908), pp. 354–5.
10. See online digital version on Early English books online: tract supplement, A5:2 [326]. The Bodleian Library Broadside Ballads electronic resource lists three versions of the ballad with the date-range 1672 to 1696, one of which forms Nanny's answer to 'The Scotch Wooing'. See http://www.bodley.ox.ac.uk/ballads/ballads (accessed February 2011).
11. See D. Daiches (ed.), *Robert Burns's Commonplace Book 1783–1785* (Fontwell: Centaur Press, 1965), p. 11. See J. Kinsley (ed.), *The Poems and Songs of Robert Burns* (Oxford: Clarendon, 1968), vol. III, pp. 1006–8.
12. There is an inconsistency in the spelling of Nannie/Nanie in the original text from the *Commonplace Book*.
13. See David Herd, *Ancient and Modern Scottish Songs*, 2 vols (Edinburgh: J. Wotherspoon, 1776). Ramsay's 'Nanny O' is found in vol. 1, pp. 264–5; and Hans Hecht (ed.), *Songs from David Herd's Manuscripts* (Edinburgh: William J. Hay, 1973).
14. See Hecht, *Songs from David Herd's Manuscripts*, pp. 247–8 (notes, p. 328).
15. See G. Ross Roy (ed.), *The Letters of Robert Burns*, 2nd edn, 2 vols (Oxford: Clarendon Press, 1985), vol. 2, letter 511, pp. 153–4, Burns to Thomson, October 1792.

16. One small music collection was produced, but without Ramsay's texts: see 'Music for Allan Ramsay's Collection of Seventy-One Scots Songs in the Tea-Table Miscellany. The Six Parts Complete [...]', set by Alexr Stuart and engraved by Robert Cooper (Edinburgh, printed and sold by Allan Ramsay, c. 1726).
17. See Roger Fiske, *Scotland in Music: A European Enthusiasm* (Cambridge: Cambridge University Press, 1982).
18. See William Stenhouse, *Illustrations of the Lyric Poetry and Music of Scotland* (Edinburgh: William Blackwood, 1853); John Glen, *Early Scottish Melodies* (Edinburgh: J. and R. Glen, 1900).
19. See John Purser, '"The Wee Apollo": Burns and Oswald', in Kenneth Simpson (ed.), *Love & Liberty: Robert Burns A Bicentenary Celebration* (East Linton: Tuckwell Press, 1997), pp. 326–33. Also John Purser and Nick Parkes (eds), *The Caledonian Pocket Companion by James Oswald*, vol. 1 (books 1–6), vol. 2 (books 7–12), available on two CD ROMs (self-published, 2006–7).
20. For scholarly discussion of Burns's songs, including text and tunes, see Dick (1903), Kinsley (1968), Donald. A. Low (ed.), *The Songs of Robert Burns* (Aldershot: Routledge, 1993) and Ericson-Roos, 'The Songs of Robert Burns: A Study of the Unity of Poetry and Music', Doctoral Dissertation from the University of Uppsala (1977). For Burns's bawdy songs, see *The Merry Muses*, ed. Valentina Bold (Edinburgh: Birlinn, 2009) after James Barke and Sydney Goodsir Smith (1968).
21. See Kirsteen McCue, 'Burns's Songs and Poetic Craft', in Gerard Carruthers (ed.), *The Edinburgh Companion to Robert Burns* (Edinburgh: Edinburgh University Press, 2009), pp. 74–85; Katherine Campbell and Emily Lyle, 'The Perfect Fusion of Words and Music: The Achievement of Robert Burns', in Kenneth Elliott et al. (eds), *Musica Scotica 800 Years of Scottish Music: Proceedings from the 2005 and 2006 Conferences* (Glasgow: Musica Scotica Trust, 2008), pp. 19–28; H. T. Kirby-Smith, *The Celestial Twins: Poetry and Music through the Ages* (Amherst: University of Massachusetts Press, 1999) and C. Ericson-Roos, 'The Songs of Robert Burns'.
22. See Mary Ellen Brown, *Burns and Tradition* (London: Macmillan, 1984).
23. See Roy, *Letters* (letter 586), vol. 2, p. 242.
24. See David McGuinness, 'Tune Accompaniments in Eighteenth-Century Scottish Music Publications', in Gordon Munro et al. (eds), *Notis Musycall: Essays on Music and Scottish Culture in Honour of Kenneth Elliott* (Glasgow: Musica Scotica Trust, 2005), pp. 221–9.
25. See Hamish Mathison, 'Robert Burns and National Song', in David Duff and Catherine Jones (eds), *Scotland, Ireland and the Romantic Aesthetic* (Lewisburg, PA: Bucknell University Press, 2007), pp. 77–92.
26. Stenhouse, *Lyric Poetry*, p. 201. See also John Purser, 'The Wee Apollo'.
27. See Kirsteen McCue, '"An Individual Flowering on a Common Stem":

Melody, Performance, and National Song', in Philip Connell and Nigel Leask (eds), *Romanticism and Popular Culture in Britain and Ireland* (Cambridge: Cambridge University Press, 2009), pp. 91–2. 'Of a' the Airts' is from Dick, *The Songs of Robert Burns*, p. 70.
28. David Johnson, *Scottish Fiddle Music in the Eighteenth Century*, 2nd edn (Edinburgh: Mercat Press, 1997), p. 3.
29. See Francis Collinson's entry for 'Strathspey', in *The New Grove Dictionary of Music*, ed. Stanley Sadie (London: Macmillan, 1980), vol. 18, p. 202.
30. David M. Bertie (ed.), *John Skinner: Collected Poems* (Peterhead: The Buchan Field Club, 2005), p. 6.
31. Roy, *Letters* (letter 147), vol. 1, p. 167; 'Tullochgorum' is from the *Scots Musical Museum*, no. 289.
32. Bertie, *John Skinner*, p. 13.
33. H. Poole, 'Masonic Song and Verse of the Eighteenth Century', *Ars Quatuor Coronatorum*, XL (1928), pp. 7–29. This quotation, p. 26.
34. See Matthew Gelbart, *The Invention of 'Folk Music' and 'Art Music'* (Cambridge: Cambridge University Press, 2007). Also McCue, 'An Individual Flowering on a Common Stem', pp. 94–6.
35. See James Hogg, *Songs by the Ettrick Shepherd* (Edinburgh: William Blackwood, 1831), pp. 1–5.
36. See Jane Millgate, 'Unclaimed Territory: The Ballad of "Auld Robin Gray" and the Assertion of Authorial Ownership', *The Library*, 8: 4 (December 2007), pp. 423–41.
37. This appeared around 1790 in a *Collection of Strathspeys, Reels, Jigs &c. for the Piano Forte, Violin & Violoncello* by Donald Grant of Elgin (p. 26).
38. Patrick Shuldham-Shaw, Emily B. Lyle et al. (eds), *The Greig–Duncan Folk Song Collection*, vols 1–8 (Edinburgh: The Mercat Press for the University of Aberdeen in association with the School of Scottish Studies, University of Edinburgh, 1981–2002).
39. The first two parts of the tune, which is in four parts, are given here.

11 – Gilbert

1. David Buchan (ed.), *Scottish Tradition: A Collection of Folk Literature* (London, Boston, Melbourne and Henley: Routledge and Kegan Paul), p. 4.
2. An Old Farmer, 'Mode of Living among Scottish Farmers during the Early Part of Last Century' [signed Selkirkshire, June 25, 1818], *Scottish Journal of Topography, Antiquities, Traditions*, 2 (1848), p. 30.
3. Janet Hamilton, *Poems, Sketches, and Essays* (Glasgow: new edn, 1885), p. 362.
4. Duncan Anderson, *Scottish Folk-Lore* (New York, 1895), pp. 90–3.
5. Anderson, *Scottish Folk-Lore*, pp. 90–3.

6. William Motherwell, *Minstrelsy: Ancient and Modern* (Glasgow: John Wylie, 1827), p. 156.
7. James Hogg, *Anecdotes of Scott*, ed. Jill Rubenstein (Edinburgh: Edinburgh University Press, 1999), p. 38.
8. J. E. H. Thomson, 'Memoir of the Ettrick Shepherd', in James Hogg, *Domestic Manners* (Stirling: Eneas Mackay, 1909), pp. 13–14.
9. Elaine E. Petrie, 'James Hogg: A Study in the Transition from Folk Tradition to Literature' (unpublished doctoral thesis, University of Stirling, 1980), pp. 45–6, 36.
10. David Buchan, *The Ballad and the Folk* (London and Boston: Routledge and Kegan Paul, 1972), p. 223.
11. See Mary Ellen Brown, 'Appendix I: Informants and Items', in *William Motherwell's Cultural Politics* (Lexington: The University Press of Kentucky, 2001), pp. 163–70.
12. T. M. Devine, *The Scottish Nation, 1700–2000* (London: Penguin Books, 2000), p. 134.
13. Buchan, *The Ballad and the Folk*, p. 184.
14. Buchan, *The Ballad and the Folk*, p. 201.
15. James Hogg, 'On the Changes in the Habits, Amusements, and Condition of the Scottish Peasantry', *Quarterly Journal of Agriculture*, 3 (1831–2), pp. 256–7, in Judy Steel (ed.), *A Shepherd's Delight: A James Hogg Anthology* (Edinburgh: Canongate, 1985), p. 41.
16. Walter Scott, *Minstrelsy of the Scottish Border* [1802–3, 1820], ed. T. F. Henderson, 4 vols (Edinburgh and London: William Blackwood and Sons; New York: Charles Scribner's Sons, 1902), vol. 1, p. 215.
17. Walter Scott, 'Memoir of His Early Years, Written by Himself' [Ashestiel, 26 April 1808], in J. G. Lockhart, *The Life of Sir Walter Scott, Bart*, New Popular Edition (London, 1893), p. 1.
18. Scott, *Minstrelsy*, vol. 2, p. 8.
19. Florence MacCann, *Sir Walter Scott's Friends* (Edinburgh: Blackwood, 1909), p. 106.
20. Scott was also getting texts second-hand. W. E. Wilson observes that 'practically all the ballads [Scott] "collected" in Liddesdale were given to him in manuscript by Dr. Elliot of Cleugh-head who thus became one of the first of many ballad-collectors who made their collections available' to Scott (quoted in W. F. H. Nicolaisen, 'Scott and the Folk Tradition', in Alan Bold (ed.), *Sir Walter Scott: The Long-Forgotten Melody* (Totowa, NJ: Vision and Barnes and Noble, 1983), p. 130.
21. Scott, *Minstrelsy*, vol. 1, pp. 164, 166.
22. James Reed, *The Border Ballads* (University of London: Athlone, 1973), p. 6.
23. Nicolaisen, 'Scott and the Folk Tradition', p. 128.
24. Irving recounts Scott's remarks on Scottish song in *Abbotsford and Newstead*

Abbey, quoted here from Charles Zug III, 'The Ballad and History: The Case for Scott', *Folklore*, 89 (1978), p. 229.
25. Review of *Reliques of Robert Burns, consisting chiefly of original Letters, Poems, and Critical Observations on Scottish Songs*, *Quarterly Review*, 1 (1809), p. 30.
26. Scott, *Minstrelsy*, vol. 1, p. 12.
27. Scott, *Minstrelsy*, vol. 1, pp. 9–10.
28. Scott, *Minstrelsy*, vol. 1, p. 7.
29. Scott, *Minstrelsy*, vol. 1, p. 7.
30. Hogg, 'On the Changes in the Habits, Amusements, and Condition of the Scottish Peasantry', p. 42.
31. James Hogg, *The Mountain Bard*, ed. Suzanne Gilbert (Edinburgh: Edinburgh University Press, 2007), pp. 249–50.
32. Motherwell, *Minstrelsy: Ancient and Modern*, p. 328.
33. Motherwell, *Minstrelsy: Ancient and Modern*, p. 230.
34. Brown, *William Motherwell's Cultural Politics*, p. 87.
35. Motherwell, *Minstrelsy: Ancient and Modern*, p. 193.
36. Motherwell, *Minstrelsy: Ancient and Modern*, p. iv.
37. Motherwell, *Minstrelsy: Ancient and Modern*, pp. xii–xiii.
38. Motherwell, *Minstrelsy: Ancient and Modern*, p. 217.
39. Motherwell, *Minstrelsy: Ancient and Modern*, p. xix.
40. Allan Cunningham, *Traditional Tales of the English and Scottish Peasantry* [1822], ed. Tim Killick (Glasgow: ASLS, 2012), p. xvi.
41. Robert Chambers, *Popular Rhymes of Scotland*, 3rd edn (London and Edinburgh: W. and R. Chambers, 1870), p. vi.
42. Brian Alderson, 'The Spoken and the Read: *German Popular Stories* and English Popular Diction', in Donald Haase (ed.), *The Reception of Grimms' Fairy Tales: Responses, Reactions, Revisions* (Detroit: Wayne State University Press, 1996), p. 71.
43. Chambers, *Popular Rhymes of Scotland*, p. 49.
44. Chambers, *Popular Rhymes of Scotland*, p. 8.
45. Thomas Carlyle, 'Sir Walter Scott', in *The Works of Thomas Carlyle*, ed. Henry Duff Traill (New York: Cambridge University Press, 2010), p. 50.

12 – Harris

1. Ronald Black (ed.), *The Gaelic Otherworld: John Gregorson Campbell's Superstition of the Highlands & Islands of Scotland and Witchcraft & Second Sight in the Highlands & Islands* (Edinburgh: Birlinn, 2005), pp. 278–9.
2. Eric J. Montenyohl, 'Andrew Lang's Contributions to English Folk Narrative Scholarship: A Reevaluation', *Western Folklore*, 47: 4 (1988), p. 270.
3. Malcolm Chapman, *The Gaelic Vision in Scottish Culture* (London: McGill-Queen's University Press, 1978), p. 114.

4. Richard Dorson, *The British Folklorists* (Chicago: Chicago University Press, 1968), p. 406, and Deborah Davis, 'Contexts of Ambivalence: The Folkloristic Activities of Nineteenth-Century Scottish Highland Ministers,' *Folklore*, 103: ii (1992), pp. 212, 214–16.
5. Alexander Carmichael, *Carmina Gadelica, Charms of the Gaels Hymns and Incantations: With Illustrative Notes on Words, Rites and Customs, Dying and Obsolete; Orally Collected in the Highlands and Islands of Scotland* [1900], ed. C. J. Moore, preface by John MacInnes (Edinburgh: Floris, 2006), pp. 24, 25, 24.
6. All citations are from J. F. Campbell, *Popular Tales of the West Highlands* [1860–1], 2 vols (Edinburgh: Birlinn, 1994), vol. 1.
7. Walter Gregor, *Notes on the Folk-Lore of the North-East of Scotland* [1881] (Nendeln: Kraus, 1967), pp. 2–3.
8. J. F. Campbell, *Popular Tales*, p. 17.
9. Carmichael, *Carmina Gadelica*, p. 31.
10. Anne MacVicar Grant, *Essays on the Superstitions of the Highlanders of Scotland*, 2 vols (London: Norwood, 1811), vol. 1, p. 134.
11. Grant, *Essays*, p. 255.
12. James Napier, *Superstitious Beliefs in the West of Scotland, Within this Century* (Paisley, 1879), p. 75.
13. Napier, *Superstitious Beliefs*, pp. 77–8.
14. Napier, *Superstitious Beliefs*, p. 182.
15. John Mackay (ed.), 'The Late Reverend Alexander Stewart, LL. D. "Nether Lochaber"', in *The Celtic Monthly: A Magazine for Highlanders* (1901), p. 81.
16. Mackay, 'The Late Reverend', p. 81.
17. Alexander Stewart, *Twixt Ben Nevis and Glencoe: The Natural History, Legends, and Folk-Lore of the West Highlands* [1833] (Whitefish: Kessinger, 2006), p. 217.
18. Stewart, *Twixt Ben Nevis and Glencoe*, p. 232.
19. J. F. Campbell qtd in Francis Thompson, 'John Francis Campbell (1821–1885)', *Folklore*, 101: 1 (1990), p. 89.
20. J. F. Campbell, *Popular Tales*, p. 2.
21. '[He] related how he suffered several hours imprisonment for fighting another boy "on account of my country"': Alfred Nutt, 'Introduction', in John Gregorson Campbell, *Clan Traditions and Popular Tales of the Western Highlands and Islands* (London: David Nutt, 1895), p. x.
22. J. G. Campbell, *Clan Traditions*, p. 56.
23. J. F. Campbell, *Popular Tales*, p. 16.
24. Hugh Miller, *Scenes and Legends of the North of Scotland or the Traditional History of Cromarty*, 7th edn (Edinburgh: Nimmo, 1969), p. 2.
25. J. F. Campbell, *Popular Tales*, pp. 15–16.
26. J. F. Campbell, *Popular Tales*, p. 10.
27. Stewart, *Twixt Ben Nevis and Glencoe*, p. 76.
28. Bold, 'Ballad Raids and Spoilt Songs: Collection as Colonization', in Thomas

McKean (ed.), *The Flowering Thorn: International Ballad Studies* (Logan: Utah State University Press, 2003), pp. 353–62.
29. Gregor is one of only two folklore collectors who gave special attention to sealore: M. Macleod Banks, 'Folklore of the Net, Fishing-Line, Baiting and the Boat on the North-East Coast of Scotland', *Folklore*, 50: 4 (1939), pp. 342–8.
30. J. F. Campbell, *Popular Tales*, p. 20.
31. Gregorson Campbell, *The Fians; Or, Stories, Poems & Traditions of Fionn and his Warrior Band: Collected Entirely from Oral Tradition, Waifs and Strays of Celtic Tradition*, 4 (London: David Nutt, 1891), p. xi. http://www.pitt.edu/~dash/scotland.html
32. Gregorson Campbell, *The Fians*, p. xii.
33. J. G. Campbell, *Clan Traditions*, p. 25.
34. J. G. Campbell, *Clan Traditions*, p. 20.
35. J. G. Campbell, *Clan Traditions*, p. 25.
36. James MacDougall, *Folk and Hero Tales* [1891], *Waifs and Strays of Celtic Tradition*, 3 (London: Strand, 1973), p. 188. Breasts and breast milk in Gaelic tales were tied to magic. Grabbing 'the end of the breast' was one of the ways to gain a prophecy from the 'washer woman', the *Bean Nighe*: "'do not let it go till thou shalt get thy first request from her'": J. G. Campbell, *The Gaelic Otherworld: John Gregorson Campbell's Superstition of the Highlands and Islands of Scotland and Witchcraft and Second Sight in the Highlands and Islands* [1900 and 1902], ed. Ronald Black (Edinburgh: Birlinn, 2005), p. 36. Changelings were covetous of human breast milk: 'exult[ing] in its lacto-vampirism after it has been found out as an impostor of the woman's child. This opportunistic changeling gleefully boasts that it has "got so much of the sap of thy breast in spite of thee" and flies out the window': Macdougall, *Highland Fairy Legends*, qtd in Jason Marc Harris, *Folklore and the Fantastic in Nineteenth-Century Supernatural Fiction* (Aldershot: Ashgate, 2008), p. 7.
37. Gregor, *Notes on the Folk-Lore of the North-East of Scotland*, p. 30.
38. Gregor, *Notes on the Folk-Lore of the North-East of Scotland*, pp. 50, 54.
39. Gregor, *Notes on the Folk-Lore of the North-East of Scotland*, pp. 123, 144.
40. Gregor, *Notes on the Folk-Lore of the North-East of Scotland*, p. 3.
41. Alexander Carmichael, *Carmina Gadelica, Charms of the Gaels Hymns and Incantations: With Illustrative Notes on Words, Rites and Customs, Dying and Obsolete; Orally Collected in the Highlands and Islands of Scotland* [1900], ed. C. J. Moore, preface by John MacInnes (Edinburgh: Floris, 2006), p. 19.
42. Carmichael, *Carmina Gadelica*, p. 361.
43. Carmichael, *Carmina Gadelica*, pp. 25, 362.
44. Carmichael, *Carmina Gadelica*, p. 30.
45. Carmichael, *Carmina Gadelica*, pp. 5–8, 265.
46. Carmichael, *Carmina Gadelica*, pp. 7–9, 269.
47. Carmichael, *Carmina Gadelica*, pp. 15–20, 429.

48. Carmichael, *Carmina Gadelica*, pp. 87–8, 431.
49. Carmichael, *Carmina Gadelica*, pp. 29–32, 484.
50. Carmichael, *Carmina Gadelica*, p. 468.

13 – Newton

1. Sheila Kidd, 'Social Control and Social Criticism: The Nineteenth-Century Còmhradh', *Scottish Gaelic Studies*, 20 (2000), pp. 67–87.
2. Malcolm MacLennan, 'Modern Gaelic Prose', in D. Rhys Phillips (ed.), *Transactions of the Celtic Congress, 1920* (Perth: Milne, Tannahill and Methven, 1921), p. 64; Sheila Kidd, 'The Forgotten First: John MacCormick's Dùn-Àluinn', *Scottish Gaelic Studies*, 22 (2006), pp. 197–219; Donald Meek, 'Gaelic Communities and the Uses of Texts', in Bill Bell (ed.), *The Edinburgh History of the Book in Scotland*, vol. 3 (Edinburgh: Edinburgh University Press, 2007), pp. 155–6.
3. Meek, 'Gaelic Communities', p. 154.
4. John L. Campbell (ed.), *Songs Remembered in Exile*, 2nd edn (Edinburgh: Birlinn, 1999), pp. 8, 17–18; Michael Kennedy, *Gaelic Nova Scotia: An Economic, Cultural, and Social Impact Study* (Halifax: Nova Scotia Museum, 2002), pp. 42–7; Michael Newton, '"Becoming Cold-Hearted like the Gentiles Around Them": Scottish Gaelic in the United States 1872–1912', *e-Keltoi*, 2 (2003), pp. 89–90.
5. Donald John MacLeod, 'Gaelic Prose', *Transactions of the Gaelic Society of Inverness*, 49 (1977), p. 209; Meek, 'Gaelic Communities', pp. 169–71.
6. Donald MacKechnie, *Am Fear-Ciùil: Original Gaelic Humorous Sketches, Poems, Songs, and Translations* (Edinburgh: Archibald Sinclair, 1904), p. x; see also MacLennan, 'Modern Gaelic Prose', pp. 51–2; Campbell, *Songs Remembered*, pp. 7, 20–1; Michael Linkletter, *Bu Dual Dhà Sin (That Was His Birthright): Gaelic Scholar Alexander Maclean Sinclair (1840–1924)*, unpublished PhD thesis, Harvard University, 2006, pp. 268–9, 297–304.
7. Kidd, 'Forgotten First', pp. 197–8, 203–4.
8. M. M., 'The Mod', in John MacDonald (ed.), *Voices from the Hills/Guthan o na Beanntaibh* (Glasgow: An Comunn Gàidhealach, 1927), pp. 198–201, 199–200. See also Kidd, 'Forgotten First', pp. 202–3.
9. Alasdair MacCaluim, 'Ruaraidh Arascain is Mhàirr', http://www.akerbeltz.org/rannsachadh/ruaraidh.htm [consulted 24 Sept. 2009].
10. Faloisg (pen-name), 'An Sgeul Gàidhlig', *An Sgeulaiche*, 3 (1911), p. 188; George Campbell Hay, 'Cor Litreachas na Gaidhlige an Albainn', *An Gàidheal*, 39 (1944), p. 104; Philip O'Leary,'The Irish Renaissance, 1880–1940: Literature in Irish', in Margaret Kelleher and Philip O'Leary (eds), *The Cambridge History of Irish Literature*, vol. 2 (Cambridge: Cambridge University Press, 2006), pp. 239–40.
11. Michael Newton, 'Gaelic Literature and the Diaspora', in Ian Brown et al.

(eds), *Edinburgh History of Scottish Literature*, vol. 2 (Edinburgh: Edinburgh University Press, 2007), pp. 353–9.
12. MacLeod, 'Gaelic Prose', p. 205; Calum Laing, 'Na Sgrìobhaidhean aig an Urr. Iain MacRuairidh', *Transactions of the Gaelic Society of Inverness*, 63 (2006), pp. 308–36.
13. Anon., 'The Gaelic Language and Anglo-Celtic Writers', *Am Bàrd*, 1 (1901), pp. 5–6; Calum MacPhàrlain, 'An Sgeul Goirid', *An Sgeulaiche*, 3 (1911), pp. 9, 18, 25; Faloisg, 'An Sgeul'; Angus Henderson, 'A' Ghàidhlig agus an Clò', *Guth na Bliadhna*, 10 (1913), pp. 133–49; Hay, 'Cor Litreachas', p. 104; Newton, 'Becoming Cold-Hearted', p. 68.
14. MacPhàrlain, 'An Sgeul', p. 15.
15. J. F. Campbell, *More West Highland Tales*, 2 vols (Edinburgh: Birlinn, 1994), p. 251.
16. Gearóid Ó Crualaoich, 'Orality and Modern Irish Culture: A Personal Strand of the Weave', in Nessa Cronin et al. (eds), *Anáil an Bhéil Bheo: Orality and Modern Irish Culture* (Newcastle: Cambridge Scholars Publishing, 2009), pp. 22–4; Michael Newton, *Warriors of the Word: The World of the Scottish Highlanders* (Edinburgh: Birlinn, 2009), p. 110.
17. MacLean, *Highlands* (Inverness: Club Leabhar, 1975), pp. xiv–xv.
18. Many of these have been published in the School's journal *Tocher*; a selection of these have also been published in Alan Bruford and Donald A. MacDonald, *Scottish Traditional Tales* (Edinburgh: Birlinn, 2003).
19. Charles Dunn, *Highland Settler: A Portrait of the Scottish Gael in Cape Breton and Eastern Nova Scotia*, 2nd edn (Wreck Cove: Breton Books, 1968), pp. 45–8; Joe Neil MacNeil, *Sgeul gu Latha/Tales until Dawn: The World of a Cape Breton Gaelic Story-Teller* (Edinburgh: Edinburgh University Press, 1987), pp. xviii–xix; John Shaw, *Na Beanntaichean Gorma agus Sgeulachdan Eile à Ceap Bretainn/The Blue Mountains and Other Gaelic Stories from Cape Breton* (Montreal: McGill-Queen's University Press, 2007).
20. MacPhàrlain, 'An Sgeul'; Faloisg, 'An Sgeul'.
21. Moray Watson, 'Argyll and the Gaelic Prose Fiction of the Early Twentieth Century', *Scottish Gaelic Studies*, 24 (2008), pp. 576–7.
22. John MacInnes, 'Short Stories', in Derick Thomson (ed.), *The Companion to Gaelic Scotland* (Glasgow: Gairm, 1994), p. 279; Kidd, 'Forgotten First', p. 214; Meg Bateman, 'The Autobiography in Scottish Gaelic', in Ian Brown et al. (eds), *The Edinburgh History of Scottish Literature*, vol. 3 (Edinburgh: Edinburgh University Press, 2007), pp. 225–30; Watson, 'Argyll', pp. 574–5, 586.
23. Kidd, 'Forgotten First', p. 204.
24. Kidd, 'Forgotten First', p. 213.
25. Lauchie MacLellan, *Brìgh an Òrain/A Story in Every Song* (Montreal and Kingston: McGill-Queen's University Press, 2000), p. 49. Original short stories appeared in *Mac-Talla* and elsewhere.

26. Donald MacAulay (ed.), *Nua-bhàrdachd Ghàidhlig* (Edinburgh: Southside, 1976), p. 46.
27. Ronald Black (ed.), *An Tuil* (Edinburgh: Polygon, 1999), p. lv; John MacInnes, *Dùthchas nan Gàidheal: Selected Essays of John MacInnes*, ed. Michael Newton (Edinburgh: Birlinn, 2006), p. 359.
28. MacInnes, *Dùthchas*, pp. 265–319.
29. Charles Dunn, *Highland Settler: A Portrait of the Scottish Gael in Cape Breton and Eastern Nova Scotia* [1968], 2nd edn (Wreck Cove: Breton Books, 1991), p. 85; Linkletter, *Bu Dual Dhà Sin*, p. 300.
30. Black, *An Tuil*, pp. lii–liv; Bill Innes, 'Poetry of the Oral Tradition – How Relevant is it to Gaelic in the 21st Century?', *Transactions of the Gaelic Society of Inverness*, 62 (2004), pp. 79–109.
31. Black, *An Tuil*, p. xxi.
32. John Shaw, 'Brief Beginnings: Nova Scotian and Old World Bards Compared', *Scottish Gaelic Studies* 17 (1996), pp. 342–55; MacInnes, *Dùthchas*, pp. 377–9; Meek, 'Gaelic Literature'.
33. Black, *An Tuil*, pp. xxii–xxiii.
34. Máire Ní Annracháin, *Aisling Agus Tóir: An Slánu i Bhfilíocht Shomhairle MhicGill-Eain* (Maynooth: An Sagart, 1992); Black, *An Tuil*, pp. xxx–xxxv; MacInnes, *Dùthchas*, pp. 380–421; Christopher Whyte, 'Cultural Catalysts: Sorley MacLean and George Campbell Hay', in Ian Brown et al. (eds), *Edinburgh History of Scottish Literature*, vol. 3 (Edinburgh: Edinburgh University Press, 2007), pp. 151–62.
35. Black, *An Tuil*, pp. xxxvi–xxxix; George Campbell Hay, *Collected Poems and Songs of George Campbell Hay*, ed. Michel Byrne (Edinburgh: Edinburgh University Press, 2003); Whyte, 'Cultural Catalysts'.
36. MacAulay, *Nua-bhàrdachd*, pp. 22, 36–8, 48, 60–2; Black, *An Tuil*, pp. xl–xliv; Michel Byrne, 'Monsters and Goddesses: Culture Re-Energised in the Poetry of Ruaraidh MacThòmais and Aonghas MacNeacail', in Ian Brown et al. (eds), *Edinburgh History of Scottish Literature*, vol. 3 (Edinburgh: Edinburgh University Press, 2007), pp. 176–84.
37. Donald Macaulay, 'On Some Aspects of the Appreciation of Modern Gaelic Poetry', *Scottish Gaelic Studies*, 11 (1966), pp. 136–45; MacAulay, *Nua-bhàrdachd*, pp. 22, 38–45, 62–8; Black, *An Tuil*, pp. liv–lv.
38. Black, *An Tuil*, p. xliv.
39. MacAulay, 'On Some Aspects'; Black, *An Tuil*, pp. xliv–lii.
40. MacInnes, *Dùthchas*, pp. 3–33, 266–73; Newton, *Warriors*, pp. 80–121.
41. Black, *An Tuil*, xxiii, xlii–xliii, lx–lxi.
42. Corinna Krause, 'Finding the Poem - Modern Gaelic Verse and the Contact Zone', *Forum: The University of Edinburgh Postgraduate Journal of Culture and the Arts*, 1 (Autumn 2005), http://forum.llc.ed.ac.uk/issue1/Krause_Gaelic.pdf, p. 10.
43. Shaw, 'Brief Beginnings'.

44. See, for example, Lewis MacKinnon, *Famhair agus dàin Ghàidhlig eile* (Sydney: Cape Breton University Press, 2008).

14 – Gibson

1. Dave Harker, *Fakesong: The Manufacture of British 'Folksong' 1700 to the Present Day* (Milton Keynes: Open University Press, 1985), p. 2.
2. Tomás Ó Deirg, as cited by Mícheál Briody, *The Irish Folklore Commission 1935–1970: History, Ideology, Methodology* (Helsinki: Finnish Literature Society, 2008), pp. 132–3.
3. Lomax's archives are part of the Library of Congress American Folklore Center (www.loc.gov/folklife/lomax/). The early field trips are detailed in John Szwed, *The Man Who Recorded the World: A Biography of Alan Lomax* (London: William Heinemann, 2010), pp. 31–76.
4. Michael Brocken, *The British Folk Revival 1944–2002* (Aldershot: Ashgate, 2003), pp. 1–11.
5. Ailie Munro, *The Democratic Muse: Folk Music Revival in Scotland* (Aberdeen: Scottish Cultural Press, 1996), pp. 9–19.
6. Neil V. Rosenberg (ed.), *Transforming Tradition: Folk Music Revivals Examined* (Urbana and Chicago: University of Illinois Press, 1993), p. 27.
7. Hamish Henderson, 'Come Gie's a Sang' (*Spectator* [25 May 1956]), in Alec Finlay (ed.), *Alias MacAlias: Writings on Songs, Folk and Literature* (Edinburgh: Polygon, 2004), p. 28.
8. Henderson, 'Enemies of Folk-Song' (*Saltire Review* [Autumn 1955]), in Finlay (ed.), *Alias MacAlias*, p. 45.
9. Henderson, 'Scots Folk-Song Today' (*Folklore*, 75 [Spring 1964]), in Finlay (ed.), *Alias MacAlias*, p. 38.
10. Adam McNaughtan, 'The Folksong Revival in Scotland', in Edward J. Cowan (ed.), *The People's Past: Scottish Folk, Scottish History* (Edinburgh: Polygon, 1980), pp. 180–1.
11. Hamish Henderson, 'Preface', in Kenneth S. Goldstein, *A Guide for Field Workers in Folklore* (London: Herbert Jenkins, 1964), p. x.
12. A vast archive of examples of this kind of practice can be heard in the collections of the School of Scottish Studies, which are now catalogued online, with audio files, as part of the *Tobar an Dualchais - Kist o' Riches* project (www.tobarandualchais.co.uk/en/).
13. Henderson, 'Folk-Singing in Auld Reekie II' (*Folk Scene* [March 1965]), Finlay (ed.), in *Alias MacAlias*, p. 8.
14. Ewan MacColl, *Journeyman: An Autobiography* (London: Sidgwick and Jackson, 1990), pp. 287–8.
15. Michael Brocken, *The British Folk Revival*, pp. 34–6.
16. Michael Brocken, *The British Folk Revival*, pp. 33–9.

17. Henderson, 'Rock and Reel' (*Scotland* [November 1958]), in Finlay (ed.), *Alias MacAlias*, pp. 19–20.
18. Henderson, as cited by Timothy Neat, in *Hamish Henderson: A Biography – Volume 2: Poetry becomes People (1952–2002)* (Edinburgh: Polygon, 2009), p. 368.
19. Henderson, '"It Was In You That It A' Began": Some Thoughts on the Folk Conference', in Cowan (ed.), *The People's Past*, p. 11.
20. Alan Lomax, 'Making Folklore Available', in Ronald D. Cohen (ed.), *Alan Lomax: Selected Writings 1934–1997* (Abingdon: Routledge, 2005), pp. 115–16.
21. Henderson, 'The Underground of Song' (*Scots Magazine* [February 1963]), in Finlay (ed.), *Alias MacAlias*, p. 34.
22. Henderson, 'Enemies of Folk-Song', p. 46.
23. Henderson, 'It Was In You That It A' Began', p. 13.
24. See Eberhard Bort (ed.), *Borne on the Carrying Stream: The Legacy of Hamish Henderson* (Ochtertyre: Grace Note, 2010), for the most recent work on Henderson, and, for his relationship with Gramsci, see, in particular, Corey Gibson, '"Gramsci in Action": Antonio Gramsci and Hamish Henderson's Folk Revivalism', pp. 239–56.
25. As cited by Henderson, 'The Edinburgh People's Festival, 1951–54', in Andy Croft (ed.), *A Weapon in the Struggle: The Cultural History of the Communist Party of Great Britain* (London: Pluto, 1998), p. 164.
26. From the programme of the inaugural ceilidh, Henderson, 'The Edinburgh People's Festival, 1951–54', in Croft (ed.), *A Weapon in the Struggle*, p. 168.
27. As cited by Ewan McVicar, *The Eskimo Republic: Scots Political Song in Action 1951–1999* (Linlithgow: Gallus, 2010), p. 41.
28. T. S. Law and Thurso Berwick (eds), *Homage to John Maclean* (Edinburgh: EUSPB, 1979).
29. Seamus Mor MacEanruig [Hamish Henderson] (ed.), *Hamish Henderson's Ballads of World War II – Collected for the Lili Marlene Club of Glasgow* (Glasgow: Lili Marlene Club of Glasgow, 1947).
30. Henderson was in fact the author of a significant proportion of the songs in the collection, though he chose not to divulge this in the publication.
31. The poems and songs in *Sangs o' the Stane* are not attributed to authors; however, Ewan McVicar has noted that half the songs were written by Morris Blythman, and of the remainder, contributers included Sydney Goodsir Smith, Norman MacCaig, Hugh MacDiarmid, John McEvoy and T. S. Law (*The Eskimo Republic*, pp. 21–2).
32. See Neil V. Rosenberg, Dave Harker and Michael Brocken.
33. Henderson, 'The Ballads' (*A Companion to Scottish Culture*, 1981), in Finlay (ed.), *Alias MacAlias*, p. 24.
34. See Mick Imlah and Robert Crawford (eds), *Scottish Verse* (London: Penguin, 2001).

35. Edwin Muir, *Scott and Scotland: The Predicament of the Scottish Writer* (London: Routledge, 1936), pp. 21–2.
36. John Speirs, *The Scots Literary Tradition: An Essay in Criticism*, 2nd edn (London: Faber and Faber, 1962).
37. Henderson, 'Folk-Singing in Auld Reekie III' (*Folk Scene* [May 1965]), in Finlay (ed.), *Alias MacAlias*, p. 10.
38. Henderson, 'The Poet Speaks' (interview by Peter Orr in *The Poet Speaks*, Routledge, 1966) in *Alias MacAlias*, p. 452.
39. Henderson, 'Enemies of Folk-Song', p. 50.
40. The 'flytings' are reproduced in Alec Finlay (ed.), *The Armstrong Nose: Selected Letters of Hamish Henderson* (Edinburgh: Polygon, 1996), pp. 117–40. These particular quotations and references are on pages 94, 134, 118, 119, 124, 126 and 122.
41. The quotation is from MacDiarmid's first contribution to the 1964 'Folksong Flyting': see Finlay (ed.), *Armstrong Nose*, p. 119. For Henderson's response see his letters in the same series of exchanges (pp. 119–20, 124–5, 131–2, 134–6, 136–8, 139–40). For a concise statement of his argument, see a note originally written in 1968 but published later, 'Freedom Becomes People', *Chapman*, 42 (1985), p. 1.
42. Henderson, 'Rock and Reel', p. 20.
43. Henderson, 'Enemies of Folk-Song', p. 50.

15 – Bennett

1. The Folklore Society supported the publication of noteworthy collectors such as the Rev. Walter Gregor from the north-east, the Rev. James Napier from Paisley, the Rev. John Gregorson Campbell from Argyllshire and Edinburgh-based Dr Robert Craig Maclagan who himself recruited a team of helpers and correspondents.
2. In 1931 it ceased to exist as such, merging into a new society, The English Folk Dance and Song Society, which, despite its title, has significant interest in Scotland. See Ian A. Olson, 'The Influence of the Folk Song Society on the Greig–Duncan Folk Song Collection: Methodology', *Folk Music Journal*, 5: 2 (1986), pp. 176–201.
3. Sharp was not, however, the first to use wax cylinder as a field-recording device as earlier examples include Zuni and Passamaquoddy voices recorded by American anthropologist J. W. Fewkes in 1890. Archived in the collection of the Center for Folklife and Cultural Heritage at the Smithsonian Institution, Washington, examples are available on the CD, *Anthology of American Folk Music*, ed. Harry Smith, Smithsonian Folkways (40539), 2006.
4. Kennedy Fraser's collection has come under frequent criticism, often from uninformed singers who have not read her biography. It is unreasonable and unfair to judge her by the standards of modern scholarship or by the values of

informed folksong collectors. To date, few of the original recordings have been accessible via commercially available productions; the voice of Peter Stewart, recorded by Marjory Kennedy Fraser in Uig, Skye (1910), can be heard on tracks 1 and 10 of *Glenlyon: A Song Cycle*, by Martyn Bennett (Footstompin CDFSR1714).

5. In 1935 Margaret Fay Shaw married folklorist and Gaelic scholar John Lorne Campbell (1906–96) and in 1938 they bought the Isle of Canna, where together they built up one of the most important archives of Gaelic tradition in existence.

6. Formed in 1839 in association with Aberdeen University Library, the Spalding Club ran till 1869, holding lectures and discussions relating to the north-east and publishing proceedings. While most of the material was of historical or literary interest, there were several ballad enthusiasts among the members. The Club reconvened as the New Spalding Club in 1886 and ran till 1928, gathering and conserving important documents and manuscripts, now part of the Aberdeen University collection.

7. Correspondence between Walker and Child began in 1890. Child's letters to Walker are archived in Aberdeen University collections; they were published in Aberdeen by Bon-Accord Press in 1930. See *Letters on Scottish Ballads from Professor Francis J. Child to William Walker*. Walker's letters to Child are archived in Harvard University, forming part of the vast manuscript collection relating to the publication of *The English and Scottish Popular Ballads*.

8. One of Walker's principal works was *Peter Buchan and Other Papers* published in Aberdeen in 1915.

9. Regarded (perhaps unfairly) as an 'armchair scholar', according to George Lyman Kittredge, Child 'made an effort to stimulate the collection of such remains of the traditional as still alive on the lips of the people in this country and in the British Islands. The harvest was, in his opinion rather scanty': George Lyman Kittredge, 'Biographical Sketch of Professor Child', in F. J. Child (ed.), *The English and Scottish Popular Ballads* (London: Houghton Mifflin, 1882–96; also London: Dover, 1965), vol. 1, p. xxviii.

10. Entitled 'The Ballad Corner', the feature ran from 1907 to 1911, encouraging readers to 'write in to the paper' with their own songs.

11. Assisted by William Walker, newspaper journalist and editor, Alexander Keith made a selection of ballads, which he referenced with Child's collection. It seems unfortunate that 'last leaves' suggests that the ballads collected by Greig and Duncan would be the last to be found. This proved not to be the case.

12. American folklorist Kenneth S. Goldstein collaborated with Arthur Argo to publish *Folk-Song in Buchan and Folk-Song of the North-East* (Hatboro, PA: 1963).

13. General editors Patrick Shuldham-Shaw and Emily Lyle laid the groundwork

for the project. They divided the collection into broad themes, then (after Shaw's death), worked with a team of assistant editors to write introductory essays and notes.
14. While based in London during his collecting years, Campbell notes in his diary: 'I met two tinkers in St James Street in February [. . .] I joined the party and one told me a version of the man 'who travelled to learn what shivering meant' while we walked together through the park to Westminster [. . .]' See John Francis Campbell, *Popular Tales of the West Highlands*, 4 vols, 2nd edn (Paisley and London: Gardner, 1893; also London: Wildwood House, 1984), vol. 1, p. xl.
15. H. Henderson, *Alias MacAlias: Writing on Songs, Folk and Literature* (Edinburgh: Polygon, 2004), p. 16.
16. The word 'cèilidh' simply means 'a visit'. See, 'Cèilidh', definition by Margaret Bennett in *The New Grove Dictionary of Music and Musicians* (London: Macmillan, 2000).
17. The event was co-organised by Henderson, along with fellow poet Hugh MacDiarmid and others, in protest at the elitist Edinburgh International Festival whose programme they saw as excluding 'our native riches of folk-song and music' and its audience excluding working-class population whose taxes subsidised high-art performances.
18. Montgomerie, a Glasgow-born school-teacher and poet, based in Dundee at the time, had already begun recording songs and children's folklore using a Wirex recorder. He and his wife Norah, an artist and folklorist, leave a significant legacy of books published from their recordings and notebook collections.
19. *The English and Scottish Popular Ballads*, vol. 1, p. 118. Child cites the example given by J. F. Campbell's *Popular Tales of the West Highlands*, vol. 4, p. 126. Child also includes tunes from three manuscript sources, vol. 5, pp. 411–12.
20. The remarkable H. M. Belden (Professor of Folklore at Indiana University), who began recording living versions of ballads in 1906, had not only amassed thousands of 'sung ballads' by the time he published his *Ballads and Songs Collected by the Missouri Folk-Lore Society* (1940), but he also annotated and cross-referenced the collection with comparative versions ranging all over the States, into Canada and also to Newfoundland, which was, at that time, a British colony. He cites, for example, over forty sung versions of Child 10.
21. The same year as Henderson recorded Jeannie Robertson, Frank and Anne Warner recorded North Carolina singer Lee Monroe Presnell singing ten verses of 'Two Sisters Loved One Man'.
22. Noteworthy also are the song collectors Greenleaf and Mansfield in Newfoundland, Helen Creighton in Nova Scotia, Edith Fowke in Ontario and, the most prolific collector of all, Quebec's Marius Barbeau, regarded as the founding father of Canadian folklore, who recorded a considerable body of folksong in English and 'First Nations' languages as well as over 7,000 French-Canadian songs.

23. A considerable number of the tunes were from Hamish Henderson's collection. After the completion of his *The Traditional Tunes of the Child Ballads*, Bronson wrote to Hamish, 'Posterity's dept to you is incalculable and will not be forgotten.' See Timothy Neat, *Hamish Henderson: A Biography, Volume 2. Poetry Becomes People (1952–2002)* (Edinburgh: Birlinn, 2009), p. 142.
24. Goldstein produced a twelve-inch vinyl recording of Lucy Stewart, as well as many other folksong records for which he wrote informative 'sleeve' notes; he also worked on the Grieg–Duncan collection, already mentioned.
25. From Nashville, Tennessee, Gower was a postgraduate student when he spent 1954 to 1956 in Edinburgh. His doctoral dissertation, *Traditional Scottish Ballads in the United States* (Vanderbilt University, 1957) was followed by publications that included *Another Harvest of Scottish Ballads, 1951–1956: Music Transcribed from Tape Recordings by George Boswell* (1957) and, editor, with James Porter, *Jeannie Robertson: Emergent Singer, Transformative Voice* (1995).
26. It was included on the first vinyl record produced by the School of Scottish Studies; Scots songs on Side A and Gaelic songs on Side B, Disc A. 0003/4, 1960.
27. To date, the most extensive collection of Jack Tales is from this area. See Richard Chase, *Jack Tales*, especially the Introduction and Notes by Herbert Halpert, who instigated this collection.
28. Recordings are deposited in the archives of East Tennessee State University. Duncan was subsequently invited to be special guest at America's biggest gathering of storytellers, the Jonesburgh Storytelling Festival in Tennessee.
29. Memorably, in 1995, director Brian McMaster programmed a series of ten concerts from the Greig–Duncan Collection, taking advice from Hamish Henderson and others on themes to include and the singers to invite.
30. Books include *Fireside Tales of the Traveller Children* (Edinburgh: Canongate, 1983), *A Thorn in the King's Foot: Folktales of the Scottish Travelling People* (Harmondsworth: Penguin Folklore Library, 1987) and *The Horsieman: Memories of a Traveller 1928–58* by Duncan Williamson (Edinburgh: Birlinn, 2012).
31. A fine storyteller and ballad singer, Betsy (née Bessie Townsley) wrote her autobiography, *The Yellow on the Broom*, followed by *Red Rowans and Wild Honey*. Several of the tales she told were also recorded, transcribed and published by Alan Bruford in *Tocher*.
32. Sheila Douglas, *Last of the Tinsmiths: The Life of Willie MacPhee* (Edinburgh: Birlinn, 2006), p. 45.
33. Eric R. Cregeen, 'Recollections of an Argyllshire Drover' and Other West Highland Chronicles by Eric R. Cregeen, ed. Margaret Bennett (Edinburgh: John Donald, 2004), p. 141. First published in *Tocher*, 18 (1975), School of Scottish Studies, University of Edinburgh, pp. 41–65.

Further Reading

Linden Bicket

Ballad Tradition

Bold, Alan, *The Ballad* (London: Methuen, 1979).
Bold, Valentina, 'Ballad Raids and Spoilt Songs: Collection as Colonization', in Thomas A. McKean (ed.), *The Flowering Thorn: International Ballad Studies* (Logan: Utah State University Press, 2003), pp. 353–62.
Brown, Mary Ellen, 'Old Singing Women and the Canons of Scottish Balladry and Song', in Douglas Gifford and Dorothy MacMillan (eds), *A History of Scottish Women's Writing* (Edinburgh: Edinburgh University Press, 1997), pp. 44–57.
—, *Child's Unfinished Masterpiece: The English and Scottish Popular Ballads* (Illinois: University of Illinois Press, 2011).
Buchan, David J., *The Ballad and the Folk* (London: Routledge, 1972).
— (ed.), *A Scottish Ballad Book* (London and Boston: Routledge, 1972).
Campbell, Katherine, 'Collectors of Scots Song', in John Beech et al. (eds), *Scottish Life and Society: A Compendium of Scottish Ethnology. Oral Literature and Performance Culture* (Edinburgh: John Donald, 2007), pp. 427–39.
Child, Francis James, *The English and Scottish Popular Ballads*, 5 vols (Boston, MA: Houghton, Mifflin and Co., 1882–98).
Coffin, Tristram Potter, 'The Traditional Ballad as an Art Form', in *The British Traditional Ballad in North America*, rev. edn (Austin and London: University of Texas Press, 1977), pp. 164–72.
Cowan, Edward J. (ed.), *The Ballad in Scottish History* (East Linton: Tuckwell, 2000).
Dugaw, Dianne, *Warrior Women and Popular Balladry 1650–1850* (Cambridge: Cambridge University Press, 1989).
Dunnigan, Sarah M., *Scottish Ballads* (Glasgow: ASLS, 2004).
Fowler, David C., *A Literary History of the Popular Ballad* (Durham, NC: Duke University Press, 1968).
Gilbert, Suzanne, 'Orality and the Ballad Tradition', in Glenda Norquay (ed.), *Edinburgh Companion to Scottish Women's Writing* (Edinburgh: Edinburgh University Press, 2011), pp. 35–43.

—, 'The Scottish Ballad: Towards Survival in the 21st Century', *Anglistik*, 23: 2 (2012), pp. 83–94.
Harris, Joseph (ed.), *The Ballad and Oral Literature* (Cambridge, MA and London: Harvard University Press, 1991).
— and Barbara Hillers (eds), *Child's Children: Ballad Study and Its Legacies*, (Trier: Wissenschaftlicher Verlag Trier, 2011).
Hodgart, Matthew John Caldwell, *The Ballads* (London: Hutchison, 1950).
Lyle, Emily, *Fairies and Folk: Approaches to the Scottish Ballad Tradition* (Trier: Wissenschaftlicher Verlag Trier, 2007).
MacCarthy, William, *The Ballad Matrix: Personality, Milieu and the Oral Tradition* (Bloomington: University of Indiana Press, 1990).
MacInnes, John, 'Twentieth-Century Recordings of Scottish Gaelic Heroic Ballads', in Bo Almqvist, Seán Ó Catháin, and Pádraig Ó Héalaí (eds), *The Heroic Process – Form, Function and Fantasy in Folk Epic* (Dun Laoghaire: Glendale Press, 1987), pp. 101–30.
Meek, Donald E., 'The Gaelic Ballads of Scotland: Creativity and Adaptation', in Howard Gaskill (ed.), *Ossian Revisited* (Edinburgh: Edinburgh University Press, 1991), pp. 19–48.
Montgomerie, William, 'A Bibliography of the Scottish Ballad Manuscripts 1730–1825', *Studies in Scottish Literature*, 4: 1 (1966), pp. 3–28.
Muir, Willa, *Living with Ballads* (London: Hogarth, 1965).
Porter, James (ed.), *The Ballad Image* (Los Angeles: University of California Press, 1983).
— (ed.), *Ballads and Boundaries: Narrative Singing in an Intercultural Context* (Los Angeles: University of California, Department of Ethnomusicology and Systematic Musicology, 1995).
—, *Genre – Conflict – Presence: Traditional Ballads in a Modernizing World*, (Trier: Wissenschaftlicher Verlag Trier, 2009).
Rieuwerts, Sigrid (ed.), *The Ballad Repertoire of Anna Gordon, Mrs Brown of Falkland* (Woodbridge: Boydell and Brewer for Scottish Text Society, 2011).
— and Tom Cheesman (eds), *Ballads into Books: The Legacies of F. J. Child*, rev. edn (Bern: Peter Lang, 1999).

Folk Narrative

Bennett, Margaret, *Scottish Customs from the Cradle to the Grave* [1993, 1998] (Edinburgh: Polygon/Birlinn, 2004).
Bold, Valentina, 'Scottish Storytelling Today: Context, Performance, Renaissance', in Bertold Schoene (ed.), *Edinburgh Companion to Contemporary Scottish Literature* (Edinburgh: Edinburgh University Press, 2007), pp. 371–80.
Brown, Mary Ellen and Bruce A. Rosenberg (eds), *Encyclopedia of Folklore and Literature* (Santa Barbara: ABC-CLIO, 1998).

Bruford, A. J. and D. A. MacDonald (eds), *Scottish Traditional Tales* (Edinburgh: Polygon, 1994).
Buchan, David, *Scottish Tradition: A Collection of Scottish Folk Literature* (London: Routledge, 1984).
—, 'Folk Tradition and Literature Till 1603', in J. D. McClure and M. R. G. Spiller (eds), *Bryght Lanternis: Essays on the Language and Literature of Medieval and Renaissance Scotland* (Aberdeen: Aberdeen University Press, 1989), pp. 1–13.
Henderson, Lizanne (ed.), *Fantastical Imaginations: The Supernatural in Scottish History and Culture* (Edinburgh: John Donald, 2009).
Henderson, Lizanne and Edward J. Cowan, *Scottish Fairy Belief: A History* (East Linton: Tuckwell, 2001).
Macdougall, James (ed. and trans.), *Folk and Hero Tales* (New York: AMS Press, 1973).
Newton, Michael, *Warriors of the Word: The World of the Scottish Highlanders* (Edinburgh: Birlinn, 2009).
Williamson, Duncan, *A Thorn in the King's Foot: Folktales of the Scottish Travelling People* (Harmondsworth: Penguin, 1987).
—, *The Horsieman: Memoirs of a Traveller 1928–58* [c. 1994] (Edinburgh: Birlinn, 2002).
—, *Fireside Tales of the Traveller Children* (Edinburgh: Birlinn, 2009).

Folk Song

Bold, Valentina, '"An Irish Boy He May Well Be but He Spak Braid Scots when He Coortit Me": Song Connections between Ireland and South West Scotland', *Traditiones*, 38. 1 (2009), pp. 131–40.
Bort, Eberhard (ed.), *'Tis Sixty Years Since: The 1951 Edinburgh People's Festival Ceilidh and the Scottish Folk Revival* (Ochtertyre: Grace Note, 2011).
Brocken, Michael, *The British Folk Revival: 1944–2002* (Hants: Ashgate, 2003).
Buchan, Norman and Peter Hall (eds), *The Scottish Folksinger* (London and Glasgow: Collins, 1973).
Campbell, Katherine and Ewan McVicar, *Traditional Scottish Songs and Music*, with accompanying CD (St Andrews: Leckie and Leckie, 2001).
Campbell, John L. (ed.), *Songs Remembered in Exile*, 2nd edn (Edinburgh: Birlinn, 1999).
Douglas, Sheila, *The Sang's the Thing: Voices from Lowland Scotland* (Edinburgh: Polygon, 1992).
— (ed.), *Come Gie's a Sang: 73 Traditional Scottish Songs* (Edinburgh: Hardie Press, 1995).
Gelbart, Matthew, *The Invention of 'Folk Music' and 'Art Music': Emerging Categories from Ossian to Wagner* (Cambridge: Cambridge University Press, 2007).
Gillies, John (ed.), *Sean dain agus orain Ghaidhealach* (Perth: 1786).

Greig, Gavin, *'The Subject of Folksong': Collected Writings on Scottish Folk Song*, ed. Stephen Miller (Isle of Man: Chiollagh Books, 2000).

Harker, Dave, *Fakesong: The Manufacture of British 'Folksong', 1700 to the Present Day* (Milton Keynes: Open University Press, 1985).

Henderson, Hamish, 'At the Foot o' Yon Excellin' Brae: The Language of Scottish Folksong', in J. Derrick McClure (ed.), *Scotland and the Lowland Tongue* (Aberdeen University Press, 1983), pp. 100–28.

—, *Alias MacAlias: Writing on Songs, Folk and Literature* (Edinburgh: Polygon, 2004).

Lloyd, A. L., *Come All Ye Bold Miners: Ballads and Songs of the Coalfields* [1952] (London: Lawrence and Wishart, 1978).

Lyric Gems of Scotland: A Collection of Scottish Songs, Original and Selected, with Music (Glasgow: D. Jack, 1856).

MacKechnie, Donald, *Am Fear-Ciùil: Original Gaelic Humorous Sketches, Poems, Songs, and Translations* (Edinburgh: Archibald Sinclair, 1904).

Macleod, Morag, 'Collectors of Gaelic Song', in John Beech et al. (eds), *Scottish Life and Society, a Compendium of Scottish Ethnology: Oral Literature and Performance Culture* (Edinburgh: John Donald, 2007), pp. 440–50.

McKean, Thomas A., *Hebridean Songmaker: Iain MacNeacail of the Isle of Skye* (Edinburgh: Polygon, 1997).

McVicar, Ewan (ed.), *One Singer One Song; Songs of Glasgow Folk* (Glasgow: Glasgow City Libraries, 1990).

Munro, Ailie, *The Democratic Muse: Folk Music Revival in Scotland* (Aberdeen: Aberdeen Cultural Press, 1996).

Ó Baoill, Colm (ed.), *Mairghread nighean Lachlainn: Song-Maker of Mull* ([Edinburgh]: Scottish Gaelic Texts Society, 2009).

Ord, John (ed.), *The Bothy Songs & Ballads of Aberdeen, Banff & Moray, Angus and the Mearns* (Paisley: Alexander Gardner, 1930).

Porter, James and Herschel Gower, *Jeannie Robertson: Emergent Singer, Transformative Voice* (Knoxville, TN and East Linton: Tuckwell Press, 1995).

Purser, John, *Scotland's Music* (Edinburgh: Mainstream, 1992).

Shuldham-Shaw, Patrick, Emily B. Lyle, et al., *The Greig–Duncan Folk Song Collection*, 8 vols (Aberdeen: Aberdeen University Press; Edinburgh: Mercat Press, 1981–2002).

Smith, R. A., *Scottish Minstrel: A Selection from the Vocal Melodies of Scotland, Ancient & Modern*, 6 vols (Edinburgh: Robert Purdie, 1821–4).

Thomson, Derick S. (ed. and trans.), *The MacDiarmid MS Anthology: Poems and Songs Mainly Anonymous from the Collection Dated 1770* (Edinburgh: Scottish Academic Press, 1992).

Literary Writers and Tradition

Bell, A. S. (ed.), *The Scottish Antiquarian Tradition. Essays to Mark the Bicentenary of the Society of Antiquaries of Scotland and its Museum, 1780–1980* (Edinburgh: John Donald, 1981).

Brown, Mary Ellen, *Burns and Tradition* (London: Macmillan, 1984).
—, *William Motherwell's Cultural Politics* (Lexington: The University Press of Kentucky, 2001).
Dunnigan, Sarah, 'The Enchanted Worlds of Scott, Scotland, and the Grimms', in Gerard Carruthers, David Goldie and Alastair Renfrew (eds), *Scotland and the 19th-Century World* (Amsterdam and New York: Rodopi, 2012), pp. 249–74.
—, 'Literary Metamorphoses and the Reframing of Enchantment: The Scottish Song and Folktale Collections of R. H. Cromek, Allan Cunningham and Robert Chambers', in Matthew Campbell and Michael Perraudin (eds), *Writing the European Folk Revival, 1760–1914* (London: Anthem, 2012), pp. 49–64.
Fowler, David C., *A Literary History of the Popular Ballad* (Durham, NC: Duke University Press, 1968).
Gilbert, Suzanne, 'James Hogg and the Authority of Tradition', in *James Hogg and the Literary Marketplace: Scottish Romanticism and the Working-Class Author*, ed. Sharon Alker and Holly Faith Nelson (Ashgate, 2009), pp. 93–109.
—, 'Alliance and Defiance: Scottish and American Outlaw-Hero Ballads', in Gerard Carruthers, David Goldie and Alastair Renfrew (eds), *Scotland and the 19th-Century World* (Amsterdam and New York: Rodopi, 2012), pp. 71–92.
Mackenzie, M. L., 'The Great Ballad Collectors: Percy, Herd and Ritson', *Studies in Scottish Literature*, 2: 4 (1965), pp. 21–33.
Malley, Shawn, 'Walter Scott's Romantic Archaeology: New/Old Abbotsford and "The Antiquary"', *Studies in Romanticism*, 40: 3 (2001), pp. 233–51.
Neat, Timothy, *The Voice of the Bard: Living Poets and Ancient Traditions in the Highlands and Islands of Scotland* (Edinburgh: Canongate, 1999).
Pound, Louise, *Poetic Origins and the Ballad* (New York: Russell, 1962).
Rieuwerts, Sigrid, 'Allan Ramsay and the Scottish Ballads', in *Aberdeen University Review*, 1: 201 (1999), pp. 29–41.
Scott, Willie, *Herd Laddie o' the Glen: Songs of a Border Shepherd*, ed. Alison McMorland (Selkirk: Scottish Borders Arts Council, 2006).
Stafford, Fiona, *The Sublime Savage: James Macpherson and the Poems of Ossian* (Edinburgh: Edinburgh University Press, 1988).
Thomson, Derick S., *The Gaelic Sources of Macpherson's 'Ossian'* (Edinburgh and London: Oliver and Boyd, 1952).
Zug III, Charles G., 'The Ballad Editor as Antiquary: Scott and the *Minstrelsy*', *Journal of the Folklore Institute*, 13: 1 (1976), pp. 57–73.
—, 'The Ballad and History: The Case for Scott', *Folklore*, 89 (1978), pp. 229–42.

Other Web Resources

Bibliography of the Scottish Ballads
http://bartleby.com/212/1700.html

Celtic and Scottish Studies, University of Edinburgh
   http://www.ed.ac.uk/schools-departments/literatures-languages-cultures/
      celtic-scottish-studies
Centre for Political Song
   http://www.gcu.ac.uk/politicalsong/
The Elphinstone Institute
   http://www.abdn.ac.uk/elphinstone/
Glasgow Broadside Ballads – The Murray Collection
   http://www.gla.ac.uk/t4/~dumfries/files/layer2/Glasgow_broadside_ballads/
Greentrax Recordings
   http://www.greentrax.com/music/artists/category/Scottish-Tradition-Series/
Grove Music Online
   http://www.oxfordmusiconline.com/public/book/omo_gmo
The James Madison Carpenter Collection Online Catalogue
   http://www.hrionline.ac.uk/carpenter/
   and
   http://www.abdn.ac.uk/elphinstone/carpenter/
Learning and Teaching Scotland, Scotland's Songs
   http://www.ltscotland.org.uk/scotlandssongs/
Learning and Teaching Scotland, Songs for Secondary Schools
   http://www.ltscotland.org.uk/scotlandssongs/secondary/index.asp
Oral Tradition
   http://www.oraltradition.org/bibliography/
School of Scottish Studies Archive
   http://www.ed.ac.uk/schools-departments/literatures-languages-cultures/
      celtic-scottish-studies/archives
The Scottish Ballads: Alive and Singing!
   http://www.springthyme.co.uk/ballads/
Scottish Storytelling Centre
   http://www.scottishstorytellingcentre.co.uk/
Society of Antiquaries of London
   www.sal.org.uk
Sruth nan Gàidheal/Gael Stream
   http://gaelstream.stfx.ca/greenstone/cgi-bin/library.cgi?site=localhost&a=
      p&p=about&c=capebret&l=en&w=utf-8
Tobar an Dualchais - Kist o' Riches project
   www.tobarandualchais.co.uk
Traditional Music and Song Association of Scotland
   http://www.tmsa.org.uk/
The Word on the Street: How Ordinary Scots in Bygone Days Found out What was Happening, National Library of Scotland, 2004
   http://digital.nls.uk/broadsides/index.html

Ballads and Songs: Discography

Bennett, Martyn, *Glenlyon: A Song Cycle* (Edinburgh: Footstompin, 2002, CDFSR1714), Compact Disc.

Campbell, Katherine, *The Songs of Amelia and Jane Harris. Scots Songs and Ballads from Perthshire Tradition* (Cupar: Springthyme Records, 2004, SPRCD 1041), Compact Disc.

Folksongs of North East Scotland: Songs from the Greig–Duncan Collection (Edinburgh: Greentrax Recordings, 1995), Compact Disc.

It Fell on a Day: Volume 17, The Voice of the People (London: Topic Records, 1998), Compact Disc.

John Mearns Sings Folk-Songs of the North-East (Aberdeen: Scottish Records, c. 1964). Extended Play Record.

MacBeath, Jimmie, *Tramps & Hawkers* (Burlington, MA: Rounder Records, 2002, CD 82161–1834–2). Compact Disc.

MacBeath, Jimmy [sic], *A Soldier's Life for Me*, The Folk Songs of Britain, vol. 8, LP (London: Topic Records, 1971,12T196, track B11); reissue of LP TC 1164 (New York: Caedmon, 1961), Long-Playing Record.

MacColl, Ewan, Charles Parker and Peggy Seeger, *Singing the Fishing* (London: Topic Records, 1999, CD TSCD 803). Compact Disc.

Mary Macqueen's Ballads (Edinburgh: Scottish Text Society, undated), Audio Cassette.

McMorland, Alison and Georgie McIntyre, with Kirsty Potts, *Ballad Tree* (Kilmarnock: The Tradition Bearers, 2003). Compact Disc.

O'er His Grave the Grass Grew Green: Volume 3, The Voice of the People (London: Topic Records, 1998). Compact Disc.

Scottish Ballads. An Interactive CD-ROM Featuring Sound, Images, Lyrics and Commentary. Directed by Ted Cowan (Glasgow: University of Glasgow, 2004).

Scottish Tradition Series, vols 1–24 (Edinburgh: Greentrax, 1992–). Compact Disc.

Stewart, Belle, *Queen among the Heather: Scots Traditional Songs and Ballads* (Edinburgh: Greentrax, 1998, CDTRAX 9055); reissue of LP 12TS307 (London: Topic Records, 1977). Compact Disc.

Stewart, Davie, *Go on, Sing Another Song* (Burlington, MA: Rounder Records, 2002, CD82161–1833–2). Compact Disc.

Stewart, Elizabeth, *Binnorrie: Songs, Ballads, and Tunes*, Traveller Traditions of North-East Scotland 1 (Aberdeen: Elphinstone Institute, University of Aberdeen, 2004, double CD EICD002). Compact Disc.

Strachan, John, *Songs from Aberdeenshire* (Burlington, MA: Rounder Records, 2002, CD 82161–1835–2). Compact Disc.

The Shepherd's Song: Border Ballads (Edinburgh: Greentrax Recordings, c. 1998). Audio Cassette.

Turriff, Jane, *Singin Is Ma Life* (Kingskettle: Springthyme, 1995, CD SPRCD 1038). Compact Disc.

Notes on Contributors

Margaret Bennett is a folklorist, writer and singer. Former lecturer at the University of Edinburgh's School of Scottish Studies, she now teaches part-time at the Royal Conservatoire of Scotland.

Linden Bicket holds a doctorate in Scottish Literature from Glasgow University where she is a teaching and research assistant. Her research interests are in Scottish Catholic fiction and particularly the work of George Mackay Brown.

Valentina Bold is director of the Solway Centre for Environment and Culture, at the University of Glasgow's Dumfries Campus. Her books include *James Hogg: A Bard of Nature's Making* (Bern: Peter Lang, 2007) and Robert Burns' *The Merry Muses of Caledonia* (Edinburgh: Luath, 2008).

Katherine Campbell is senior lecturer and ethnomusicologist in Celtic and Scottish Studies, University of Edinburgh, specialising in fiddle and Scots song. She is general editor of the Scottish Tradition Series of recordings from the School of Scottish Studies Archives.

Robert Dunbar is the Chair of Celtic Languages, Literatures, History and Antiquities at the University of Edinburgh. His interests include Gaelic in Canada, Gaelic poetry overseas, nineteenth-century Gaelic culture and society, and Gaelic sociolinguistics and language policy.

Sarah Dunnigan is senior lecturer in English Literature at Edinburgh University. Her research interests include medieval and early modern Scottish literature, Scottish women's writing, fairy tales and children's literature.

Corey Gibson is a postdoctoral fellow at the Institute for Advanced Studies in the Humanities at the University of Edinburgh.

Suzanne Gilbert, senior lecturer in English at Stirling University, publishes on eighteenth- and nineteenth-century Scottish literature, ballads and chapbooks. She and Ian Duncan are general editors of the Stirling/South Carolina Research Edition of *The Collected Works of James Hogg* (Edinburgh University Press).

Anja Gunderloch is a lecturer in Celtic in the department of Celtic and Scottish Studies at the University of Edinburgh. Her research interests lie in the development and literary characteristics of Scottish Gaelic poetry before 1900, with particular focus on the heroic ballads and the work of Donnchadh Bàn MacIntyre.

Jason Marc Harris is the author of *Folklore and the Fantastic in Nineteenth-Century British Fiction* (Aldershot: Ashgate, 2008).

Lizanne Henderson is lecturer in History at the University of Glasgow (Dumfries Campus). Her main research areas are the European and African witch-hunts, the folklore and cultural history of animals, slavery and abolition, and the Scottish diaspora in North America, Australasia, Africa and the Caribbean.

Emily Lyle is a senior research fellow in the Department of Celtic and Scottish Studies at the University of Edinburgh. Her long-term interests in oral culture have led to many publications, most recently, *Ten Gods: A New Approach to Defining the Mythological Structures of the Indo-Europeans* (Newcastle upon Tyne: Cambridge Scholars Publishing, 2012).

Kirsteen McCue is head of Scottish Literature and co-director of the Centre for Robert Burns Studies at the University of Glasgow. She has written on Romantic song culture and is currently completing new editions of *Songs by the Ettrick Shepherd* and a companion volume of *Contributions to Musical Collections and Miscellaneous Songs* for the *Collected Works of James Hogg*.

John McNamara teaches the medieval languages and literatures of England, Scotland and Ireland at the University of Houston. His recent research and publications have been on Anglo-Saxon, Anglo-Latin and Middle Scots literature and folklore.

Michael Newton is assistant professor in the Celtic Studies Department of St Francis Xavier University in Nova Scotia. He has written several books and numerous articles on many aspects of Highland tradition and history in Scotland and North America.

James Porter is professor emeritus, University of California, Los Angeles and honorary professor, University of Aberdeen. He has published widely in the fields of ethnology and musicology.

Ian Russell is professor and director of the Elphinstone Institute at the University of Aberdeen and has written extensively on folksong, traditional drama, folk dance and traditional humour at home, in Europe and the USA.

Index

Aarne, Antti, 5, 27, 117
  The Types of the Folktale, 21
Aberdeen University, 93
Acair, 125
Acallam na Senórach, 75
Adair, John, 88
Adamson, Patrick, 28
Adomnán, *Life of St Columba*, 50
Aelred of Rievaulx, 49
Aeneid, 66
Aesop, 10, 42, 46
agriculture, 4, 22, 107
Aiken Drum, 32–3
Ailean Dall (Allan MacDougall), 55
Alasdair, Alasdair mac Mhaighstir *see* MacDonald, Alexander
Am Baile, 19
'Am Brón Binn', 80
America, North, 3, 9, 13, 3, 79, 107, 123–5, 127, 130, 133, 134–5, 137, 140, 147–9
American Folklore Society, 144
Amodio, Mark C., 67
An Comunn Gàidhealach, 124–5, 130
Anderson, Duncan, 105–6
Andrew, St, 11, 46, 50
Andrew of Wyntoun, 45
Angus, Marion, 5
Antiquarian Repertory, The, 91
antiquarianism, 85–93, 94, 108
Appalachians, 148–9
Arabian Nights, 63, 126
Argo, Arthur, 146
Argyle, 8th Duke of, 9
Armour, Jean, 99, 100
Armour, Matt, 149
  'Generations of Change', 149–50
Armstrong, John, 69
Arnim, Achim von, 64
'A-Rovin on a Winter's Night', 149
Arthur, King, 79–80
'As I Came in by London O', 97–8
Athenaeum, The, 144

Atholl, John, 7th Duke of, 61
Aubrey, John, 86
audience, 3, 5, 20, 23, 33, 48, 55, 67, 71, 75, 78, 80, 124–7, 150
  international, 145
  participation, 18–19, 129
  poetry, 129–32
'Auld Maitland', 106
authenticity, 137, 151
authorship, 23–4, 26–7, 124
  attribution, 102–3

Bacach, Eachann, 55
Bakhtin, Mikhail, 38
Baldred, St, 49
ballads, 5, 36, 141
  adventure, 81
  Border, 8, 68–9, 108–9
  bothy, 4, 22, 24, 149
  classical, 14–18
  collection, 8, 13, 15–16, 43, 53, 76–9, 106–13, 145–6
  death in, 83
  description, 91–2
  dialogue in, 82–3
  early modern, 65
  Gaelic, 1, 53, 74–6
  heroic, 74–84
  historical, 68–71
  international, 13
  motifs, 17
  narrative, 1, 5, 15, 16, 17, 43, 53, 76–9, 106–13
  origins, 43
  Ossianic, 53, 55, 56, 75–6
  refrain, 18
  revival, 135–6
  Romantic, 111
  stanza, 16–17
  themes, 79–84
  variants, 3, 16, 17, 111–12
  women and, 60, 70–1, 80, 86
Bannatyne manuscript, 65, 66
Barbour, John, *The Bruce*, 42, 43–4, 45
Bàrd Thighearna Cholla *see* MacLean, John

Barden, Jean, 106
bardic verse, 1, 76
Barker, Elspeth, 5
Barry, Jonathan, 72
'Bàs Chonlaoich', 79
'Battle of Otterburn, The', 43
Bawcutt, Priscilla, 47
BBC, 137
Bell, A. S., 91
Bennett, Margaret, 15, 206
'Berry Fields of Blair, The', 23
Bertie, David M., 102
Bible, 11, 45, 57
Bicket, Linden, 206
'Big Lad of Dervaig, The', 117–18
Birlinn (publisher), 62
Black, Ronald, 130, 131
'Black Bull o Norroway, The', 63, 112
Blackadder, Jenny, 112
'Blacksmith's Wife of Yarrowfoot, The', 31
Blair, Hugh, 92
Blair, John, 45
Blairgowrie Festival, 5
'Blooming Caroline o Edinburgh Toon', 22
Blythman, Morris (Thurso Berwick), 138, 140
Boece, Hector, 86
Bold, Valentina, 119, 206
'Bonny Earl of Murray, The', 69, 87
Book of the Dean of Lismore, 76–7, 78, 79, 80, 83
books, 7, 112
  Bible, 11, 45, 57
  chapbooks, 4, 37, 94, 95
  songbooks, 94, 140
Border ballads, 8, 68–9, 108–9
Boswell, James
  Account of Corsica, 87
  Journal of a Tour to the Hebrides . . ., 87
  Journey to the Western Isles of Scotland, 87

209

Bothwell, James Hepburn, Earl of, 69
bothy ballads, 4, 22, 24, 149
Bower, Walter, *Scotichronicon*, 45
Boyman, Jonet, 28
Bracciolini, Poggio, 12
Bremner, Robert, 100
Brentano, Clemens, 64
'Bridegroom Greets when the Sun Gaes Doun, The', 102, 103
Brigid, St, 49, 50
British Empire, 3
British Museum, 93
broadsides, 4, 23, 37, 94, 95, 149
Brocken, Michael, 135
Brocket, Lord, 140
Bronson, Bertrand H., 16, 148
  The Traditional Tunes of the Child Ballads, 16
Brown, Anna (née Gordon), 3, 36, 86, 106
Brown, Mary Ellen, 65
brownies, 32–3
Bruce, Robert, 43–4
Bruford, Alan, 19
Brunvand, Jan Harold, 20–1
Buchan, David, 23, 27, 36, 107
Buchan, David Steuart Erskine, 11th Earl of, 86, 87, 91, 92
Buchan, Norman, 3, 25, 138
Buchan, Peter, 8, 107, 135, 145
Buchan Field Club, 145
Buchan Observer, 145–6
Buchanan, Dugald, 55
  Laoidhe Spioradail, 55
Buchanan, George, 86
Burke, Peter, 65, 72
Burns, Robert, 1, 2, 7, 91, 94, 96–7, 98–9, 100–1, 108
  'As I Came in by London O', 97–8
  Commonplace Book, 96–7
  'Halloween', 91
  The Merry Muses of Caledonia, 101
  'My Love is Like a Red, Red, Rose', 100, 149
  'Of a' the Airts', 99, 100
  songs, 23
  'Tam o Shanter', 34, 91
'Butcher Boy, The', 22
Bute, John Stuart, 3rd Earl of, 91

Camden, William, 85
Cameron, Alexander, 60
Cameron, John, *Lyric Gems*, 12
Campbell, Alexander, 54
  Albyn's Anthology, 54
Campbell, James, 88
Campbell, John Francis ('Iain Òg Ìle'), of Islay, 9, 10, 13, 28, 60, 62, 78, 84, 114, 115, 116, 117, 118, 119, 151
  Leabhar na Féinne, 79
  Popular Tales of the West Highlands, 19, 62, 78, 118, 146
Campbell, John Gregorson, 60, 61, 62, 114, 117–18, 119
Campbell, John Lorne, 51, 127, 135
Campbell, Katherine, 206
Campbell, Mrs (of Asheville), 148
Canada, 3, 123, 128
  Nova Scotia 19, 51, 55, 57, 127, 129, 133
'Captain Car', 17
Caraid nan Gàidheal *see* MacLeod, Neil
Carlyle, Thomas, 112
Carmichael, Alexander, 51–2, 60, 61, 62, 78, 79, 84, 114, 115, 116, 120–2
  Carmina Gadelica, 78, 120–2
Carmichael, Ella, 62
Carter, Angela, 1
Casket, 129
'Cath Rìgh na Sorcha', 80–1, 82
Catholicism, 72, 121
ceilidhs (cèilidhs), 51–2, 62, 124
  Edinburgh People's Festival, 2, 138, 139, 147
Celtic Monthly, The, 61, 117
Celtic Review, The, 62
Celtic Twilight, 124, 131
Chalmers, George, 85
Chambers, Robert, 8, 9–10, 23, 27, 112
  The Popular Rhymes of Scotland, 8, 19, 27, 63, 112
  Scottish Jests and Anecdotes, 19
chapbooks, 4, 37, 94, 95
'Charlie, He's My Darling', 91
'Charm for the Face of a Maiden', 121
charms, 120–1
Chesnutt, Michael, 43
Child, Francis James, 13, 15–16, 27, 107, 145, 147–8
  The English and Scottish Popular Ballads, 13, 16, 107, 147
children, 39, 141
Cholla, Bàrd Thighearna, 56
Christianity, 75, 76, 121
  Catholicism, 72, 121
  clergy, 1, 52–3, 59, 60–1
  Protestantism, 53, 56, 71–2
Christiansen, Reidar, 27
'Christis Kirk on the Grene', 65
clans, 59
  legends, 12
  lore, 52
Clarke, Stephen, 99
Clarke, William, 99
Clàrsach an Doire, 56
clergy, 1, 52–3, 59, 60–1
Clerk, Sir John, 86, 87
Club Leabhar, 125
Cochruinneacha Taoghta de Shaothair . . ., 56–7

Cogitosus, *Life of Brigid*, 50
Collection, 8–10, 19, 21–3, 94, 111
  of ballads, 8, 13, 15–16, 43, 53, 76–9, 106–13, 145–6
  of folklore, 26, 27, 33
  Gaelic, 51–62
  tales, 112
Collection of Gaelic Proverbs and Familiar Phrases, A . . ., 60
collectors, 9, 12, 13, 52–4, 58–61, 76–9, 89, 91, 114–19, 136, 136
  twentieth century, 127
Columba, St, 49, 50
Columbia Records, 24, 147
'Come A' Ye Fisher Lassies', 24
common places, 112
communication, 35, 39–41
communities, 42, 132, 136
Complaynt of Scotland, The, 63, 64, 65, 66, 72–3, 112
context, 22, 38, 136, 145, 149
Cook, Captain James, 92
Cormack, Art, 62
'Coronation Coronach', 140
court, 1, 15, 47–8, 66–7, 70, 71, 72
Cowan, Edward, 64
Craig, David, 142
Crawford, David, 86
Crawford, Thomas, *Society and the Lyric*, 94
Crawfurd, Andrew, 16
Creech, William, 92
Cregeen, Eric, 152
Creighton, Helen, 19
Critic's Group, 137
Cromek, Robert Hartley, 29–30
  Remains of Nithsdale and Galloway Song, 29, 30
'Cruel Brother, The', 18
Cù Chulainn (Cuchullin), 11, 121, 128
Cuairtear nan Gleann, 61
cultural transmission, 40, 51
Cumming, James, 77
Cunningham, Allan, 28, 29–31, 33, 112
  The Songs of Scotland, Ancient and Modern, 29
  Traditional Tales of the English and Scottish Peasantry, 29, 30
Curleton, Walter, 88
Cuthbert, St, 49

Dalrymple, Sir David, Lord Hailes, 86, 87
Dalyell, John Graham, 33
'Dàn an Deirg mhic Drabhaill', 81–2, 82–3
Dante, 142
Darnley, Henry Stuart, Lord, 69
Dasent, Sir George Webb, 9
death, in ballads, 83
Deirdre, 11

INDEX

Devine, T. M., 107
dialects, 2, 42, 61, 74
dialogue, 38, 62, 82–3, 123
Diarmaid and Gràinne, 11–12, 74, 81
Dick, James, 97
Ding Dong Dollar, 140–1
Dòmhnall nan Òrain *see* MacLeod, Donald
Donn, Rob (Robert Mackay), 53
Donnchadh Bàn (Duncan Ban MacIntyre), 4, 53, 55
Donnchadh nam Pìos (Duncan MacRae), 52
Dorson, Richard, 91
Douglas, Gavin, 49, 66
 The Palis of Honoure, 65–6
Douglas, Sheila, 25, 151
 Last of the Tinsmiths, 151
Drummond, William, 92
Duanaire An, 57
Dun, Finlay, *Orain na h-Albain*, 54
Dunbar, Robert, 206
Dunbar, William, 47–8, 66
 'Dance of the Sevin Deidly Synnis', 48
 Flyting betwyxt Kennedie and Dunbar, 48
 'Tretis of the Twa Mariit Wemen and the Wedo', 48
Duncan, James Bruce, 21–2, 145–6
 Greig-Duncan Folk Song Collection, 25, 103, 145–6
Duncan, Jock, 150
Dundes, Alan, 21
Dunlop, Bessie, 28
Dunn, Charles, 127
Dunnigan, Sarah, 206

Eachdraidh Mhic-Cruislig, 60
Earle, John, *Micro-Cosmographie*, 87
Easton, Gordon, 150
Easy Club, 8, 89
Edinburgh
 Arthur's Seat, 28
 Scottish Storytelling Festival, 19
 Surgeon's Hall Museum, 93
Edinburgh International Festival, 146, 150
Edinburgh People's Festival, 134, 142, 147
 Ceilidhs, 2, 138, 139
Edinburgh University, 7, 62, 88, 92
 School of Scottish Studies, 2, 11–12, 19, 25, 51, 127, 134, 135, 138, 147
 Scottish Ethnology, 147
editors, 54, 58–9, 70, 78, 86, 94, 104, 107, 111, 112, 117
education, 20, 23, 27, 77, 107, 115–16, 124
'Eigg Collection', 56
English language, 128, 132–3

Enlightenment, 29, 88, 108
epics, 36, 43–5
Erskine, Ruaraidh, 125
ethnography, 39–41
ethnology, 111
Ever Green, The, 8, 65
exiles, 130

fables, 10, 46–7
'Fair Annie', 110
fairies, 28–9, 32
Fairport Convention (band), 1
fairy tales, 1, 21, 29
Fear-Tathaich nam Beann, 61
Fergusson, Robert
 'Elegy on the Death of Scots Music', 102
Fernaig Manuscript, 52
Fhianuis, An, 61
fiction
 1820s, 112
 twentieth century, 123, 124–5, 128
fiddles, 99, 115
Fionn mac Cumhaill, 3, 11–12, 74, 75, 76, 79, 80, 83, 114, 119–20, 121
Fletcher, Andrew, 138
'Flower of Scotland', 23
folk beliefs, 26–34, 115, 116–17, 120–2
folk culture, 43, 64, 135, 136, 137, 140, 141
folk literature, 26–7, 34
folk music, 134, 135
folk narrative, 18–21, 26, 27
 collections, 19
 see also folktales; legends
folk revival, 2, 134–43, 146
 and literature, 141–3
 politics, 138–41
Folk Tales and Fairy Lore . . ., 60
folklore, 26–7, 34–5, 112, 144
 collectors, 26, 27, 33
 migratory, 114
 nineteenth century, Highlands and Islands, 114–22
Folklore Society, 58, 115, 144
folksong, 8, 12, 21–5, 135, 136–8
 authorship, 23–4
 collections, 25
 and literature, 141–3
 military, 24
 variants, 21–4
Folk-Song Society, 144
folktales, 5, 8–9, 10, 31
 genres, 26–7
 international, 9
Ford, Robert, 37
Foulis, Sir James, 56
Fowlis, Julie, 62
Fox, Adam, 4, 64
'Fox and the Crow, The', 10
Fraser, Marjory Kennedy, 145
 Songs of the Hebrides, 145

Fraser, Simon, 54
 The Airs and Melodies . . ., 54
Frazer, James, 115
Freud, Sigmund
 Jokes and their Relation to the Unconscious, 21
'Friday, Saturday', 151–2
Frog King story, 9

Gàidhealtachd, 88, 129
 North American, 125
Gaeldom, 29, 123, 125, 130, 131–2, 145
Gaelic, 1, 116, 117
 ballads, 1, 53, 74–84
 Bible, 57
 Classical Common, 74, 76
 culture, eighteenth century, 89–90
 fiction, 62, 128
 panegyric code, 129
 periodicals, 61–2
 poetry, 52, 53, 56–7, 59, 129–33
 printing, 55, 60, 61
 Scottish, twentieth century, 123–33
 songs, 54, 55, 57–61, 130, 145
 stories, 152
 suppression, 115, 124
 translation: from Gaelic, 9, 60, 116, 117, 122, 145; into Gaelic, 126
 Vernacular tradition, 51–62
Gaelic Books Council, 125, 131
Gaidheal, An, 61
Gàidheal, Caraid nan, 62
Gairm, 131
Galloway, 30, 32
Gazin-Schwartz, Amy, 90
genre, 38, 124
Gesto Collection of Highland Music, The, 58
Gibson, Corey, 206
Gibson, Edmund, 85
Gilbert, Suzanne, 207
Gillies, John, 56
Gillies Collection, 77
'Girl with the Mantle, The', 80
Glasgow, 11, 50, 138, 140
 Unity Theatre, 147
 University, 77, 93, 125
Glen, John, 98
Glenbuchat Ballads, The, 16
Goldstein, Kenneth S., 148
Goodrich-Freer, Ada, 61
Gordon, Alexander, 87
Gordon, Anna (Mrs Brown), 3, 36, 86, 106
Gough, Richard, 85
Gower, Herchell, 148
Gramsci, Antonio, 139, 141
Grant, Anne MacVicar, 115, 116
 Essays on the Superstitions of the Highlanders of Scotland, 116
Grant, Katherine W., 126

INDEX

Grant, Peter, 56
Greentrax, 25
Gregor, Walter, 28, 114, 116, 119, 120
  An Echo of the Olden Times . . ., 119
  Notes on the Folk-Lore of the North-East . . ., 120
Gregorson, J. G., 115
Gregory, David, 88
Greig, Gavin, 21–2, 135, 145–6
  Folk-Song of the North-East, 146
  Greig-Duncan Folk Song Collection, 25, 103, 145–6
  Last Leaves of Traditional [Ballads and] Ballad Airs, 136, 146
'Grey Paw, The', 114
Grimm, Jacob and Wilhelm, 8, 9, 65
  Die Kinder- und Hausmärchen, 8–9, 21
Grose, Francis, 91
  Ireland, 91
Gude and Godlie Ballatis, The, 72
Gunderloch, Anja, 207

haddock, 11
haiku, 132
Hailes, Sir David Dalrymple, Lord, 86, 87
Halley, Mrs (of Aberdeenshire), 103
Hamilton, Janet, 105
Hamilton, Mary, 70
Hamilton, Nancy, 15
Harker, Dave, 134
Harris, Jason Marc, 207
Harris, Tim, 71
Hary (Blind Harry), 45–6
  The Wallace, 42, 43, 45–6
Hay, George Campbell, 131
Hebrides, 51–2, 55, 78, 145
Henderson, Hamish, 2, 19, 23, 24, 40, 43, 64, 68, 69, 135, 136, 137, 138–9, 141–2, 143, 146–7, 148
  Alias MacAlias, 146–7
  'Ballad of the Men of Knoydart', 140
  Ballads of World War II, 140
Henderson, Lizanne, 207
Henryson, Robert, 46
  Moral Fables, 42, 46–7
  'The Preaching of the Swallow', 47
Herd, David, 13, 97, 108, 135
  Ancient and Modern Scottish Songs, 90, 97
Herder, Johann Gottfried, 40, 64, 90
  Von Deutscher Art und Kunst, 90
heroes
  in ballads, 3, 53
  Celtic, 11–12

heroic ballads, 74–84
  in tales, 3, 52, 119–20
Hicks, Ray, 148–9
Highland History and Culture website, 19
Highlander, The, 61
Highlands, 9, 52, 54, 56–7, 58, 76, 78, 84, 90, 114, 116–18, 124
history, 76
  historical ballads, 68–71
History of the Feuds and Conflicts among the Clans, 56
Hobbs, Sandy, 21
Hodgart, John, 18
Hogg, James, 8, 13, 33, 102, 106, 107–8, 110, 112–13
  The Brownie of Bodsbeck, 32
  'Donald McDonald', 102
  Jacobite Relics, 12
  'On the Changes in the Habits . . .', 110
Hogg, William, 106–7
Homage to John Maclean, 140
Hull, Thomas, 14
Hunter, William, 93
'Hunter and the Fairy Woman, The', 121–2
Huntly, George Gordon, 6th Earl of, 69

identity, 42, 123
industrialisation, 3, 38, 105, 107, 116, 136
informants, 118
Inverness Collection, 57
Ireland
  ballads, 74, 75, 83–4
  horses, 85
  legends, 11
  tales, 50
Irish Folklore Commission, 127, 134
Irish language, 125
Irvine, Alexander, 54
Irving, Washington, 109
Isle of Lewis, 11, 115, 121, 129, 131

Jack, R. D. S., 67
'Jack Tales', 1, 148
Jackson, Kenneth, 127
Jacobite Risings, 77
Jacobitism, 89, 140
James III, King, 46
James IV, King, 47, 48, 66
James V, King, 69
James VI, King, 69
  Daemonologie, 28
James Madison Carpenter Collection, The, 25
'Jamie Telfer of the Fair Dodhead', 108
Jamieson, John, 85
  The Etymological Dictionary of Scotland, 85
Jamieson, Robert, 108

Jocelyn, *Life of Kentigern,* 42, 49–50
John MacLean Memorial Rally, 140, 142
'John of Hazelgreen', 149
'Johnie Scot', 111
'Johnnie Lad', 103
Johnson, James, 1, 98
  The Scots Musical Museum, 1, 86, 90–1, 98–9
Johnson, Samuel, 87
Jung, Carl, 21
Junnor, Bill, 37

Kames, Henry Home, Lord, 92
Karpales, Maud, 148
Kellock, William, 139, 141
Kennedy, William, 48
kennings, 59
Kentigern, St, 49
Killick, Tim, 112
King, Elspeth, 45
'King Berdok', 66–7
Kinsley, James, 97
Kirk, Robert, 28, 29, 34, 52–3
  The Secret Common-Wealth . . ., 2, 53
Kittredge, G. L., 36
Knox, John, 70, 71
Krohn, Kaarle, 117

'Labour Provost, The', 140
Laidlaw, William, 8
Laidlaw Hogg, Margaret, 106–7
'Laird of Logie, The', 69–70
Lamb, Mary Ellen, 64, 71
Lamb, William, 58
Lamond, Mary Jane, 62
Lang, Andrew, 115
  Blue Fairy Book, 72–3
  The Book of Dreams and Ghosts, 115
language, 1, 2, 8–9, 13, 19, 42–3, 141
  English, 128, 132–3
  sociolinguistics, 35, 46–7
  see also dialects; Gaelic; Latin; Scots; Vernacular
'Laoidh Dhiarmaid', 81
'Laoidh Fhraoich', 81, 83–4
'Lass of Roch Royal, The', 36
Latin, 42, 45, 46–7, 49, 76, 101
Lawrie, Kate, 84
Leach, MacEdward, 127
Learning Teaching Scotland website, 25
Ledwick, Edward, 91
legends, 10–12, 20–1, 26, 31, 33–4, 44
  clan, 12
Leland, John, 85
Leyden, John, 8, 63, 65, 108
Lhuyd, Edward, 53
Library of Congress, 135
Lindahl, Carl, 42

Lindsay, Lady Ann, 102–3
  'Auld Robin Gray', 102, 103–4
literacy, 36, 105, 124, 128
Literary and Antiquarian Society, 92
literature, 2–3
  folk, 26–8, 34
  and folksong, 141–3
  in medieval period, 42–50
  prose, 62
  twentieth century, Gaelic, 123–32
  see also fiction; poetry
Livingstone, William, 56
Lom, Iain (John MacDonald), 22, 23, 53, 55
Lomax, Alan, 12, 24, 134–5, 138, 141, 146–7
Lomax, John, 134–5
Lord, A. B., *The Singer of Tales*, 36
'Lord Gregory', 149
Low, Donald, 91
Lyle, Agnes, 3, 107
Lyle, Emily, 64, 207
Lyndsay, David, 66
  'The Dreme', 66
lyrics, 5, 15, 22, 67, 90, 91, 94–104

Mac an Ollaimh, Giolla Coluim, 79
Mac-an-Tuairneir, Pàruig Peter Turner), 57
mac Fhionnlaigh, Dòmhnall, 56
mac Mghaighstir, Alasdair *see* MacDonald, Alexander
MacArthur, Allan, 12–13
MacBeath, Jimmy, 5, 24, 139
MacCallum, Duncan, 57
McCarthy, William, 36
MacCodrum, John, 55, 56
MacColl, Evan, 56
MacColl, Ewan, 2, 24, 137
MacCormick, John, 128–9
  Dùn Àluinn, 129
  Gun Tug Mi Spéis do'n Àrmunii, 128
McCue, Kirsteen, 207
MacDiarmid, Ewen, 53, 60
MacDiarmid, Hugh, 141, 142–3
  'Second Hymn to Lenin', 142
MacDonald, Alexander (Alasdair mac Mhaighstir Alasdair), 7, 53, 55, 60, 89
MacDonald, Alexander ('the Ridge'), 129
MacDonald, Allan, 60, 62
MacDonald, Cicely ('Sìleas na Ceapaich'), 53, 59
MacDonald, Donald, 88
MacDonald, John ('Iain Lom'), 22, 23, 53, 55
MacDonald, Keith Norman, 58
MacDonald, Patrick, 54
  A Collection of Highland Vocal Airs, 54

MacDonald, Ranald ('Raghnall Dubh'), 56
MacDonell, Margaret, 127
MacDougall, Allan ('Ailean Dall'), 55
MacDougall, James, 60, 115, 116
  Folk and Hero Tales, 120
MacEacharn, Dòmhnall, 124
McEwen, Elspeth, 32
MacFadyen, John, 128
MacFarlane, Malcolm, 126
MacFarlane, Peter, 57, 75
MacGill-Eain, Somhairle *see* MacLean, Sorley
McGowan, John, 87
MacGregor, Duncan, 76–7
MacGregor, James, 76–7
MacInnes, John, 4, 11, 78–9
Macintosh, Donald, 60
  A Collection of Gaelic Proverbs . . ., 60
Macintyre, Donald, 78–9, 130
MacIntyre, Duncan Ban ('Donnchadh Bàn'), 4, 53, 55
Macintyre, James, 56
MacKay, Isabella, 78
Mackay, Robert ('Rob Donn'), 53
Mackenzie, George, 88
Mackenzie, John, 60
  Sàr-Obair, 12
MacKenzie, Kenneth, 55
MacKinnon, Alasdair, 55
MacKinnon, Donald, 62
MacKinnon, Jonathan, 61
MacKormick, Donald, 58–9
MacLachlan, Ewen, 55
MacLachlan, John, 56
MacLagan, James, 53, 54, 77, 89
  Manuscript Collection, 89
MacLaine, Allan H., 6
MacLean, Alasdair, 147
MacLean, Calum, 19, 127, 138, 147
Maclean, Hector, 54, 55, 57, 78
MacLean, John ('Bàrd Thighearna Cholla'), 55, 56, 57
Memorial Rally, 140, 142
  Orain Nuadh Ghaedhlach, 55
MacLean, Sorley ('Somhairle MacGill-Eain'), 130–1, 142, 147
  Dàin do Eimhir, 130–1
MacLellan, Angus
  Raonull Bùàn Mac Eoghain Òig, 129
MacLeod, C. I. N., 127
MacLeod, Donald ('Dòmhnall nan Òrain'), 55
  Orain Nuadh Ghaeleach, 55
MacLeod, George, 77
MacLeod, Kenneth, 145
MacLeod, Kitty, 139
Macleod, Mary ('Màiri nighean Alasdair Ruaidh'), 53
Macleod, Morag, 58

MacLeod, Neil ('Caraid nan Gàidheal'), 56
  Clàrsach an Doire, 12
Macleod, Norman, 61
Macleòid, Fionnlagh, *Gormshuil an Rìgh*, 62
MacMhuirich, Lachlan, 56
MacMhuirich, Niall, 53
MacMillan, Angus 'Barrach', 127
McNamara, John, 207
McNaughtan, Adam, 24, 136
MacNeil, Flora, 150
MacNicol, Donald, 4, 53, 55, 56
MacNiel, Joe Neil, 128
  Sgeul gu Latha, 128
MacPhee, Willie, 5, 151
  'Friday, Saturday', 151–2
MacPherson, Donald, 57
Macpherson, James, 75–6, 77
  Fingal, 89
  Fragments of Ancient Poetry, 89
  Ossian, 30, 75–6
  Temora, 89
MacPherson, Mary (*née* MacDonald; 'Màiri Mhòr nan Òran'), 56
MacRae, Duncan ('Donnchadh nam Pìos'), 52
MacRury, John, 61, 126
Mac-Talla, 61, 126, 127, 129
'Maddeis Lamentatioun', 71
Mairghread nighean Lachlainn, 55
Màiri Mhòr nan Òran (Mary MacPherson), 56
Màiri nighean Alasdair Ruaidh (Mary Macleod), 53
Major, John, 86
Malinowski, Bronislaw, 40
Märchen, 1, 21, 26
Marshall, William, 99, 100, 101
Martin, Martin, 28, 29, 34, 85, 88–9
  Description of the Western Isles of Scotland, 19, 28, 88, 89
Marwick, Ernest, *The Folklore of Orkney and Shetland*, 21
Mary, Queen of Scots, 69
'Mary Hamilton', 15, 70
Masonic song, 102
Matheson, William, 54
Mathison, Hamish, 99
Mayakovsky, Vladimir, 142
Mearns, John, 24
Meek, Donald, 57, 60
memoirs, 105
memorisation, 36
memory, 111–12, 136
Miller, Hugh, 28, 33–4, 114–15, 118
  Scenes and Legends of the North of Scotland, 19, 33
Millgate, Jane, 102
Modern Gaelic Bards, 130
modernism, 17, 141
modernity, 131, 136

Moluag, St, 11
Montgomerie, Alexander, 67–8
Montgomerie, William, 147
Montrose, James Graham, 4th Duke of, 91
More West Highland Tales, 62
Morison, John, 56
Motherwell, William, 13, 27, 108, 110–12
  Minstrelsy: Ancient and Modern, 106, 107, 110–11
motifs, 5
  ballad, 17
  Motif-Index of Folk-Literature, 21
  poetry, 59
  songs, 22
  stories, 10
Muir, Edwin, *Scott and Scotland*, 141
Muir, Willa, *Living with Ballads*, 141
Munro, Ailie, 135
Murray, Lady Evelyn Stewart, 61
museums, 93
music
  folk, 134, 135
  Gaelic, 58
  see also céilidhs; tunes
musicians, 12, 115
  fiddle composers, 99–100
  travelling minstrels, 149
'My Nanie O', 96, 98
myths, 10

'Nanny O', 95, 96
Napier, James, 28, 115, 116–17
Napoleonic wars, 59, 128
narrative, 1, 5
  ballads, 8, 13, 15–16, 17, 43, 53, 76–9, 106–13
  folk-, 18–21, 26, 27
  oral, 52, 62, 126–9
  twentieth century, Gaelic, 126–9
  see also stories; tales
nationalism, 2, 42, 108, 131, 136
Newman, Steve, 95
Newton, Michael, 207
Nicholson, William, 'The Brownie of Blednoch', 32–3
Nicol, James, 107
Nicolaisen, W. F. H., 109
Nicolson, Alexander, 60
Nilsen, Ken, 127
Ninian, St, 49
Nithsdale, 30–1
Norn language, 8
North East Folklore Archive, 19
Northern Chronicle, The, 61, 126
Nova Scotia, 19, 51, 55, 57, 127, 129, 133
novels, 128
nursery stories, 8, 73, 112
Nutt, Alfred, 115

Ó Crualaoich, Gearóid, 127
o' Phaup (Laidlaw), Will, 20
Oban Times, 61
Òg Ìle, Iain *see* Campbell, John Franncis
Oisean, 74, 75
Olrik, Axel, 27
oral composition, 36
oral literature
  transmission, 36–7, 40–1
  twentieth century, Gaelic, 123–5
oral narrative, 52 62, 126–9; *see also* storytelling
oral tradition, 1, 23, 36, 68–9, 72, 123–5
  Gaelic, 51–3
oral transmission, songs, 22–3, 36–8, 40–1, 112
orality, 1, 22–3, 34, 36, 64, 67, 123, 128
'Òran na Comhachaig', 56
origins, 26–7
Oswald, James, 98, 102
  Caledonian Pocket Companion, 98, 99
  'Scots Recluse', 99

Pagan, Isobel, 86
Paine, Tom, 107
Patrick, St, 49, 75, 76
'Pawkie Auld Kimmer, The', 31–2
Pearl website, 19
Peirson, Alison, 28
Pennant, Thomas, 84, 87
  Tour in Scotland . . ., 90
People's Journal, 124, 128–9, 130
Percy, Thomas, 14, 64, 87
  Reliques of Ancient English Poetry, 30, 43, 87, 90, 108
performance, 3, 20
  ballads, 17, 18
  folk song, 23
  oral, 36, 38–9
  poetry, 67–9
  theory, 38–9
periodicals, 52, 59, 123–5, 128–9
  Gaelic, 61–2
Perspectives on Contemporary Legend, 21
Peter, St, 11
Philosophical Transactions, 88
place-names, 83–4
Pleyel, Ignace, 98
poetry, 52, 53–60
  bardic, 1
  court, 48
  early modern, 66–8
  Gaelic, 52, 53, 56–7, 59, 129–33
  lyric, 94–104
  oral, 67–9, 112
  performance, 67–9
  political, 59
  praise, 59
  song-poetry, 52, 130–2, 142

township verse, 59
  women's, 60
  see also ballads; lyrics
Poet's Box press, 22
politics, 3, 18, 21, 42–3, 59, 68–9, 71–2, 125, 130–1, 134
  The Complaynt of Scotland, 63, 64, 65, 66, 72–3, 112
  of folk revivalism, 138–41
  satire, 140–1
Pope, Alexander, minister, 53, 77
popular culture, 2, 39, 64, 66–8, 71–3
Popular Tales of the West Highlands, 19, 62
Porter, James, 17–18, 207
praise poetry, 59
'Prayer', 121
Pringle, Sir John, 92
print, 4, 12–13, 52, 94
  broadsides, 4, 23, 37, 94, 95, 149
  chapbooks, 4, 37, 94, 95
  culture, 22–3, 116
  Gaelic, 55, 60
Propp, Vladimir, 27
  Morphology of the Folktale, 21
Protestantism, 53, 56, 71–2
Puirt-a-Beul, 58
Purser, John, 67

Quarterly Journal of Agriculture, 110
'Queen's Maries, The', 8

Raghnall Dubh (Ranald MacDonald), 56
railway, 116
Ramsay, Allan, 7, 8, 13, 23, 65, 69, 86, 87, 89, 90, 94
  Collection of Scots Proverbs, 89
  The Ever Green, 8, 65, 89
  Fables and Tales, 89
  'The Gentle Shepherd', 8, 95
  'Nanny O', 95, 96
  Scots Songs, 89, 95
  The Tea-Table Miscellany, 7, 8, 89, 95, 98
Rebels' Ceilidh Song Book, 139, 140–1
recording, 13, 127, 136, 144, 151
  recordings, 25, 136–7, 147, 152
Reid, Anne, 150
Reid, Tom, 150
Renaissance, 64, 67, 142
revivalism, 24, 86, 134–43
  politics of, 138–41
riddles, 12
Ritchie, Jean, 148
Ritson, Joseph, 87, 109
  Scottish Songs, 87
  Select Collection of English Songs, 87
Robert, King, 43, 44, 45
Robertson, Jeannie, 3, 5, 20, 147, 148

INDEX

Robertson, Stanley, 18, 20, 151
romance, 43–4, 69–70
Romanticism, 64, 105–13
Rosenberg, Neil V., 135
Ross, Elizabeth Jane, 54
Ross, Wester, 52
'Roving Ploughboy, The', 22, 23
Roy, William, 86
  Military Antiquities of the Romans in North Britain, 86
Royal Danish Society, 92
Royal Society, 86, 88
Royal Society of Edinburgh, 92
Ruaidh, Màiri nighean Alasdair, 56
Ruddiman, Thomas, 86
Rule, St, 50
Russell, Ian, 208

saints, 11, 42, 49–50
Sandyknowe, 7
Sangs o' the Stane, 140
'Sash, The', 140
satire, 28, 47, 48, 59, 71, 129
  political, 140–1
schools, 115–16, 124, 138
Scot, Sir John, 86
'Scotch Wooing of Willy and Nanny, The', 16, 24, 89. 95–6, 97
Scots language
  Middle, 42
  'native', 89
  'thin', 16
  see also Gaelic; Vernacular
Scots Magazine, The, 144
Scots Musical Museum, 1, 86, 90–1, 98–9, 101, 104, 136
Scotsman, 142
Scott, Sir Walter, 13, 27, 33, 34, 64, 65, 69, 70, 92–3, 106, 108–10, 111, 112
  childhood, 7
  youth, 8
  The Antiquary, 87
  Ivanhoe, 87
  'Jock of Hazeldean', 149
  Minstrelsy of the Scottish Border, 8, 12, 43, 63, 85, 108, 109, 110
  Rob Roy, 93
Scottish Storytelling Centre, 19, 151
  Website, 20
Scottish Storytelling Festival, 19
Scottish Storytelling Forum, 151
Scottish Tradition, 25
SCRAN website, 19
script, 76
Sean Dain, 56
'Seathan Son of the King of Ireland', 122
second sight, 29
Sempill, Robert, 28, 71
Sharp, Cecil, 135, 144–5

English Folksongs of the Southern Appalachians, 148
Sharpe, Charles Kirkpatrick, 8, 33, 108, 112
Sharpe, Richard, 50
Shaw, John, 19, 52, 127
Shaw, Margaret Fay, 145
  Folklore and Folksongs of South Uist, 145
Shell, Alison, 64, 72
Shenstone, William, 14
Short, James, 86
Shortreed, J. E., 109
Shortreed, Robert S., 109
Sibbald, Sir Robert, 86, 88
  An Account of the Scottish Atlas, 88
Sìleas na Ceapaich (Cicely MacDonald), 53, 59
Sinclair, Alexander Maclean, 54, 57–8
Sinclair, Archibald, 57
Sinclair, Donald, 11, 152
  An t-Òranaiche, 12
Sinclair, George, *Satan's Invisible World Discovered*, 28
Sinclair, Sir John, 92
singers, 3, 4–5, 7, 12, 15–16, 18, 22–5, 36, 37
singing, 52, 54, 58–9, 105, 107–8
  ballads, 18, 105, 106
  games, 24
  styles, 136–7
Singing the Fishing, 24
Sinton, Thomas, 61
'Sir Patrick Spens', 108
Skinner, John, 94, 101–2, 103
  'Tullochgorum', 101–2
  'Widow Greylocks', 102, 103–4
Sloane, Hans, 88
Smellie, William, 92
Smith, Donald, 151
  Storytelling Scotland, 19
Smith, Iain Crichton, 131
Smith, Sydney Goodsir, 142
Society of Antiquaries of London, 86–7
Society of Antiquaries of Scotland, 86, 91–3
sociolinguistics, 35, 46–7
'Solemn League and Covenant, The', 91
songbooks, 94, 140
song-poetry, 52, 130–2, 142
songs, 1, 3–4, 7–8, 62
  Burns, 23
  Gaelic, 52–3, 54, 58–60, 61, 130, 145
  learning, 12
  lyric, eighteen century, 94–104
  Masonic, 102
  printed, 12–13, 104
  variants, 23–4
  waulking, 4, 56, 58–9, 59–60
  see also ballads; folksong

Spalding Club, 145
Speirs, John, 141
Statistical Accounts of Scotland, 92, 105
Stenhouse, William, 98
Stewart, Alexander, 4, 20, 57, 115, 117, 118–19, 120
  Twixt Ben Nevis and Glencoe, 117, 118–19
Stewart, Belle, 4, 5, 23
Stewart, Davie, 24
Stewart, Elizabeth, 22
Stewart, Essie, 151
Stewart, James, 2nd Earl, 69
Stewart, Lucy, 148
Stewart, Margaret, 62
Stewart, Sheila, 4, 20, 23
Stine Bheag (witch), 33–4
Stirling Bridge battle, 46
Stone, Jerome, 53
stories, 10, 11–12, 14–15, 20–1, 105–6, 117, 148–9
  Early Modern, 63
  1820s, 112
  nursery, 8, 73, 112
  printed, 128
  transmission, 33
  see also ballads; narrative; tales
storytellers, 19, 20, 81, 106, 119, 126, 150–2
storytelling, 4–5, 6, 9–10, 20, 34, 105–6, 110, 116, 145
Strachan, John, 24
strathspey, 100
Stuart, Gilbert, 92
supernatural, 7, 26–9, 52, 60, 86, 106, 114, 116, 120
  in ballads, 5, 14
  legends, 10, 12
  tales, 21
  see also witches
superstition, 26, 29, 112, 115–17, 120, 152
Sutherland, Christina, 77–8
Sweet, Rosemary, 86, 87–8
Sydow, Carl von, 38
Symond, Deborah A.
  Weep Not For Me, 70–1

tales, 1
  collection, 112
  fairy, 1, 2, 21
  of heroes, 3, 52, 119–20
  Irish, 50
  Jack, 1, 148
  types, 5, 114
  wonder, 21, 26, 60, 73
  see also folktales; legends; narrative; stories
'Tam Lin', 1, 14
Tannahill, Robert, 24
'Tarves Rant', 24
Teachdaire Gae'lach, An, 61
Teachdaire nan Gaidheal, 61
Tea-Table Miscellany, 7, 8

technology, 116
Temperley, Alan, *Tales of Galloway*, 21
textile industries, 107
textuality, 36
'Thánaig Adhbhar mo Thuirse', 79
Thompson, Stith, 5, 21, 27, 117
    Motif-Index of Folk-Literature, 5, 21
    The Types of the Folktale, 21
Thoms, William, 26
Thomson, Derick, 77, 131
Thomson, George, 98
    Original Scotish Airs, 98
Thomson, William, 98
    Orpheus Caledonius, 89, 95, 98
Thorkelin, Grímur Jónsson, 92
'Three Who Went to Discover What Hardship Meant, The', 126–7
Tobar an Dualchais, 19, 25
Tocher (journal), 19
Tolmie, Frances, 58
Topic Records, 25, 134
t-Oranaiche, An, 57, 58
Torrie, Donald, 78
tradition, 38, 140–1, 143
    ballad, 4
    continuing, 144–52
    in medieval period, 42–50
    early modern period, 63–6, 72–3
    oral, 1, 23, 36, 68–9, 72, 123–5
    and Romanticism, 105–13
    roots, 1–6
    Scottish Gaelic, twentieth century, 123–33
    Vernacular Gaelic, 51–62, 123–5
tradition-bearers, 3, 5, 28, 77–8, 106–7, 116, 136, 137, 145, 148
    and ethnography, 39–41
Traditional Music and Song Association, 5, 134
traditionality, 36

Transactions of the Gaelic Society of Inverness, 61
translation
    from Gaelic, 9, 60, 116, 117, 122, 145
    into Gaelic, 66, 126
transmission, 3, 4, 35–41, 127, 136, 137–8
    oral, 22–3, 36–8, 40–1, 112
    print, 22–3
Travellers, 23, 34, 36, 40
travelling minstrels, 149
travelling people ('tinkers'), 5, 146, 147, 148, 149
Tulloch, Tom, 6
'Tullochgorum', 101–2
tunes, 4, 94, 95–6, 97–8, 99–104
    ballad, 17, 36
    'The Bridegroom Greets', 102, 103
    'My Nanny O', 96
    'Of a' the Airts', 100
    published, 58
    'Tullochgorum', 101–2
Turner, Peter ('Pàruig Mac-an-Tuairneir'), 57
Turriff, Cameron, 37
'Twa (Two) Sisters, The', 17, 147–8

Ulster Cycle, 74, 79, 81
University of Glasgow, 77, 93, 125
urban myths, 20–1
urbanisation, 136
Ur-text, 27

Vernacular, 22–4, 42, 64–6, 89, 102
    Gaelic tradition, 51–62, 123–5
    poetry, 129–33, 141
violin, 99, 115
'Vixen, The', 121
Voice of the People, The records, 25

Waifs and Strays of Celtic Tradition, 115

Walker, William, 145, 146
Wallace, William, 44–6
Warner, Marina, 21
Watson, Jim, 127
Watson, William J., 57
    Specimens of Gaelic Poetry, 57
waulking, 4, 56, 58–9, 59–60
'Weary Coble o Cargill, The', 110–11
Wedderburn, Robert, 63, 72
Weekly Magazine, 102
Weekly Scots Magazine, 102
Wemyss, John, 69
Western Australian Folklore Archive, 19
'White Cockade, The', 140
Whyte, Betsy, 20, 24, 151
'Wild Mountain Thyme, The', 23–4
Williamson, Duncan, 5, 20, 148–9, 150–1
Williamson, Linda, 151
Williamson, Roy, 23
witches, 28, 30–2, 33–4
    trials, 28, 29
'Witches' Tryst, The', 30
Withers, Charles, 91
women
    antiquarians, 86
    authors of ballads, 60
    subjects of ballads, 70–1, 80
work
    communal, 116
    industrialisation, 3, 38, 105, 107, 116, 136
    songs, 4, 56, 58–9, 59–60, 149–50
workers, 23
    gatherings, 37
Workers' Music Association, 134
writing, 4, 36–7, 124; *see also* print

'Yellow of the Broom', 24
Yoo Sun Lee, 88

EU representative:
Easy Access System Europe
Mustamäe tee 50, 10621 Tallinn, Estonia
Gpsr.requests@easproject.com

www.ingramcontent.com/pod-product-compliance
Lightning Source LLC
Chambersburg PA
CBHW062224300426
44115CB00012BA/2206